Charles John Andersson

The Okavango River; a narrative of travel, exploration and adventure

Charles John Andersson

The Okavango River; a narrative of travel, exploration and adventure

ISBN/EAN: 9783337208608

Printed in Europe, USA, Canada, Australia, Japan

Cover: Foto ©Andreas Hilbeck / pixelio.de

More available books at **www.hansebooks.com**

THE OKAVANGO RIVER:

A NARRATIVE

OF

TRAVEL, EXPLORATION, AND ADVENTURE.

BY

CHARLES JOHN ANDERSSON,
AUTHOR OF
"LAKE NGAMI."

WITH NUMEROUS ILLUSTRATIONS
AND A MAP OF SOUTHERN AFRICA.

NEW YORK:
HARPER & BROTHERS, PUBLISHERS,
FRANKLIN SQUARE.
1861.

PREFACE.

The traveler in Africa had formerly a very simple task to perform when he came before the public to give an account of his adventurous inroads into that most repulsive and least accessible quarter of the globe. Readers were then satisfied with a few details of mere discovery—with a few latitudes and longitudes as correctly set down as might be. At present they demand much more. He is now expected to be competently versed in many sciences, and in much knowledge out of the beat of ordinary accomplishment. He is supposed to understand meteorology, hygrometry, and hydrogeny; to collect geological specimens, to gather political and commercial information, to advance the infant study of ethnology, to sketch, to write a copious journal, to shoot and stuff birds and beasts, to collect grammars and vocabularies, and frequently to forward long reports to the Royal Geographical Society. Now, without pretending to have reached, or to have at all closely approached this standard of an explorer's qualifications, I have certainly touched, in the following pages, on several of the topics just enumerated. My humbler object, however, has been merely, by a plain narrative of my adventures, accompanied by the remarks they have suggested, so to mingle information with amusement as to make a pleasant and somewhat instructive book.

Five years have now elapsed since my former work on South Africa was published. I have, since then, become much better acquainted with that country than I was at that time. The denizens of its wilds and deserts have especially, as a sportsman, engaged my attention, and I think the parts of this volume devoted to my hunting excursions will be found particularly interesting and exciting. Africa, in fact, may be said, even up to the present day, to be principally inhabited by wild beasts. Its savage human natives only afford a study of rational life on so low a scale as hardly to justify the epithet I have just made use of, whereas one may, in the regions I have frequented, luxuriate in the contemplation of pure animal existence in its fullest and freest developments. To do so has been to me a great source of enjoyment. Living pictures of the *feræ naturæ* in multitudes, in endless variety, oftentimes, too, of beauty and of happiness, have a wonderful attraction to the reasoning intellect looking *down* upon them, yet mightily *humbled* by its sense of superiority! In brief, Africa is a vast zoological garden and a vast hunting-field at the same time. Let us visit it, reader, and let us hunt over it together. Our drier explorations, and our companionship through them, will be all the pleasanter for this recreation.

A word more before I conclude. As I have found it currently believed, both on the Continent and at home, that the Royal Geographical Society or that the British government has paid the costs of my several explorations in the interior of Africa, I must, in justice to myself, contradict this statement in the most unqualified manner. The expenses of all my African expeditions have been defrayed entirely by myself.

In this volume I have seen reason to alter the spelling of a few places mentioned in Lake Ngami.

CONTENTS.

CHAPTER I.

Project of an Expedition into the Interior with Mr. Green.—Mr. Green's Expedition to Libèbè.—Professor Wahlberg killed by an Elephant.—Another Expedition of Mr. Green in search of the River Cunenè.—Two Rhenish Missionaries, Messrs. Hahn and Rath, join Mr. Green.—Visit to the Ovambo.—Treachery of King Nangoro.—The exploring Party attacked by his Orders by a large Body of Natives.—The Victory of the Europeans.—Six hundred fighting Men beaten by thirteen.—The accidental Discovery of a Fresh-water Lake called Onondova.—The farther Prosecution of the Expedition renounced.—I determine on resuming it in Person.—Difficulties to be overcome.—Traveling Equipment and Suite.—Particular Objects of the Expedition.—Motives for choosing my Route through Western Damara Land................................Page 21

CHAPTER II.

Departure.—Leave-taking.—Slow Progress.—Live-stock.—Omaruru River.—Scenery.—Cutting a Way through the Bush.—Escape and Capture of my Horse.—A serious Accident.—A Forest of Trees *without Thorns.*—A delightful Surprise.—The Damara Parent-tree.—Tracks of Elephants.—Magnificent Range of Hills.—Periodical Water-course.—A Mountain Gorge.—Difficulty of finding a Route.—The Passage for the Wagon impracticable.—The Wagon smashed to Pieces.—Narrow Escape of the Oxen-driver.—Wagon repaired and reladen.—Route in a new Direction.—Encampment.—Country densely bushed................ 32

CHAPTER III.

Another Limestone Range of Hills.—Passage through it at last found.—Clearing a Road through Rocks.—The Wagon like a Ship in a heavy Cross-sea.—The Fountains of Otjidambi.—Traces of human Habitation.—The Ovaherero and the Namaquas.—The Hottentots and Damaras.—Cattle and Sheep stealing.—Guides at a Loss.—Two Natives captured.—One of them forced to become a Guide.—The Natives of a Village flee away in alarm.—A few Presents reconcile some of them to become Guides.—An Accident: a Dog killed instead of a Hyena.—A grand Illumination: Fields on Fire.—A Hurricane.—The Passage of a Defile.—Game rare.—Long Shots.—The Guide escapes.—Several Werfts (Hamlets) and Vleys (Wells).—Scarcity of Water.—Quest of Water.—Kind-heartedness of Damara Women.—No Guides.—No Water, and Country parched and desolate.—One more Attempt to go forward.............Page 52

CHAPTER IV.

The Guides lose their Way.—The Lives of the whole Party at stake.—A search for Water in all Directions.—In vain.—Necessity of returning without Delay.—Two Men exploring the Country for Water left behind.—The Sufferings of the Men and Animals from Thirst.—Retreat resolved upon.—A grand and appalling Conflagration.—The Magnificence of the Spectacle.—The Cattle one hundred and fifty Hours without a single Drop of Water.—The two Men left behind make their Appearance.—The Water so long searched for found.—Okaoa reached in Safety.—Ondjuona the favorite Resort of Elephants.—The annual Pilgrimage of these Animals to another Station.—The Damara Mode of Elephant-hunting.—View from the Summit of Okonyenya.—Country surveyed.—A Thunder-storm under Foot............ 68

CHAPTER V.

A singular Mirage.—Arrival on the Omaruru.—I resolve on crossing over to the Omuramba, viâ Matako, while the Wagon is undergoing a complete Reparation.—Two Lions attack the Dogs.—Wild Beasts abundant.—Lion Man-eaters.—Their stealthy Mode of Attack.—A horrid Dream.—The physical Features of Damara Land.—Granite, Limestone, and Sandstone.—Carboniferous Formations.—Scented and aromatic Plants and Trees.—Scenery.—Mines......Page 84

CHAPTER VI.

My traveling Stud.—Game plentiful.—Giraffes, Zebras, Gnus, and Koodoos.—Two Giraffes killed.—Lions, Hyenas, Jackals, and other Beasts of Prey.—Great Numbers of Natives. —Honey in great Quantities.—Visitors from the civilized World.—A Night Watch for Game.—Elephants descried. —An Elephant Hunt.—Two Elephants killed.—The Rejoicings of the Damaras on the Prospect of a Gorge.—A Breakfast on an Elephant Foot and a Dish of Honey... 95

CHAPTER VII.

Night Watches and Day Trackings.—A great English Sportsman and a great English Traveler's Opinion of Dr. Livingstone.—A Moonlight Ambush.—Living Pictures of Animal Life.—Nature's Menagerie.—Two more Elephants killed.— A Night Assemblage of a large Herd of one hundred and fifty Elephants at a drinking Tank.—The furious Trumpetings of the Herd when fired at.—Female Elephants particularly vicious.—A Cow Elephant-hunt.—The Hunter hunted.—Narrow Escape.—Following the Spoors of a Herd.— The Emigration of Elephants.—Paterfamilias, or General of Division.—An unsatisfactory Shot.—A Tree torn up.—A Picture of Rage and Grandeur.................... 109

CHAPTER VIII.

A Herd of Camelopards or Giraffes.—One Shot.—A comic Scene.—A Lion wounded.—The Antelope.—The Eland.—The Numerousness of this ruminant Tribe.—The Springbok, its extraordinary Agility.—A Damara trading Caravan destined for Ovambo Land.—Retainers of Afrikander.—I refuse to join the Caravan.—Dearth of Water.—Rejoined by the Wagon.—Start again to the Eastward.—Lion Man-eaters, a Native carried off by one of them.—Mr. Green's Narrative.—Lion Chase.—Fragments and Bones of the Native discovered.—Another Visit from a Lion.—Dismay in the Encampment.—Wild Boars.—Dogs no Match for them. —I overtake the Caravan, and determine to accompany it for a while............................Page 128

CHAPTER IX.

A Retrospect.—Omanbondè a Sheet of Water.—Rhinoceroses, Hippopotami, and other large Game in Abundance. —A beautiful Landscape.—Elephants numerous.—Fatigues and Dangers of Elephant-hunting.—Hints to Elephant-hunters.—Extreme Thirst.—Extreme Exhaustion.—A Man killed by a Rhinoceros.—A Creeping Stalk of a Rhinoceros. —Attack of a Rhinoceros.—An adventurous Chase.—Discovery of the Man killed.—Accidental Death.—Damara Grave, and Rites of Sepulture.—The Feast after the Funeral.—Lions attack a crippled Rhinoceros........... 145

CHAPTER X.

A Troop of Lions.—A Watch by Night.—Wild Animals at a Vley.—A Duel between a Lion and Lion-hunter.—Dogs and Damaras.—An exciting hunting Scene.—One hundred Damaras in the Field.—Another wounded Lion.—Dinner on Beefsteak *au Lion* and Hump *de Rhinocéros*.—Lion's Flesh very palatable.—The Ovambo Caravan still in the Neighborhood.—The Feeding-time of the Ovambos after a

Day's successful Sport.—A disgusting Spectacle.—Change of Route.—A Bevy of black Damsels.—Advice about Marriage.—A Road practicable for the Wagon.—News from Europe.—How I dispose of my Ivory.—A Collection of Insects and Birds.—Swifts and Swallows.—Tremendous Storms of Thunder and Lightning.—The peculiar Beauty of the Sunsets.................................Page 160

CHAPTER XI.

The Damara Caravan forbidden by Chipanga, the successor of Nangoro, to enter Ondonga.—The Ovambo's superstitious Dread of Fire-arms.—The Party belonging to the Caravan steal the Cattle and Property of the Ovambo.—A Descent made upon the Ovambuengo by the Makololo.—A Guide with a Harem of Wives.—A Battle between two Bushmen Werfts.—Dr. Livingstone's Opinion that Bushmen never quarrel about Women.—A Native Woman wounded by poisoned Arrows.—I endeavor to capture the Offenders.—Two of their Party made Prisoners.—Not guilty.—Effect their Escape 175

CHAPTER XII.

The Rate of Absorption and Evaporation of Moisture in the dry Season.—The Return of the Party sent to Otjimbingué.—Preparations for a fresh Start.—We make for the Omuramba U'Ovambo.—Reasons for this Choice.—Bid Farewell to Omanbondè.—Description of my Suite.—The Guide ignorant of the Route.—A Passage through a Forest.—The Guide allowed to depart.—Difficulty of finding Water.—Indications of Bushmen Villages.—A small Well discovered.—Bushmen make their Appearance.—Their contradictory Descriptions of the Omuramba, supposed by Travelers to be a Branch of the Cunenè 182

CHAPTER XIII.

Comparatively good Road.—Pretty Scenery.—Fruit and Forest Trees.—A sandy Soil.—Thorn Jungles.—Scarcity of Water.—Vleys dried up.—The Heat intense.—Guides declare there is no Possibility of proceeding farther.—Delight on finding Water.—An Accident happens to the Wagon.—The Axle-tree renewed six Times.—The Acacia Giraffe and the White Ant.—Monotony of Toil, Anxiety, and Hardship .... Page 189

CHAPTER XIV.

Gadflies.—Another Elephant Hunt: interrupted by a Storm of Rain.—A very jeopardous Position.—An arduous Chase.—An Elephant charges his Pursuer.—Wounded severely.—Brought down after a long Hunt.—Another Elephant bagged.—Plenty of Provision.—The Natives flock together to devour the Carcasses.—Jerking and Drying.—Slow Progress.—The Number of Bushes and Trees cut down to clear a Passage.—One hundred and seventy Bushes felled every three hundred Yards.—The incredible amount of Labor to advance one Mile.—Description of the Country.—Variation of the Compass.—Some Alteration in my Course 196

CHAPTER XV.

All Hope of finding the Omuramba described by Travelers renounced.—Doubts about its being a Branch of the Cunenè.—The River pointed out by the Bushmen quite distinct from the Cunenè.—A sandy Country, a continuous Forest.—An unexpected Visit from a Bushman, an old Acquaintance of Messrs. Green and Hahn.—He consents to be our Guide for some Distance.—I promise to kill an Elephant for him and his People.—Encampment by a fine Vley of Water.—A benevolent Bushman.—An Elephant struck dead by Lightning.—Fruit-trees and Forest-trees.—Their Description.—A Forest-tree of huge Dimensions and spreading Foliage.—Another Elephant-hunt.—Elephants in Herds as numerous as Cattle, like a large Army.—Their shrill Trumpetings at Night.. 204

CHAPTER XVI.

The Difficulty of finding Way and Water increased.—Guides decamp.—Conflicting Opinions about the Road to the River.—I leave the Wagon to explore the Country.—The Capture of a whole Werft of Bushmen.—Two of them compelled to be Guides.—Tied together as Prisoners.—A Native Woman captured.—A Werft of twenty or thirty Huts.—Conversation with the Chief of the Hamlet.—Reach Ombongo.—A periodical Water-course.—Great Anxiety as I approach the Water, Bushmen have often so contradictorily described.—Was it merely a Valley periodically filled with Water, or a mighty River?—Our Guides hide their Arrows in the Trees from fear of Robbery by the Ovaquangari.—I perceive on the far-away Horizon a distinct dark blue Line.—I recognize at once a great River.—This River called by the Natives the OKAVANGO.—Reflections, Description, Conjectures...P. 214

CHAPTER XVII.

The Terror of the Ovaquangari on our Approach.—The Natives cross the River in several Canoes, armed to the Teeth.—Ordered to lay aside their Weapons and talk peaceably.—The Difficulty of communicating with them in the Ovambo Language.—They are made to understand the Object of our Visit.—The Chief sends us Food.—I make known my Intention to visit the paramount Chief, Chikongo by name.—Dispatch a Messenger to him.—He intimates a Wish to see me.—A suitable Conveyance refused.—Procured at last by threatening to leave the Country.—A Sail on the Okavango.—The Boatman a great Blackguard.—Shows the white Man as a wild Beast to crowds of Natives.—The Women exceedingly ugly.—The River described.—Hippopotami and Alligators.—Picturesque Landscape.—Modes of catching Fish.—Bivouac under a Tree, with the Wind for a Bedfellow.—Description of a Werft.—All the Chiefs of the Nation assemble to meet me.—Portrait of Chikongo.—

His Hospitality.—The Makololo.—Dr. Livingstone's Attempts to civilize this People unsuccessful.......Page 222

CHAPTER XVIII.

The Mambari.—Traders from the Confines of the Kingdom of Benguela.—Visit the Ovaquangari every Year.—Peddler Expeditions as far as Libèbè.—Much valuable Information, especially respecting the North and its Natives, to be derived from these Traders.—They convey a Letter for me to the Governor of Benguela.—They also forward one to the R. G. S. of London.—I think of returning to my Men left with the Wagon.—Chikongo objects to this Proposal, as his People have not yet "had time to stare at me."—The Savages quite on a Par, in Point of Intelligence, with the Ovambos.—Agricultural Pursuits.—Trades of the Ovaquangari.—Various Tribes to the Northeast of this People.—No permanently settled Nations.—Only Bushmen.—Rejoin my Wagon.—Tremendous Penalty for my successful Enterprise.—Attacked by a malignant Fever.—Five of my Men prostrated by the same Disease.—Anticipate a like Fate for the Remainder of my Party.—I hesitate about incurring the Responsibility of persisting in my Enterprise.—Determine, on Reflection, to do so........................ 236

CHAPTER XIX.

A Leopard hunted by Dogs.—An extraordinary Leap.—Leopards and Panthers.—Their stealthy, fawning Mode of attacking their Prey.—The Chetah.—An Antelope Hunt.—Among the Elephants again.—A Presentiment and a Prophecy.—An exciting Chase.—A Night Hunt.—A pastoral Picture of Elephants enjoying themselves.—A dangerous Position.—A Mistake.—Two Elephants shot instead of one.—A glorious Day's Sport.—Three Elephants bagged.—A new Attack of Fever............................. 243

CHAPTER XX.

On the Okavango again.—The Numbers on our Sick-list increase.—Partial Recoveries and Relapses.—The numerous Species of Fish in the River all edible, and some delicious.—Fishing.—Singular Contrivances for catching Fish.—Alligators and Hippopotami, Otters.—My original Project of proceeding northward.—Generosity of Chikongo.—Pereira and Mortar take the Fever.—Obliged to abandon my long-cherished Scheme.—A precipitate Retreat.—The Okavango perfectly unknown to Europeans.—An Excursion toward its Source recommended.—The native Portuguese not aware of the River's Existence.—The Unhealthiness of the Climate confined probably to the Spring Season.—Malaria from the Lagoons . . . . Page 255

CHAPTER XXI.

Departure from the Okavango.—Very slow Progress.—The Country retraced devoid of natural Springs.—No Water to be procured for Cattle on our Retreat.—Obliged to halt till the rainy Season set in.—A Return to Ombongo in prospect.—Live-stock getting very low.—Too ill for Elephant-hunting.—Pereira recovers.—He is dispatched with an Attendant or two to Otjimbingué, to inform Friends of my awkward Position, and to procure Provisions.—Visit from Bushmen sent by a Party of the Ovambo encamped about two Days' Journey from us.—Suspicions of the Intentions of this Party.—Spies in the Camp.—Dangers threaten.—The Camp fortified.—Description of fortified Camp in the Desert. 262

CHAPTER XXII.

Tidings of Pereira.—He falls in with a suspicious-looking Party of Ovambo.—The Country all around on Fire.—Suspect the Ovambo wish to burn me out.—Visit from Chikongo, an Ovambo Chief, Brother of the Chief of the same Name before mentioned.—The whole Neighborhood again in a Blaze within a hundred Yards of the Camp.—Interview with Chikongo, escorted by sixty Attendants fully armed.—The Chief's Professions most friendly.—On my Guard against Treachery.—Showed him I had nothing to fear from him, but he had much to fear from me.—Chikongo's Invitation.—Presents interchanged.—My Illness continues.—Study of Natural History.—A Collection of Birds and Insects.—Partridges. — Antelopes. —Another Elephant shot. — Anticipation of a Feast.................................. Page 270

CHAPTER XXIII.

Anxiety about Pereira.—His safe Return.—Rejoicings.—He brings Intelligence that Mr. Frederick Green is on his Way to join me.—The extreme Precariousness of my Situation.—Native Politics.—A "Commando" with a numerous Escort dispatched from Ondonga to destroy me.—This fearful Intelligence brings Mr. Green to my Rescue.—An heroic Act of Friendship.—The Expedition sent against me arrives.—The murderous Project abandoned.—The Dangers escaped by Pereira.—Green's Difficulties in advancing.—I go to meet him.—A rather arduous Enterprise.—The joyful Meeting.—Prospects not much mended by it.—Resolved, after much Hesitation on my Part, to proceed to Mr. Green's Encampment on the Omuramba.—Singular Hardships and Fatigues of this Journey.—Scarcity of Water.—Thirst.—Suffering from excessive Heat........................ 280

CHAPTER XXIV.

Homeward Course pursued.—The Omuramba Water-course.—Whence, being sometimes dry, does it derive its frequent Flood of Water?—The rainy Season.—Sufferings from Wetness and Wind.—A Bushman devoured by a Lion Man-eater.—A Lion Hunt.—A marvelous Shot in the Dark.—A Duel in the Desert.—A Lion killed.—A perilous Position.—A wonderful Escape.—A Lion's Grief for the Loss of his Friend.—The History of two Lions, the Terror of the District.—Three Men carried off in the Night from a Village by the Man-eaters.—A hundred human Beings fall a Prey to them.—The Country thereabouts abandoned by human Beings..Page 289

CHAPTER XXV.

More Lion Adventures.—A Cow carried off.—An Ambush, baited by a Goat, laid for the Thief.—A Lion Hunt.—Beating up the Country.—Retreat of the Enemy in a Brake.—Courage of a Dog.—The Animal driven out of the Brake by setting it on fire.—Cowardice of most of the Party in running away as soon as the Lion appears.—The Lion attacks his Assailant.—A Shot takes no Effect.—Bodily Encounter with the Lion.—He receives a Shot in the Shoulder while struggling with his human Antagonist, who escapes.—Is precipitated to the Ground by an Accident.—Tussle with the Lion while on the Ground.—Terribly mutilated.—The Lion shot by D—— while mangling his Victim.—The Narrator's Account confirmed by his runaway Party...... 304

CHAPTER XXVI.

Introduction. — Saldanha Bay. — St. Helen's Bay. — The Berg River.—Lambert's Cove.—Cape Donkin and Donkin's Bay. —The Oliphant River.—Mitchell's Bay.—Hondeklipp Bay. —The Koussie River.—Cape Voltas.—Homewood and Peacock Harbors.—Alexander Bay.—The Orange River: Description, Scenery, precious Stones; central Course unknown. —Boundary of British Dominions.—Angras Juntas.—Possession Island.—Elizabeth Bay.—Angra Pequena.—Pedestal Point.—Robert Harbor.—Ichaboe.—Hottentot Bay.—Rae's Bay. — Spencer's Bay. — Mercury Island. — Hollam's Bird Isle.—Sandwich Harbor...................... 318

CHAPTER XXVII.

The Swakop River.—Half-moon Bay.—The Omaruru River. —Cape Cross.—The wrecked Vessel.—Mount Messum.—

B

Berg Damaras.—Hogden's Harbor.—Cock's Comb and Sugar Loaf.—Supposed permanent Stream.—Fort Rock Point.—Cape Frio.—The Cunenè, or Nourse River.—Great Fish Bay.—Formation and Disappearance of Bays, etc.—Excursion inland from Great Fish Bay.—The Nourse River again.—Bembarougi.—Port Alexander.—The River Flamingos.—The Natives.—Fossil Shells.—Summary.—Concluding Remarks: Rivers, Harbors, Islands, etc.; Winds, Temperature, Rollers; Scarcity of Rain.................Page 341

CHAPTER XXVIII.

A Contrast.—Discouragement with respect to Settlement in one Part of Africa counterbalanced by the Encouragement it meets with at 250 miles from Table Bay.—Establishment on the River Knysna.—Dangerous Entrance to the Harbor.—A tremendous Surf.—Perils incurred in getting into safe Water.—Description.—Fine Scenery.—A fatal Act of Daring.—A noble and diversified Prospect.—Delicious Climate.—Description of Landscape.—Salt Marshes.—Government Dock-yard.—A Night Scene.—European Visitors.—An English Gentleman-Farmer.—Plattenburg's Bay.—Forest Scenery.—Birds of gorgeous Plumage not Vocalists.—General Prospects of the Settlement.................. 373

CHAPTER XXIX.

The Guano Trade.—When Guano was first used in Agriculture.—Its Discovery in Africa.—The Island of Ichaboe: its Anchorage; Rollers.—The Treasures of Ichaboe made known by Mr. Livingstone.—First Attempt to reach the Island a Failure; a second succeeds.—Vessels arrive in Numbers.—Immense Deposits of Guano.—The Penguin.—The Penguin's Lament.—Stages for loading Vessels.—The "Flying Railway."—Committee of Safety.—Guano Pits.—Squabbles among the Captains and others.—The Guano Fever versified.—The Island is properly divided.—Ichaboe presents an animated Scene.—Bad Doings on the Island.—Sir J. Marshall.—Guano Pits exhausted.—Concluding Remarks. 388

ILLUSTRATIONS.

1. THE AFRICAN ELEPHANT.................*Frontispiece.*
2. PORTRAIT OF THE AUTHOR (ENGRAVED ON STEEL FROM A PHOTOGRAPH).............*Vignette.*
3. FIRST PROGRESS ....*To face page* 35
4. CROSSING A BURNING SAVANNA .... " " 75
5. A WELL-STOCKED SHOOTING-GROUND ... " " 96
6. A RIGHT ROYAL FRONT............. " " 116
7. FURIOUS CHARGE OF A PATERFAMILIAS " " 127
8. CHASE OF THE WILD BOAR.......... " " 143
9. DISAPPOINTED LIONS .... " " 159
10. DEATH OF A LION .... " " 165
11. PURSUIT OF AN ELEPHANT........... " " 209
12. THE WHITE MAN A SHOW........... " " 229
13. THE LEOPARD AND HIS PREY .... " " 247
14. A HORRIBLE SURPRISE.............. " " 299
15. DEATH-GRAPPLE WITH A LION .... " " 317
16. GROUP OF NATIVES NEAR GREAT FISH BAY............................... " " 358
17. ISLAND OF ICHABOE .... " " 399
    MAP OF SOUTHERN AFRICA........... " " xx.

NOTE TO THE AMERICAN EDITION.

The English edition of the Okavango River contains no Map or Table of Distances. The American Publishers have endeavored to supply this deficiency by inserting the accompanying map, originally prepared for Livingstone's Travels. The principal points ascertained by Mr. Andersson having been added, this is the best accessible map of Southern Africa.

Mr. Andersson furnishes few dates or distances. The following summary will enable the reader to follow him on his journeys toward the Okavango.

He left Otjimbingué (about lat. 22° S., long. 15° W.) March 22, 1858, reaching the Omaruru River in a fortnight; thence set off through the Kaoko, by way of Okoa, which place was reached early in May. After trying different routes for three weeks, he was compelled to turn back by the want of water, reaching Okoa May 25, and the Omaruru July 1. Here he remained till the 20th; then set off to the northeast, by way of the Omuramba, having sent his wagon to Otjimbingué to be repaired. He remained on the Omuramba till August 29, when, the wagon having returned, he set out northward, reaching Lake Omanbondé September 16. He remained in the region of the lake till January, 1859, when he started for a river which the Ovambo call the Mukuru-Mukovanga.

Reaching it, he found that instead of running west to the sea, it flowed east, directly into the heart of the continent. The natives call this river the OKAVANGO. He does not give the date of his reaching the river, but it must have been in March, 1859, a year after he started on his journey. He remained in the neighborhood of the river nearly three months, but was unable to make any extensive explorations, on account of the sickness of himself and his men. He started homeward June 6, 1859, but, it being the dry season, was detained for months in the country of the hostile Ovambo. Having dispatched a messenger setting forth his peril, his former traveling companion, Mr. Green, set out for his relief, and reached him toward the end of November. They arrived at the missionary stations in the spring of 1860, the journey to and from the Okavango thus occupying two years.

THE OKAVANGO RIVER.

CHAPTER I.

Project of an Expedition into the Interior with Mr. Green.—Mr. Green's Expedition to Libèbè.—Professor Wahlberg killed by an Elephant.—Another Expedition of Mr. Green in search of the River Cunenè.—Two Rhenish Missionaries, Messrs. Hahn and Rath, join Mr. Green.—Visit to the Ovambo.—Treachery of King Nangoro.—The exploring Party attacked by his Orders by a large Body of Natives.—The Victory of the Europeans.—Six hundred fighting Men beaten by thirteen.—The accidental Discovery of a Fresh-water Lake called Onondova.—The farther Prosecution of the Expedition renounced.—I determine on resuming it in Person.—Difficulties to be overcome.—Traveling Equipment and Suite.—Particular Objects of the Expedition.—Motives for choosing my Route through Western Damara Land.

TOWARD the end of 1856 I found myself once more back at the Cape, having, in the interim between this period and my last exploring expedition, been on a visit to Europe, partly with a view to see my relations, friends, and acquaintances, and partly in order to publish my travels ("Lake Ngami"). I had no fixed plan for the future; but, previous to my departure from the Cape, I had promised a friend—Mr. Frederick Green—to join him on an exploring and hunting tour into the distant interior. Mr. Green, who had in the mean time undertaken an expedition to some extent on his own account, had not yet returned to the Cape on my arrival at that place, nor could I hear of his movements or exact whereabouts. This left me rather in a fix. For two months I waited patiently, but with no better result. At the end of this period I was offered the management of certain mines on the borders of Great Namaqua and Damara Land, and as I could ill afford to idle away my time, Mr. Green's return seeming so uncertain, I accepted, after some little hesitation, the proffered post, which was one of considerable difficulty and responsibility. Scarcely was this arrangement concluded when my friend suddenly made his appearance at the Cape. On hearing of my new engagement he was naturally disappointed; the regret was mutual.

In company with a Mr. Wilson, Mr. Green had, on the expedition above alluded to, penetrated from the Lake regions to Libèbè, up to that time an almost *terra incognita*. They had accomplished this exploration partly by water and partly by land, but the undertaking encountered the most serious obstacles and terrible hardships. Mr. Green has published a short account of it in the Cape "Eastern Province Magazine," for which narrative I beg to refer the curious to the June and July numbers of that periodical for 1857.

Subsequently Mr. Green joined the late esteemed and much lamented Professor Wahlberg in an excursion to the eastward of Lake Ngami, chiefly with a view to hunting. This proved a most disastrous expedition, for it ended in the death of the professor, who was killed by an enraged and wounded elephant.

Nothing daunted, however, by his friend's frightful fate, or by his own sufferings and hardships, Mr. Green determined once more to take the field, this time in a direction totally different to his former wanderings, viz., in search of the River Cunenè, a point that Mr. Galton and myself had failed in reaching in the year 1850.

Our arrangements were soon completed, and in the course of a week or so we found ourselves on our way to Walwich Bay; I for the purpose of undertaking the management of the mines above mentioned, and Mr. Green to prosecute his journey into the interior. This journey had a threefold object—exploring, hunting, and bartering. It was, however, not until some months had elapsed after our arrival at Walwich Bay that Mr. Green was able to take, in the month of April, 1857, his final departure. The route he intended to pursue was somewhat doubtful; but for a certain distance he purposed following the course of the Omuramba Ua' Matako, taking *en route* Otjimbingué, Barmen, Schmelens Hope, etc.

At this period two Rhenish missionaries—the

Rev. Messrs. Hahn and Rath, residing respectively at Barmen and Otjimbingué—also proposed visiting the Ovambo, whence, if practicable, to penetrate to the Cunenè. They left some weeks after Mr. Green had passed their stations, but, owing to various delays, overtook my friend (after about a month's journeying) at a fountain called Otjituo, situated on a branch of the Omuramba Ua' Matako. Previous to their arrival here Mr. Green had made a short exploring tour to the eastward, but, not finding a sufficiency of water, he deemed the road in that direction impracticable for attaining his object. In consequence of this failure, it was agreed that they should all form one party, and first visit the Ovambo, with the intention of proceeding thence on to the Cunenè.

To shorten a long story, I will merely say that the travelers arrived in safety in the Ovambo country, and were at first exceedingly well received by King Nangoro. This good reception, however, turned out at last to be but treacherous; for, as the party were one morning about to retrace their steps from Ondonga, they were suddenly attacked by his orders. Fortunately they were not altogether unprepared, having received frequent hints of the kind intentions of their *friends*, as they called themselves. By a most determined and judicious resistance, they not only secured their own safety, but completely defeated the Ovambo, with the loss of but one native attendant, who was stabbed by the side of Mr. Hahn's wagon previous to the commencement of the affray. The Ovambo, on the other hand, had many killed and wounded. Among the former was one of Nangoro's sons. Indeed, the king himself met his death on this memorable occasion; for, on hearing the repeated discharges of fire-arms, he became so terrified that his bowels burst asunder, and he fell down dead on the spot. It was supposed, at the lowest calculation, that at one time the assailants of the English party must have amounted to six hundred fighting men, all well armed with kieries, assegais, bows and arrows, while the travelers could only muster *thirteen* men capable of bearing arms, some of whom, moreover, had other duties to attend to, such as driving wagons, cattle, etc. In short, their victory was most wonderful, and deserves to be chronicled among heroic deeds. Shortly after I heard of it I sent an account of the event to the Cape "Monthly Magazine," to which I beg to refer the readers, should they feel interested in its details.

After such a tremendous lesson, my friends, as may be well imagined, gave up all farther hopes of reaching the Cunenè, and forthwith retraced their steps to their respective homes, Mr. Green lingering somewhat behind his fellow-travelers.

I have omitted to mention one interesting fact connected with this expedition, and which, in some measure, redeems the credit of the undertaking. This was the discovery of a fresh-water lake, called

Onondova, which the explorers actually stumbled upon; for, though they had people with them perfectly well acquainted with the country, they were not aware of its existence until they actually and *accidentally caught sight of the water.* This lake, as far as it is possible to judge either from the west or east—and I have been within a couple of days' journey of it—is situated in about lat. 21°, and long. 19°. The travelers did not go round it, they merely saw it at its eastern extremity; but water appeared as far as the eye could reach all round, and they estimated its circumference at from twenty-five to thirty English miles. Mr. Galton and myself, in the year 1850, actually passed within one day's march of this superb inland sea without —such is the difficulty of obtaining information from the natives—having the slightest suspicion of its existence.

By the time Mr. Green had returned to Otjimbingué my engagement with the Walwich Bay Mining Company had nearly expired, and as it had given but little satisfaction to either party, we were neither of us willing to renew it.

On this expiration of my contract it was my original intention to have returned forthwith to the Cape, but I felt *so* disappointed at my friend's failure in not reaching the Cunené (to which enterprise, besides, I had devoted considerable pecuniary assistance) that, after some little hesitation, I determined to solve, if possible, the difficult problem in person. There was, however, considerable difficulty in realizing my plan without first visiting the Cape, for I was totally destitute of the necessary outfit, even down to my personal wearing apparel. On the other hand, a journey to the Cape would in all probability have involved so much loss of time that I might thereby have run the risk of losing the *season*, *i. e.*, a whole year, a consideration of no small importance to a poor fellow like myself. Yet I did not remain long undecided. After carefully considering all the *pros* and *cons*, I determined to proceed on the journey without delay; and as there is always a way where there is a will, I succeeded, by dint of patience and perseverance, in collecting a fair assortment of the most needful and important prerequisites, begging or buying some article of clothing here, borrowing a gun there, and so on, till, after five weeks of incessant application, working, so to speak, night and day, I was ready to take my departure. But here let me pause for a moment, that I may return my sincere thanks to the kind friends who aided me in my equipment. I will not mention individual names, since each and all of those to whom I allude vied with each other in rendering assistance to the solitary traveler. *Without their cordial co-operation my plan must have failed.*

Now for a few words before I proceed with my narrative about my traveling establishment. My servants were as follows: one cook, acting as confidential servant; one general attendant, who also superintended my native "personnel;" one wagon-driver, one leader, one guide, two herds, two interpreters, and one or two lads whose duty consisted in making themselves generally useful—that is, eleven men *in toto;* no great force, certainly, to enter upon the exploration of a wild and unknown region. Of all this little band of followers, John Mortar and John Pereira, the first two on my list, were the only persons on whom, in a case of emergency, I could rely. Those who have perused "Tropical South Africa" and "Lake Ngami" will at once recognize in the first of these names Mr. Galton's cook, who, through a difficult and harassing expedition, proved himself so faithful and trustworthy. Mortar had, when he entered mine, just left Mr. Green's service, where he had earned for himself a similarly good character. I considered myself most fortunate in securing so tried and valuable a servant. It will be remembered that this man was a native of Madeira, and consequently well acquainted with the Portuguese language. John Pereira was of Malabar descent. He had received a most liberal, and, for his station in life, unusual education. He wrote a fair hand, spoke and wrote English, Dutch, and Portuguese fluently, understood Chinese and several Hindostanee dialects, and could translate Latin, which is more than I can do myself.

The rest of my servants being all native attendants, and distinguished for no remarkable quality (except Kamapjie and Tom, both capital "trackers" and interpreters), I pass them over in silence. I have only to add, that besides several other barbarous tongues, my men spoke Damara, Hottentot, Sichuana, and Portuguese, languages most likely to come into requisition.

The remainder of my establishment consisted of one wagon, thirty first-rate trek oxen, five draught and carriage oxen, eleven young oxen, four donkeys, one old horse, seventy sheep and goats, chiefly for slaughter, and, lastly, but not the least important, about a dozen dogs of a somewhat mongrel description, though good enough as watch-dogs, for which service they were principally required.

The chief object of the expedition was, as already stated, to penetrate to the Cunenè; and farther, supposing a safe arrival on the banks of that river, to explore it either toward its source or toward its embouchure, according to the point where I might happen to strike it. Moreover, if time and means admitted, I intended thence to make an excursion to some Portuguese settlement on the west coast, such as Mossamedos, Benguela, etc.

If I succeeded in accomplishing these purposes the following results would be obtained, viz.: the great blanks in the maps between Damara and Ovambo Land, and in Dr. Livingstone's remarkable journey from the banks of Seshcke to St. Paul de Loanda, would be filled up, while vast, and probably rich regions would be opened to the influence of commerce and civilization.

It was only a few days previous to my departure from Otjimbingué that I could make up my mind as to what route to select in order to reach the Cunené River. I had the choice of two: either through the Kaoko (Western Damara Land), or *viâ* Omuramba Ua' Matako, the track pursued for a considerable distance by Mr. Green. The first of these routes was unquestionably the most direct, but then the country to be traversed was entirely unknown. Moreover, should I choose it, I should have to pass through tribes akin to the Ovambo—a by no means agreeable prospect, since it was impossible to know in what mood these people might be found, or, rather, what influence the disastrous encounter of the Ovambo a few months before, already alluded to, might have had upon them. The Omuramba Ua' Matako, on the other hand, though a more circuitous route, afforded for a long distance a safe passage, yielding during two thirds of the year an abundant supply of water and game—considerations of the most vital importance. Besides, having reached Mr. Green's farthest easterly point, I should, in all probability, not have above a fortnight's journey to the Cunené, or at least some river connected with it. I was, therefore, strongly urged to select this route. We generally, however, prefer our own counsel to that of disinterested friends, so I at last determined on striking through Western Damara Land.

I had some strong reasons for adopting this course. I had been given to understand that the Kaoko abounded in elephants and other large game, and that of water there was there no positive dearth. I reasoned in this way: it is now the very best part of the rainy season, consequently drought can not prove a hinderance; a couple of months' traveling or less will in all probability bring me to the borders of the different Ovambo territories, and if I then find the country impracticable in that direction, I shall still have sufficient time to try my luck in another quarter before the dry season sets in. On the other hand, if I succeed in getting through in safety (after having ascended the Cunenè toward its source), the Omuramba Ua' Matako will afford a convenient and safe route by which a weary traveler may retrace his steps to Damara Land. I was sadly disappointed in all my anticipations, as the sequel will show.

CHAPTER II.

Departure.—Leave-taking.—Slow Progress.—Live-stock.—Omaruru River.—Scenery.—Cutting a Way through the Bush.—Escape and Capture of my Horse.—A serious Accident.—A Forest of Trees *without Thorns.*—A delightful Surprise.—The Damara Parent-tree.—Tracks of Elephants.—Magnificent Range of Hills.—Periodical Water-course.—A Mountain Gorge.—Difficulty of finding a Route.—The Passage for the Wagon impracticable.—The Wagon smashed to Pieces.—Narrow Escape of the Oxen-driver.—Wagon repaired and reladen.—Route in a new Direction.—Encampment.—Country densely bushed.

On the 22d of March I left Otjimbingué, accompanied by the good wishes of an assemblage of numerous friends and acquaintances. There was much shaking of hands, many a "God speed you," many a "God bless you" uttered. The women wiped their eyes—

"The April's in her eyes;
. . . .
Her tongue will not obey her heart, nor can
Her heart inform her tongue. . . . ."

The children cried because ma did so; the little urchins shouted, and the men greeted me with tremendous and repeated volleys of fire-arms; in short, it was a complete "scene;" my departure occasioned as much noise and bustle as a visit from the Queen of England to this country would have done.

FIRST PROGRESS.

Taking leave of a place which has been one's abode for some time, though neither one's home, nor associated with any particular or fond recollection, is always a sad and solemn incident in life. In the present instance I felt the woman more than once rise to my eyes, and why not? How was I to know that this was not my last farewell? my last link of connection with a people capable of sympathizing with, and caring for the stranger? while an unknown, inhospitable region of indefinite extent lay before me, inhabited by savage beasts and still more savage men.

At first our progress was exceedingly slow, being sometimes delayed for days by deluging rains. The soil became by these torrents in places so soft and yielding that the wheels of our wagon frequently sank into it above their naves, whence they could only be extricated by immense exertions, and, what was worse, at the cost of some important part of the vehicle. Indeed, I had some serious wheelwright work to perform. The wagon, being very heavily laden, yielded but slowly to our efforts. The draught oxen, too, though of the very best description, sometimes got discouraged by the excessive badness of the country. After the lapse of nearly a fortnight, however, I found myself on the banks of the Omaruru River, or about seventy English miles, as the crow flies, from my starting-point.

Up to this period nothing worth recording had

occurred, if I except an accident to myself. I was stalking some giraffes, and, while pushing a heavy elephant rifle before me, something caught the trigger and caused the piece to explode. Unfortunately, the full force of its recoil struck the inside of my naked right arm near the elbow, and occasioned a severe jagged wound.

Of game, contrary to my expectation, we had seen little or nothing, and I began to have the most serious forebodings for the future. A person not acquainted with the voracity of native attendants can scarcely understand why I should so early have felt uncomfortable on this head, as I have mentioned that I started with about seventy sheep and goats; but this would scarcely afford provision for a hundred days to my party, and, for aught we knew, the expedition might extend over a period of twelve, eighteen, or even twenty-four months. The reader will now perhaps better understand my anxiety.

The Omaruru River is the second in size and importance of the great arteries which intersect Damara Land. It drains a considerable extent of country, and is nearly as large as the Swakop, but inferior to that stream in the quality of its water, especially for pasturage purposes. Where I crossed it its bed is nearly a quarter of a mile broad, and its banks are studded with fine groups and groves of various acacias and mimosas, plants indigenous to the soil. The river commands, moreover, at this point, some of the finest hill-scenery in Damara Land. Its periodical flow had just ceased, but little rills were seen still meandering here and there through its extensive channel. As the Omaruru approaches the sea, its aspect, however, greatly changes for the worse. At about this time on the preceding year I had occasion to journey up its course as far as two days' distance from its embouchure, and a more desolate and sterile expanse than the country presented can scarcely be conceived. The river had forced a passage through low broken ranges of primary rock of a very dark color, with occasional streaks and dikes of white quartz and granite. This greatly increased the general hideousness of the scene, while outside these rocky defiles immense barren flats extended as far as the eye could reach.

I find the following note in my journal descriptive of this tract: "When a heavy sea-fog rests on these uncouth and rugged surfaces—and it does so very often—a place fitter to represent the infernal regions could scarcely, in searching the world round, be found. A shudder, amounting almost to fear, came over me when its frightful desolation first suddenly broke upon my view. "Death," I exclaimed, "would be preferable to banishment to such a country."

After a few days' stay on the Omaruru River we took our departure again for the north. The rains had now ceased to annoy us, or, at least, fell only in such limited quantities as not to impede our progress. But this was only changing one evil for another, for harassing thorn jungles at present beset us on every side. Hitherto we had, by chopping away an occasional bush or two, managed to get through comfortably enough, but now the country had become densely wooded, and continued to be so for a very considerable distance. Indeed, for *upward of one hundred miles we had literally to cut our way step by step;* it was not mere bushes either that we had to clear away, but trees also, varying from a few inches to as much as two feet in diameter. Pick and crowbar [for fortunately I had taken the precaution to be pretty well provided with roadmaking implements] were, besides, frequently put into requisition—in short, it was chop, pick, and heave the livelong day, from sunrise to sunset. It was most severe and harassing work. The wagon sail, which was made of the best ship's canvas, was torn to shreds—a good criterion of the terrible uncouthness of the country. For fear of being without a roof altogether, we were obliged to patch up, as we went along, the ragged sail with the skins of the slaughtered sheep and goats.

A few days after leaving the Omaruru River an accident occurred that put me to some inconvenience. I was riding leisurely along in advance of the wagon, hoping to fall in with some game, when, while passing through a thick brake, I espied a giraffe. I at once gave the spurs to my steed, but the quarry was almost immediately lost to view. Pulling up at the nearest tree, I sprang to the ground, leaving the horse standing with the reins on his neck, as I had often left him before. I then began climbing the tree, that I might have a good roundabout view; but, when half way up, to my surprise and extreme annoyance, I saw the horse coolly turn on his heels and canter off. I could not help exclaiming to myself, "A fig for my gun now!" for, as ill luck would have it, a valuable double-barreled smooth-bore Westly Richard was in the gun-bag on the horse's back. It was, in fact, the only gun (barring a large elephant rifle) that I could depend upon; the mischief therefore done was very great. Once before the horse had made off, but then fortunately without any thing but his saddle. However, taking for granted that the brute would make for the nearest water, which we had only just left, I put the best face I could on the matter, and forthwith rejoined the wagon, whence I dispatched several men in pursuit of the fugitive, the wagon in the mean time proceeding slowly on its way. It was not until the third day that the runaway was secured, when his capture was purely accidental. He had evidently meant to return to Otjimbingué, but had been met and attacked by a troop of hyenas, which he had, it appeared, after a desperate struggle, succeeded in beating off. In the scuffle the saddle had got under his belly; one of his fore legs, too, had got afterward entangled in the girths, and this had fortunately brought him to a stand-still. The gun was recovered, but broken short off in the stock, and otherwise most seriously injured. With considerable difficulty I succeeded in repairing the damage, but never quite to my satisfaction.

"Misfortune," says the adage, "never comes alone," and it was strikingly verified in my case; for, on the very day after the mishap just alluded to had occurred, another accident of even a more serious character befell me.

We had encamped for the night in the neighborhood of a place called Ongarivanda, and I had proceeded on foot to the hamlet to ascertain whether water was to be had for the cattle. On my return, passing at a rapid pace over a large mass of rugged granite, my foot slipped, and I was precipitated headlong to the ground. When suddenly and severely hurt, a person is often all but insensible to the pain—at least such is my experience; but in this instance I felt at the instant an agonizing chilliness creep over my body as the warm blood kept oozing through my linen and trowsers. On recovering from the shock, I discovered that large pieces of flesh had been literally torn away from both my arms, while my left knee (the right was also slightly hurt) was most severely lacerated. The sun was just setting, and I was three or four miles from camp. I knew perfectly well that unless I got back while the wounds were still moist and warm,

I should have to bunk it out on the cold naked rock. With an effort, therefore, I rose and made the best I could of my way to the wagon, which I at last reached, somewhat after dark, the wound in my knee being by no means improved by the exertion.

This accident was a most unfortunate one: it was not the pain, though severe enough, that I dreaded, but the inconveniences attending it, for at no period of my travels were my strength and energy more needed. I could not afford to wait until my wounds were healed, nor had I the slightest idea of returning by the route in which we were now traveling. Consequently, it was of the utmost importance to me to make all my observations as I went along. There were astronomical observations to be made, bearings to be obtained, and a knowledge to be acquired of the physical features of the country, to say nothing of a host of duties of a secondary importance, such as providing for the larder, frequently repairing the wagon, and looking out for and making roads, etc., etc. These things *were*, however, all attended to.

Here I may as well mention that while, owing to the injuries I had received, I could not bear any tight-fitting garment, an old dressing-gown that I happened to have by me proved quite a treasure. At night it served as a blanket; in a raw, chilly morning it made a comfortable wrapper; while in cases of sickness it is to a traveler circumstanced as was a luxury and comfort which can not be too highly appreciated.

On the 14th of April, shortly after leaving the fountain of Otjongoro, we suddenly found ourselves traveling in a forest of tall, handsome trees, *without thorns!* I do not think that I was ever more agreeably surprised in my life—not even on my first entrance on the plains of Ondonga. The change was so unexpected—a wood of beautiful foliage is so rare in this wretched country—that for a moment I hesitated to trust my senses. Even the dull faces of my native attendants seemed for a few seconds to relax from their usual heavy unintelligent cast, and to express joy at the novel scene.

The forest we were now passing through was composed entirely of the tree called, in the Damara language, omutali. This tree has a dark olive-green leaf, in shape like a cloven heart, and emits, when rubbed between the fingers, an agreeable aromatic scent. On the under surface of its leaves are innumerable little insect-cells, of a sweet, sugary substance. These cells are said to be much relished by the natives, who collect them in great quantities as an article of food. The bark of the omutali is of a yellowish-white, while its heart is of a light mahogany color, and, as far as I can judge, capable of receiving a very high polish. This part of the tree is very closely grained, and so hard as sometimes to blunt, at a single stroke, the best-tempered tools. When a strain is applied to it longitudinally it appears exceedingly strong, but a sudden jerk or heavy transverse pressure will shiver it in an instant. Being straight and slender, I tried it for disselbooms, but, having demolished three of them in the course of a single day's journey, I gave the experiment up. For building purposes and household utensils it seems that this wood is well adapted; it is exposed, however, to the attacks of that destructive little insect, the white ant.

Another tree, the omomborombonga, *i. e.*, the Damara parent-tree, became also, in a little time, pretty abundant; it is only found along river courses, where it sometimes attains to most gigantic proportions. The omomborombonga is very rare in southern Damara Land, but is (as I have already mentioned in my former work) common enough to the eastward, on the direct route to Lake Ngami—a circumstance which led me to believe that the Damaras originally entered their present abodes from that quarter.

The following rude lines pretty well describe the qualities and peculiarities of this tree:

> My name is omborombonga;
> I flourish south of Ondonga
> (The country of agricultural Ovampo);
> My land of birth is that of the past'ral 'Herero
> (Better known as the race
> Called Cattle Damaras),
> Who claim me as their ma and pa,
> And sure I do not know what a';

To me this 's strange and odd,
For I yield nothing but wood.
But why blame people's fancy?—
Their parent I am and must be.

I am slow of growth,
Like gnarled oak,
Which I rival in girth,
And much outstrip in height,
Overtopping all forest trees.

My wood, hard, brittle, and cross,
Unfriendly to all edge tools,
Is light yellow at the outer rind,
But my stout heart is as red
As the sand of river-bed
By which I best thrive.

Centuries affect me but little—
The elements assail me unavailingly—
In short, my age is a page
In Time's Being.

The day after our agreeable surprise we arrived at a very large fountain called Ondjuona (Little Elephant). There I saw, for the first time on this journey, fresh footprints of elephants—another delightful surprise! Cripple as I was, I managed to drag myself to the water on the ensuing night for the purpose of lying in ambush for the mighty game; but I waited to no purpose. The night turned out cloudy, with a slight drizzling rain, and no elephants visited the place. I could not afford to delay, and so, on the next morning, we proceeded on our journey.

The road, hitherto bad enough, now became execrable. Thorn jungles, stones, ruts, ravines, water-courses, etc., seemed all to unite to hinder our farther progress. The labor, consequently, of finding and clearing a passage became extremely severe and harassing, and the risk, moreover, of having the wagon capsized or smashed gave additional anxiety. Fortunately, it was an exceedingly good vehicle. "God," said Pereira to me one day, "watches over that wagon;" and, truly, without speaking irreverently, there seemed something providential in its numerous escapes. However, it did not escape without injuries of various kinds, which I managed, nevertheless, generally to repair in a satisfactory manner.

On the 19th of April we found ourselves at the base of a magnificent limestone (chalk) range, forming part of an extensive mountain system. It presented the finest and most peculiar hill-scenery I have ever seen. For upward of fifty miles it formed a perfect table, with perpendicular side-cliffs many hundred feet high.* Toward its western extremity the range was broken into detached "tables," as beauteous and varied in aspect as can possibly be conceived. There were extensive fortifications, with gigantic buttresses exquisitely "worked" in their details; crumbling pieces of Gothic architecture, with

---

* Those of my readers who may have seen those remarkable formations in Sweden called *Halle* and *Hunneberg*, may form a tolerably correct notion of the range now alluded to, for they resemble it closely both in aspect and character.

all the delicate outlines, touches, characteristics, and finish of that beautiful art; splendid Italian villas, with terrace-like slopes, besprinkled with decaying sculptures, variegated marbles, huge sepulchral-like caverns, stuccoed grottoes, and many other singular and fantastic pageant forms.

At the foot of this interesting range a noble periodical water-course shaped its way, its banks clothed with a rich verdure of every hue, while here and there sprang up stately groups of acacias, interspersed with pleasant shrubs and sweet-smelling plants. Grass, also, of the rankest and most luxuriant description, fragrant with odors, reached, as they labored along with the huge and cumbersome vehicle behind them, the oxen's bellies. In the background, and, indeed, almost every where around us, the scene was bounded by extensive and lofty mountain ranges, the magnificent and almost faultless granite cone Okonyenya rising in a distant corner, in isolated grandeur, to a height of about 2200 feet above the neighboring country. Altogether it was a striking and imposing spectacle, wanting only a large body of permanent water to make its beauty perfect.

On the ensuing night we bivouacked on the river in question, just at a point where, creating a tremendous chasm, it had forced a passage through a projecting angle of the mountain. On one side this mountain or rock rose nearly perpendicularly to a height of at least 1000 feet, enveloping every object in darkness under its vast shadow, and giving to the place an indescribably cheerless and gloomy aspect. This picture, however, soon underwent a change; for the moon presently shone out in all its brilliancy, diffusing a glorious light throughout the whole gorge, the instant before so drear and dismal.

The evening was calm and balmy, and the atmosphere steamed with sweet aromatic scents rising from the grateful earth, just refreshed by heavy thunder-showers. The solemnity of the hour and of the scene, with all the circumstances of my position, plunged me into a reflective mood; and reflect I did more than was my wont, for I had ample cause to do so.

When yet at a distance I had carefully reconnoitred this range through the telescope, and when sufficiently near to scan it with the naked eye had anxiously pried into its every crevice, every cranny, every slight indentation, in the hope of finding some break or opening to get across the mountain—all in vain. To add to my perplexity, I could elicit no satisfactory information from my guide, who had only once, and then on foot, crossed the range before us. He was at all times singularly dull and incommunicative, except when women and cattle were spoken of, when he was talkative enough and quite at home. He had previously assured me that we should come to a place where it would take at least "ten days to find a passage for the wagon."

Now whether this was the spot or not I could not ascertain. Patience, consequently, was my only stay just at this time, though the morrow's sun would probably put an end to my doubts. It was, I own, then, with a heavy heart that I betook myself to rest that night. I had a vague presentiment of some difficulty or danger, but was determined, come in what shape it might, to brave it out.

The next day, at an early hour, we again moved forward. The guide led us at first down the river in a westerly direction, but, after a short ride, turned abruptly to the northward, at the same time entering another defile running at right angles to the course we had hitherto followed. This defile I had been unable to see before on account of intervening rocks. Well, up it we at first proceeded pretty comfortably; gradually, however, it became narrower; hundreds of little ravines intersected it in every direction, considerably retarding our progress, and finally bringing us to a dead stop. Retreat was impossible, unless we had taken the wagon entirely to pieces—a most inconvenient and disagreeable alternative. The guide declared again and again that there was not any other exit. In this extremity, we renewed the attempt at pushing forward, and so far, with great trouble and exertion, succeeded that we had only about one hundred and fifty yards to get over to reach a country apparently open and less beset with difficulties. Small, however, as this distance was, it offered a most formidable resistance. On our left was a ravine fifty feet deep, while the rock to our right rose high, and was almost perpendicularly steep. After a hurried survey, I determined, nevertheless, to risk the passage, and at once busied myself with axe, shovel, pick, and crowbar in removing sundry stones, trees, and boulders that impeded our progress. In proportion as we succeeded in clearing a way, the driver had orders to follow cautiously with the wagon.

Under these circumstances, having just turned a small angle of the rock, which hid me from my party, I was actively working away with the crow, when there suddenly arose behind me a confused shouting, evidently meant as a check to the oxen, then a harsh grating sound, then a dead pause, then thump, thump, thump, followed by a frightful crash and a heart-piercing cry from a bevy of women who were following in our wake. The crowbar fell from my powerless hands, and I sank down on the rock, the cold drops of perspiration trickling down my cheeks, while I exclaimed to myself, "Good God! there goes my wagon and some poor fellow with it." For a second or two, not a sound being audible, I felt too agitated to move—in short, dared not proceed farther for fear of seeing my worst fears realized. At last, feeling suspense more dreadful than a knowledge of the true state of affairs, and hearing the women in the rear set up a chorus of distressing lamentations, I rose and hurried to the scene of the disaster as fast as my crippled condition, for

D

I was still suffering from the wound in my knee, would permit.

Near the bottom of the ravine lay the prostrate vehicle, seemingly a heap of ruins, the oxen struggling wildly to free themselves from their uncomfortable position, and hard by the driver, stunned and bleeding, sprawling on the ground. The latter, however, thank God! soon got up, not having sustained any very serious injury. When the wagon first began to slide off the slippery ledge it was crossing, the poor fellow was on the side nearest the precipice, endeavoring to keep up the "after" oxen; but, on seeing all his efforts unavailing, he had the presence of mind to dive under the disselboom, and thus, though knocked down by the pole, probably saved his life.

Dismal and discouraging as things now looked, I did not give way to useless lamentations. In a few minutes every available hand was hard at work. The oxen were soon set free, and I was truly delighted to find that the axles had sustained no injury. By arduous efforts, in which all zealously joined, we not only succeeded in righting the wagon and replenishing it with its usual stores, but, just as the sun was diffusing its last golden rays over the picturesque broken tables that surrounded us, we were once more able to move forward.

Of course our former route was out of the question, but we managed successfully to ascend the opposite side of the ravine, which, though far from affording either an easy or safe passage, still enabled us to extricate ourselves from our perilous position without farther accident. The last streaks of daylight disappearing in the encroaching darkness saw us pitching our tents in an open and convenient spot, grateful to be allowed a quiet night's rest after a hard day's work.

The real extent of the damage sustained I did not ascertain until some days later, when I was particularly glad to find that my instruments and guns, my chief cares, had received but trivial injuries.

The following morning we continued our journey, and arrived on the same evening at a fountain called Okahongottie, situated in a small river bed. The country, like that we had traversed on many a previous day, was exceedingly unfavorable for wagon traveling. It was densely wooded, and besprinkled with huge flint-like fragments of limestones, which sadly cut and lacerated the feet of both men and beasts. The bush was in some places so dense that a man on foot could not force a passage through it without having recourse to a hatchet. In this day's march we probably cut down 1500 trees and bushes.

CHAPTER III.

Another Limestone Range of Hills.—Passage through it at last found.—Clearing a Road through Rocks.—The Wagon like a Ship in a heavy Cross-sea.—The Fountains of Otjidambi.—Traces of human Habitation.—The Ovaherero and the Namaquas.—The Hottentots and Damaras.—Cattle and Sheep stealing.—Guides at a Loss.—Two Natives captured.—One of them forced to become a Guide.—The Natives of a Village flee away in alarm.— A few Presents reconcile some of them to become Guides.—An Accident: a Dog killed instead of a Hyena.—A grand Illumination: Fields on Fire.—A Hurricane.—The Passage of a Defile.—Game rare.—Long Shots.—The Guide escapes.—Several Werfts (Hamlets) and Vleys (Wells).—Scarcity of Water.—Quest of Water.— Kind-heartedness of Damara Women.— No Guides.—No Water, and Country parched and desolate.—One more Attempt to go forward.

We were now fairly through the limestone table which for some time had given me so much uneasiness, and I was flattering myself that the difficult place pointed to by my guide was passed; but in this hope I was deceived.

Immediately fronting us was another line of limestone ranges of a different description and character—carboniferous, rugged, and peaked. They did not look very formidable at a distance, but on a nearer approach were really found to be so.

Two parties I had posted off in different directions, in search of a passage through this range, returned after some days' absence without any success. It was, they said, utterly impossible for a wagon to cross the mountain. Even a man on foot had to pick his way. A third party, however, was more successful; for, after skirting the hills for a considerable distance, they at last found a pass which they deemed practicable. It was considerably out of the direct route, but I felt thankful for any chance that offered itself, and lost no time in setting out.

We entered the defile in question on the second day after our departure from Okahongottie. The greater portion of the passage was accomplished without much inconvenience, and I was congratulating myself on the worst being over, when suddenly our progress was checked by a ravine choked with huge boulders, fragments of rock, quartz stones, trees, bushes, etc. Unyoking the oxen, I at once set every man and woman to work, leading the way myself with a powerful crowbar. After six hours of unremitting exertions, I had so far succeeded in opening a pass that I ventured on proceeding, though it was still on break-neck and cut-throat looking ground. On, on crushed the huge vehicle, thumping and creaking very much like a vessel buffeting a strong cross-sea, and marking its progress with sparkling streams of fire as the wheels came into collision with the more than iron-tempered surface of the rock. It was devil-a-care, let go; and I felt quite frightened, often holding my breath in anxious suspense. Indeed, I did not breathe freely until we were fairly across the ridge, when, to my great delight, I found the country suddenly change for the better.

Both soil and vegetation were now different, our progress for some days was comparatively easy, and on the morning of May-day we found ourselves at the fine fountains of Otjidambi.

Otjidambi is a collection of wells and pits (fed by powerful springs) partly dug in the sandy soil of the banks of a periodical rivulet, and partly scooped out of limestone. The place had a pleasant but curious aspect—rock and plain alternating. The former was a succession of parallel ridges of granite, cone-shaped, running about east and west, each ridge being composed of innumerable blocks, some fifty to one hundred feet high, piled up, as if systematically, on one another.

Hitherto we had scarcely seen a human being, but that the country was inhabited was evident from the occasional footprints met with in the sand. At one time the Kaoko, like the rest of Damara Land, must have been fairly besprinkled with homesteads of the pastoral Ovaherero, who possessed numerous herds of cattle. But of these they had been gradually deprived by their unscrupulous neighbors the Namaquas. It was only, indeed, the year previous to my visit that a party of Hottentots had extended their forays to these distant tracts, and had succeeded in carrying off a considerable number of cattle and sheep. This, however, was not accomplished without severe losses; for, contrary to their wont, the Damaras had ventured to resist the intruders. A desperate fight, which resulted in the Namaquas losing above one half of their total number, was the consequence. The few surviving Damaras still possessing cattle then fled in a north and northwest direction. They are represented as braver and more warlike than the rest of their brethren, yet no one acquainted with this country can for a moment doubt that ere long they must share the fate of their countrymen. It was, then, with feelings of pain that I wandered over these extensive regions, once resounding with the lowings and bleatings of herds and flocks, and the merry voices of a happy and careless race, now a waste, tenanted by a handful of poverty-stricken wretches, gaining a precarious subsistence by the chase and uncertain crops of wild roots and berries.

My guide's information now flagged. Hitherto he had shown a fair knowledge of the country, gained chiefly, I found, by marauding and cattle-lifting forays against his countrymen. At first his ignorance of our whereabouts did not give me much anxiety, as I thought we should be sure to stumble upon water here and there, the rainy season being apparently just over; but, alas! I was in this anticipation very much deceived, as the sequel will show.

The day before reaching Otjidambi we had perceived recent spoors of human beings in the sand, and even columns of smoke in the distance. In the hope, therefore, of securing a fresh guide, I dispatched a few men to reconnoitre this company of natives; but they fled on our first approach, and my messengers were not able to overtake them. Nothing then remained but dependence on our own efforts. A party was accordingly organized for the purpose of exploring the country ahead, and much surprised and pleased I was when, early the next day after their departure, they returned, bringing with them a Damara man and woman whom they had captured. The poor devils were dreadfully frightened, but a gorge on fat mutton and plenty of backshish soon allayed their fears. By a strict cross-questioning I learned from the man something about our route, finding, nevertheless, afterward serious flaws in his statements. He assured us that at about a day's journey from Otjidambi lay a werft of his friends, who would direct us farther. Of course I meant him to bring us to this place, but kept my own counsel until the following morning, when, every thing being in readiness for a start, I ordered him to lead the way. He had evidently expected to be let off with mere words, and showed himself reluctant to obey. However, I cut the matter very short by giving him the choice of an ounce of lead through his brains, or a handsome remuneration if he guided us satisfactorily.

For the first hour or two we made good progress, the country being unusually favorable for wagon-traveling; but suddenly we arrived at the spur of one of those irregular cone-shaped granite ridges above mentioned, which occasioned us much delay and trouble. However, after a few hours' hard work, we succeeded in clearing the rocks; and having once more a fair road to travel on, we reached, a few minutes before sunset, a small fountain called Okava—the spot indicated by our guide as the abode of his friends. This statement proved correct; yet before we got to the place the birds had flown, alarmed, probably, by the noisy approach of our wagon and the cracking of the driver's whip.

The next morning I sent parties out in search of the runaways, with orders to bring them back if possible. After long tracking, one of these parties came upon some men, who would not allow my people, although in company with our new guide, to approach them. It was in vain to assure them that my object was quite pacific; they would listen to no overtures. At last a woman, who had been absent from home on our arrival, and was thus unconscious of our presence, was pounced upon and secured while walking leisurely up to the water to quench her thirst. She was a young and comely damsel, and I lavished upon her, besides all sorts of coaxing and winning expressions, beads, meat, tobacco, etc. Fortunately, we needed not her assistance; for on the third day all the fugitives unexpectedly stood before us of their own accord. I was both pleased and surprised at this sudden turn of affairs. It was owing to the representations of my new guide's companion, a woman whom I had dismissed with a present and friendly assurances a short time before.

The chief of our new acquaintances was a well-fed and rather good-looking young fellow. Sundry uninteresting remarks and a present of tobacco having been interchanged, I requested him to furnish me with guides to the Ovagandjera—the nearest tribe. He appeared reluctant to comply with the proposal, but said he would consider. I was determined, however, to have guides at any cost.

That same evening a melancholy incident occurred. I was "observing" at a little distance from my wagon, when suddenly my attention was drawn to a peculiar grating sound, as of some animal gnawing or crunching bones. Walking back to the bivouac fire, I asked my servants in a distinct voice, "Are all our dogs here?" "Yes, all are here," was the prompt reply. "Quite sure?" "Yes, sir, quite sure." Taking for granted, therefore, that a hyena, or some other beast of prey, was intruding upon us, I picked up my gun and proceeded in the direction still indicated by the grating sounds. At last I perceived a dark, conspicuous-looking object, and when within a few paces leveled and fired. The bullet sped true; but, alas! instead of having destroyed an obnoxious animal, I found, to my dismay, that I had shot my best and favorite dog, Cæsar. I recognized him at once by the cry of pain he uttered on receiving the fatal lead. Calling one of my men, I had the poor brute carried to the fire to see what could be done for him; but a glance at the wound at once convinced me that his life could not be saved. In order, therefore, to put an end to his misery, I drew my revolver and lodged a bullet in the head of the faithful creature. The scene sickened and saddened me indescribably. Those who know what it is to lose a beloved dog, especially under such distressing circumstances, who has been their faithful companion and guardian during many a dark and dismal night, will easily understand my grief. Poor Cæsar!

The next day the chief again made his appearance, and at an early hour, but no guides were visible. I at once demanded why the latter had not arrived, when he replied rather sulkily, "None of my people will go." "Well, then," I sternly rejoined, "if that's the case, *you yourself must go.*" This led to a fresh consultation, which ended in two individuals presenting themselves as willing to guide me to the nation lately alluded to. Of course, as there was no natural inclination on their part for this service, but quite the contrary, I felt that the game I was playing was a hazardous one, and that, consequently, it behooved me to be more than usually on my guard.

I started the same day for Okaoa. On demanding how far it was to the nearest water, some said two, others ten days' journey; but, on being pressed and cross-questioned, they unanimously declared that a man on foot would have to sleep two nights on the way, which would be equal to three days' journeying with a wagon. In this instance I believed our informants, yet took every precaution I could to insure our safety.

The first night we bivouacked at the foot of an elevated limestone range (facing another which we had crossed in the course of the day) of precisely the same nature as those which had already proved so troublesome, and on this night I witnessed one of the finest natural illuminations I remember to have seen in Africa. The whole of the range facing us—*i. e.*, the one we had traversed—exhibited one magnificent blaze of fire, kept vividly alive by a high wind. The flames crossed and chased one another like furies—here rising high above the inflamed substances, as if unsatisfied with their low prey and career—there rushing in snake-like folds, as if writhing under some agonizing torture—now smouldering for a moment as if gasping for breath, then shooting up into the heavens with redoubled vigor; in short, assuming all sorts of brilliant and fantastical shapes. Yet, splendid as this conflagration was, it fell far short of one I beheld afterward, and which, associated as it was with circumstances most peculiar and painful, will never be obliterated from my memory.

At an early hour on the following morning we were on the move. A regular hurricane swept the country, accompanied with a chilliness quite wintry. My hands became in a short time so benumbed that it was with difficulty I could carry my gun. The natives suffered intensely. Almost immediately after our departure we entered a defile infinitely more formidable than any we had hitherto traversed. On viewing the huge boulders and sharp rock-ledges that obstructed our passage, my blood almost ran cold with discouragement. But I will not trouble the reader with details. Suffice it to say, that after due delays and hard work we accomplished our object, though the wagon, in addition to the chance of being capsized or smashed, barely escaped destruction by fire.

In their usual thoughtless manner, the natives had, to our horror, suddenly set fire to the grass; and as the pass through which we were progressing was narrow, and the wind high, the whole mountain was soon enveloped in flames and smoke, from which we only extricated ourselves with extreme difficulty; indeed, this was a danger to which we now found ourselves daily exposed. Wherever we went, smoke and fire were before, around, and behind us; for it is customary with the tribes of South Africa to fire the grass when it has arrived at a certain state of maturity and dryness.

A short time before sunset we reached a small vley, where a werft of Ovatjimba, or poor Damaras, had established themselves. The water we here found, being quite unlooked for, was especially welcome, so that we began to think the natives had again deceived us; but in this conjecture we were mistaken. We bivouacked in this place the next day, and, having duly pastured and watered our cattle, etc., continued to travel on.

Game, which throughout our journeys had been scarce, now became still more so. A dead gemsbok, which we found in a state of decomposition, and evidently destroyed by a poisoned arrow, was hailed with joy as a God-send; and no less so were two or three ostriches which I succeeded in knocking over. One of these birds I killed at the long range of 374 yards. I stepped the distance carefully twice, and as the locality happened to be perfectly level, there could be little or no error in the measurement. My friend Green would treat this feat as a bagatelle, but I felt proud of the performance.

I never could from experience understand how, at immense distances of from 500 to 1000 yards, great Nimrods frequently kill, or are said to kill, their game. They laugh at you when you call 200 yards a long range. But their vaunts remind me of the answer given by a certain fusileer to one who asked him how a 24-pounder at the battle of —— could have been propelled over a four-feet-high wall at a gallop. "Speed does it, sir; but, Lor', *that* is nothing," was his reply.

In the afternoon of the second day after leaving the vley we had fairly left all landmarks behind us, and the hills began to assume that azure tint which is so indicative of distance. Nothing was seen ahead but immense grass savannas, dotted with occasional clumps of trees and low brushwood. The soil was the same—red sand—but the grass, though as luxuriant as ever, was of an inferior quality. The fine sweet grasses, so peculiar to Damara Land, had given place to equally rank, but sour and brackish pasturages.

A short time before sunset I observed the guide loitering behind. Hitherto I had never allowed the fellow to go out of my sight; but as he was waiting for his wife, who was coming up in a sickly state to join us, I left him alone. This was a fatal mistake. I never saw the scoundrel afterward. Nevertheless, we were again, at an early hour the next morning, moving ahead in the direction pointed out by him on the preceding day.

After a few hours' journeying we came all at once upon several werfts, some of which had evidently not been long evacuated. There were numerous vleys in the neighborhood. One or two of these vleys appeared not to have been dry above a week. The people who had dwelt in the neighborhood evidently possessed cattle and goats; and as their folds were of a description resembling those constructed by the Ovambo, I concluded that the owners were Ovagandjera—the tribe we were in search of. All these signs we thought favorable; and so, despite the absence of our guide, we felt inspired with fresh hopes. Still thinking it possible the absentee would overtake us, I outspanned a second time, and proceeded without delay to reconnoitre. I also dispatched several parties in different directions in quest of water, but all returned, after many hours of fatiguing search, without finding the slightest indication of any. Thirst in the mean time began to tell dreadfully on our party; the cattle were also sorely distressed for want of drink.

Under these circumstances it would have been madness to advance; nothing therefore remained to us but to retrace our steps in double-quick time; and, fortunately, there was a crescent moon, by the light of which we succeeded in gaining the bivouac we had left that very morning.

A fire had passed over the spot, and the ground was in places so hot — indeed, there were still smouldering embers here and there—that it singed and scorched our shoes. This was easily accounted for; for when leaving the place in the morning I observed Mortar piling all the superfluous wood on the fire. From a vague impression that it might possibly one day be needed, I remarked, "Don't do so, John." "Oh, surely," he replied, "we shall never have occasion to bivouac here again." "I trust not," I rejoined; "yet who knows?" My forebodings, alas! proved but too true.

The next day a pleasing incident occurred, which I find thus recorded (I copy word for word) in my diary: "Observed an agreeable trait in the character of our Damara women, which forcibly bespoke the heart of *the woman*, let the color of her skin be black or white. Several of the men in charge of the loose cattle had remained behind to dig up some moist and palatable roots and bulbs, which appeared rather plentiful in a particular spot. On repassing us, the wagon-driver and the leader, both suffering intensely from thirst, asked these men for a taste of the roots they had already possessed themselves of, but were flatly refused. A few minutes afterward, two of the women (not in any way connected with the soliciting party), who had also remained behind to procure a few of the juicy herbs, passed us, and, without being asked, handed a couple of roots to each of the men who had just begged for a taste of one in vain from their boon companions. 'Kindness, thou hast built thyself a noble temple—woman!'"

On the night of the fourth day we reached the vley where, on traveling northward, we had found the werft of Ovatjimba. Unfortunately, the water, or rather the muddy slime, was only sufficient for a small portion of our cattle, and I had therefore to post them off to the fountain Okaoa—another day's journey—making in all five entire days that the poor brutes had been without a drink. I and Mortar remained with the wagon.

E

The question that arose now was, Was I to give up all farther hopes of penetrating to the Cunenè? The mere idea was agonizing; yet, from what I had seen of the country, it was impossible to proceed farther unless assisted by efficient guides. Natural springs there appeared to be few or none, and all the temporary rain-water pools were exhausted—in short, the country was dry and parched in the extreme. From this I inferred that the rains in these parts either fell much earlier than in the southern portion of Damara Land, or had been unusually scanty during the last season. The chief at Okaoa had assured me before parting that the road to the Ovagandjera, with cattle, was only practicable in the wet season. I did not give full credit to his statement at the time, but that it was true experience afterward fully proved.

After some little hesitation I resolved on one more attempt, provided I could obtain fresh guides, and, if then unsuccessful, to make my way back to the precincts of Damara-Land civilization, whence to accomplish, if possible, my object by a more eligible, though perhaps more circuitous route. Of course this would involve much loss of time, and require an extra stock of patience and perseverance. But I had set my heart on the undertaking, and nothing but insurmountable physical difficulties, sickness or death, could deter me from making every effort to carry it into effect. I find the following remarks about my present perplexity jotted down in my journal on the very day I began to retrace my steps:

"Will the cattle, etc., hold out? God grant they may; but it will be a hard push. Is this, then, to be the upshot of an expedition I have had so much at heart, and for which I have sacrificed every thing—happiness, comforts, security, in short, all that makes life tolerable? Is it for this I suffer the extremes of cold and heat, hunger and thirst—for which I brave every danger attendant upon traveling in a barbarous country? No, it can not. it must not be! . . . . "

Having come to the resolution thus expressed, I sent Pereira to Okaoa to treat with the Damara chief for fresh guides. I directed him to threaten and coax alternately, according as he found the party he had to deal with stubborn or yielding. His efforts were happily crowned with success, for late in the evening of the second day he returned, bringing with him two men, of whom one was said to know the country to the northward exceedingly well. On engaging them, I entered into a compact with myself never to allow them to get out of my sight either by day or by night, and I was faithful to my word. But, alas! all my care and trouble proved entirely unavailing, and that from a cause, as will be seen in the following chapter, quite unexpected.

CHAPTER IV.

The Guides lose their Way.—The Lives of the whole Party at stake.—A Search for Water in all Directions.—In vain.—Necessity of returning without Delay.—Two Men exploring the Country for Water left behind.—The Sufferings of the Men and Animals from Thirst.—Retreat resolved upon.—A grand and appalling Conflagration.—The Magnificence of the Spectacle.—The Cattle one hundred and fifty Hours without a single Drop of Water.—The two Men left behind make their Appearance.—The Water so long searched for found.—Okaoa reached in Safety.—Ondjuona the favorite Resort of Elephants.—The annual Pilgrimage of these Animals to another Station.—The Damara Mode of Elephant-hunting.—View from the Summit of Okonyenya.—Country surveyed.—A Thunder-storm under Foot.

During the first day's march on this new start we followed the spoor of our wagon in our first attempt, but afterward inclined more to the eastward. Our troubles very soon commenced. On the second evening, or on the third after leaving Okaoa, I saw the guides suddenly halt and look about them, as if undecided how to proceed. They had a short time previously declared that we should reach water that night. My suspicions were therefore at once aroused, or rather my heart misgave me. "Surely," I muttered to myself, "the fellows are trying to deceive us, or they have lost their way!"

The one conjecture was as bad as the other. For a few seconds I remained silent; but, seeing them still wavering, I advanced, and in a voice trembling with rage and distress, thundered out, "Where is the water, men?" adding, with my fowling-piece presented at the head of the acting guide, "If you don't bring us to water before noon to-morrow, you die. Proceed." It soon became obvious, however, that they had *lost themselves*, and that, under such circumstances, threats would only tend still more to confuse them. I consequently, as they were wandering to and fro like men groping in the dark, and the night was fast closing upon us, sounded a halt to bivouac. *That night was perhaps the most painful one in my life.* I felt most keenly that not only the issue of the undertaking, but the lives of my party, were at stake. The agony I suffered is indescribable; yet, lest I should frighten my attendants, I did not betray the deep emotions that agitated me. They had, nevertheless, already taken the alarm; dismay—nay, despair—was depicted on every countenance; but, be it said to their credit, not a murmur escaped them. Supposing the place we were in search of should not be found, the nearest water, Okaoa, was three long days' journey off. Could this place be reached in safety in our present weak state? I dared scarcely answer the question. The possible answer seemed too awful to dwell upon.

Sleep was that night, of course, out of the question, and before break of day I was in the saddle in search of water, having first dispatched three different parties on the same errand in as many directions. I returned to the camp after eight hours' sharp riding and walking, my horse completely done up—unsuccessful! My approach was watched by the men at the wagon with feverish anxiety; there was no need of words; my face told but too plainly my complete failure. Kamapjie, who had also been absent on a similar mission, soon joined us, equally successless. Two parties were still absent, and on their efforts rested now all our hopes; but hour after hour elapsed without any news. The sun set, yet no men. The shadows of evening crept upon us, yet no men. The moon rose, yet no men. Our anxiety was at its height. Had the men found the water, or had they lost themselves in this fearful and death-boding wilderness? Should I wait for the return of daylight before finally deciding on what course to pursue, or should I face back at once? These and many other were the distracting thoughts that crowded in rapid succession on my giddy brains. The delay of a night would occasion the loss of another day, and then, just suppose the absent parties unsuccessful in finding water, what would be the result? Apparently inevitable destruction. The oxen had now been four days without water, and their distress was already very great. Their hollow flanks, drooping heads, and low, melancholy moans, uttered at intervals, told but too plainly their misery, and went to my heart like daggers. My poor horse was no longer an animated creature, but a spectre of himself—a gaunt, staggering skeleton. The change that had come upon him during the last twenty-four hours was incredible. From time to time he would put his head into the wagon, into any one's hands, and, looking wistfully and languidly into his face, would reproachfully (his looks conveyed as much) seem to say, "Cruel man, don't you see I am dying; why don't you relieve my burning thirst?" The dogs, again, ceased to recognize my caresses. Their eyes were so deeply sunken in their sockets as to be scarcely perceptible. They glided about in spectral silence; death was in their faces. The wagon was heavily laden, the soil exceedingly heavy, the sun in the daytime like an immense burning-glass, and the oppressiveness of the atmosphere was greatly increased by the tremendous "veldt" fires, which, ravaging the country far and wide, made it like a huge fiery furnace.

Under such circumstances the oxen could never hold out for seven days—the time which must, I calculated, elapse before I could reach Okaoa—without water! Well, then, with all these ominous facts and forebodings before me, would it be advisable to await the return of the absent men? A few moments of anxious self-communion determined me not to do so, but to retrace my steps without farther delay. This resolution was, of course, the death-blow to the expedition. Before starting on our backward course I fired a number of shots, which received no answer, to attract the notice of the absentees.

I had yet a small supply of water in the wagon, having taken the precaution at starting to take the entire stock under my immediate charge. I now served out a few mouthfuls to each individual, left a small quantity, together with a few biscuits, on a bush for the absent men, should they find their way back, and then began the return journey at a brisk pace, but with a heavy heart.

Health and strength, time and the season, had been thus wasted and lost, heavy pecuniary sacrifices made, the life of men and valuable beasts jeopardized, bright prospects blighted, and all—all to so little purpose! My feelings on this memorable occasion may be more easily imagined than described.

We had proceeded but a comparatively short distance, and were just escaping out of a thorn-thicket, when we were suddenly startled by a grand, but to us appalling sight.

The whole country before us was one huge lake of flames. Turning to Mortar, I exclaimed, "Good God, our return is cut off!" I had seen many wood and grass fires, but nothing to equal this. Immediately in front of us lay stretched out like a sea a vast pasture prairie, dotted with occasional trees, bounded in the distance by groves of huge giraffe thorns, all in a blaze! Through the very midst of

CROSSING A BURNING SAVANNA.

this lay our path. By delaying a few hours the danger would have been considerably diminished, if not altogether over; but delay in our case seemed almost more dangerous than going forward, and so on we pushed, trusting to some favorable accident to bring us through the perils we had to face. As we advanced we heard distinctly the sputtering and hissing of the inflamed grasses and brushwood, the cracking of the trees as they reluctantly yielded their massive forms to the unrelenting and all-devouring element, the screams of startled birds and other commingling sounds of terror and devastation. There was a great angle in our road, running parallel, as it were, to the raging fire, but afterward turning abruptly into a burning savanna. By the time we had reached this point, the conflagration, still in its glory on our right, was fast receding on our left, thus opening a passage, into which we darted without hesitation, although the ground was still smouldering and reeking, and in some places quite alive with flickering sparks from the recent besom of hot flames that had swept over it. Tired as our cattle were, this heated state of the ground made the poor brutes step out pretty smartly. At times we ran great risk of being crushed by the falling timbers. Once a huge trunk, in flames from top to bottom, fell athwart our path, sending up millions of sparks, and scattering innumerable splinters of lighted wood all around us, while the numerous nests of the social grossbeaks

—the *Textor erythrorhynchus*—in the ignited trees looked like so many lamps suspended in designs at once natural, pleasing, and splendid. It was altogether a glorious illumination, worthy of Nature's palace with its innumerable windows and stately vaulted canopy. But the danger associated with the grand spectacle was too great and too imminent for us thoroughly to appreciate its magnificence. Indeed, we were really thankful when once our backs were turned on the awful scene.

At break of day we halted for a few minutes to breathe and to change oxen, then continued to journey on. I dispatched all the loose cattle ahead, giving the men orders to return with a fresh team as soon as they had drunk, fed, and rested a little. We arrived at the vley a little before midnight on the 24th of May, but on attempting to kraal the trek oxen, notwithstanding their fatigue, the thirsty brutes leaped over the stout and tall thorn fences as if they had been so many rushes, and with a wild roar set off at full speed for Okaoa fountain, which they reached the following day, having then been more than *one hundred and fifty hours without a single drop of water!*

Before reaching the water the men in charge of the loose cattle had become so exhausted with long and incessant marching, suffering all the time from burning thirst, that one by one they had sunk down. The cattle, unherded, found their way to the fountain without much difficulty; but the wretched horse missed his, and kept wandering about until he dropped from sheer exhaustion. Some Ovatjimba fortunately found the brute, and reporting the discovery to their chief, he good-naturedly brought the dying beast some drink and fodder, by which means he gradually recovered. The animal, when found, had been *seven days without water.* I had no idea that a horse was capable of enduring fatigue and thirst to the extent experienced by this hack of mine.

The poor dogs were by this time in a fearful state. What was once a clear perspicuous eye now appeared like a mere lustrous speck under a shaggy brow. Blood flowed at times from their nostrils; and it was with difficulty they dragged along their worn and emaciated carcasses. Sometimes they tried to give vent to their great sufferings in dismal howls, half stifled in the utterance. Some of the men were nearly as much affected. Poor Mortar was more than once speechless from thirst, and it was quite pitiful to see him, like a man despairing of life, chew old coffee-tobacco and withered tea-leaves. For my own part, I am thankful to say I suffered on this trying occasion, in a bodily sense at least, less perhaps than the rest of my party.

The day after our arrival at the vley the lost men suddenly and unexpectedly made their appearance, and, to my great surprise, I learned that they had accidentally stumbled upon the very water we had so long searched for in vain. In retracing their steps to the wagon to report the good news they had unfortunately lost their way, and, after a fruitless search, were obliged to bivouac on the waste. Like myself, they had repeatedly discharged guns, but as this was done long after dark, it is probable the wagon had by that time taken its departure, so that their signals were unheard and unanswered.

On the eighth day, late in the evening, I reached Okaoa in safety, without the loss of a single man or beast, all, however, being in a dreadful state of prostration, not only from fatigue and hardship, but from torn and lacerated feet. This, coupled with the impossibility of procuring trustworthy guides, with the evident dearth of water, the absence of game, and many other formidable hinderances, induced me to face homeward without any farther delay than was necessary to recruit in a measure the strength and vigor of bipeds and quadrupeds.

By a careful computation, I found that from this place (Okaoa) to Otjimbingué the distance was 115 hours' actual travel, which is equivalent to 300 English miles in round numbers, while in our last two fruitless attempts to push northward we had traveled *one hundred and twenty hours, that is, about three hundred and thirty English miles*—a distance more than sufficient to have brought us to the Cunené—nay, there and back again—had we been able to hold our course directly for that river. I need scarcely say, therefore, that the decision I had come to cost me some pain and regret. However, as I said before, though at present foiled, I by no means intended to abandon the undertaking as hopeless, for I consider him but half a man who gives up every thing for lost because a spoke has chanced to start in his fortune's wheel.

On the 29th of May we bid adieu to Okaoa. As we traveled by exactly the same line of route as that with which the reader is already acquainted, it would be tedious to go over the ground afresh. I will merely, then, allude to a few of the most important events of this retrograde march.

On the 10th of June we were once more at Ondjuona—a favorite resort of elephants, and having scarcely had any opportunity of enjoying my gun, I looked forward with eagerness to a week or two of exciting sport; but I was doomed, it seemed, to nothing but disappointments. The elephants had, we found, not only abandoned Ondjuona, but every other resort within a hundred miles of that place. Some natives, whom we met and fraternized with, suggested that the herds had probably migrated to the Omanini River and the Omuramba Ua' Matako —a pilgrimage they were, we were told, accustomed to perform annually at a certain season. At a later period I had personal experience of the truth of this statement.

The Damaras in these parts, since they have become impoverished, occasionally attack and kill elephants. When a hunt is decided on they muster in force, usually, I believe, dividing themselves into two parties. The object of this division is that, while one party approach the elephant and discharge their missiles on him, the other endeavor to divert the attention of the enraged beast by shouting and beating on sticks. Old male elephants, being less active and dangerous than young ones and cows, are, in these hunts, the particular marks of the sportsmen. The chase, full of excitement and peril, very frequently results in the destruction of one or more of the hunters. The ivory obtained is in the course of time brought to the Ovagandjera, from whom its vendors receive in exchange assegais, hatchets, daggers, iron and copper, beads, etc. Ultimately, however, it finds its way to the Portuguese market on the west coast.

Though disappointed with respect to sport, I determined, as the cattle stood much in need of rest, and Ondjuona abounds with good water and grass, to make a halt here for a couple of weeks.

By the failure of the expedition, or rather by going over its ground a second time, I had gained one point, viz., I had been enabled to complete my map very satisfactorily. With the best will and the most strenuous exertions, it is utterly impossible to acquire a thorough knowledge of the physical features of a country on a first and hurried visit to it. I had hitherto spared no trouble or pains, ascending conspicuous hills and other landmarks, often very many miles out of my way, in order to obtain valuable and useful bearings, and, though I had succeeded, there still remained much to be done besides improving a prismatic compass triangulation begun in the 25° N. and extended to near the 19° of S. lat. Therefore Okonyenya, the beautiful granite cone already alluded to in these pages, being now not very distant, I determined to visit it. From its central, isolated, and prominent position, I judged a good view might be obtained from its summit over a great portion of western Damara Land, and that, consequently, an excursion to the site would well repay the trouble. Thought matured to action. Accordingly, having hastily made a few arrangements, and provided myself with the necessary instruments, I set out on this exploration. The guide managed, however, to miss the way, and we did not reach the base of the mountain until the morning of the third day from our departure from Ondjuona.

After partaking of some refreshment, and providing ourselves, in case of being obliged to spend the night on the mountain's top, with a few necessaries and comforts, we began the ascent, which, from the steepness of the rock, proved a very laborious and fatiguing one. My native attendants, unused to climbing hills, were completely done up long before we had gained its crowning height. Indeed, mountain climbing in this scorching climate, even to the most practiced and elastic foot,

F

is an arduous enterprise. As I had anticipated, the prospect from the summit was extensive and magnificent, though somewhat circumscribed by the haziness of the atmosphere. Hoping for a clearer sky the next day, I resolved to bivouac on the spot. In the mean time I employed myself in obtaining what observations and bearings I could, and in sketching a picture of the scene before me, to which I find I have thus alluded in my diary:

"The country all around and beneath me has a singularly odd appearance. The ground, being much cut up and intersected by innumerable little periodical water-courses, looks a good way off, and from a height, very like a large town—the principal water-courses representing the chief thoroughfares, and the smaller ones, usually joining them at right angles, the lesser streets; while the trees, some towering apart, and some in lower clusters, with the bushes, make out a very fair pageant of churches, buildings, and houses.

"As the shadows of night stole upon us a furious wind arose, which continued to blow with unabated violence until the next day. It was with difficulty we could keep our footing; and fuel being scarce, we spent a rather comfortless night. A grand natural spectacle, a thunder-storm, brought us some relief in this unpleasant situation. This war of the elements was not overhead, but under our feet. It resembled greatly the subterraneous rumbling which often precedes an earthquake, for which, indeed, I mistook the first clap.

"The return of daylight brought no improvement to the atmosphere, but the view was less obscured in a particular direction, and, on the whole, I obtained a valuable and useful set of bearings. Having done all that could be done, I began the descent, and before noon had rejoined my camp at the base of the mountain. Three huge lions had passed within gunshot of the carriage oxen during the night, but without any attempt at molestation. The next morning at at early hour we retraced our steps to the wagon, which we reached at dusk.

"We had been twelve hours on the move, compassing a distance, by road, of rather more than thirty miles—a sharp day's march, in the course of which I killed a couple of gemsboks, and saw, for the first time, a fair sprinkling of game, such as giraffes, gemsboks, zebras, springboks, etc."

CHAPTER V.

A singular Mirage.—Arrival on the Omaruru.—I resolve on crossing over to the Omuramba, viâ Matako, while the Wagon is undergoing a complete Reparation.—Two Lions attack the Dogs.—Wild Beasts abundant.—Lion Man-eaters.—Their stealthy Mode of Attack.—A horrid Dream.—The physical Features of Damara Land.—Granite, Limestone, and Sandstone.—Carboniferous Formations.—Scented and aromatic Plants and Trees.—Scenery.—Mines.

On the 25th of June we again moved forward, or, rather, it would be more proper to say, backward. Early one morning, a day or two afterward, we were regaled with the sight of a pretty and very singular mirage, remarkable on account of its rich, warm, transparent *pink* color, produced, as I found immediately afterward, by the reflection of a huge mass of red granite which happened to intercept the sun's rays.

The 1st of July found us safe on the banks of the Omaruru River. The wagon had by this time become all but a wreck. Every bolt was broken or damaged, and scarcely a single piece of wood sound. It required all my care and ingenuity to make it keep together.

I had already formed my plans for the future. Mortar and Pereira, with a complement of natives,

ARRIVAL ON THE OMARURU.

were directed to bring the wagon to Otjimbingué, in order to get it repaired, if possible, and to obtain a few necessaries; while I myself, attended by some of my Damaras, proceeded up the Omaruru toward its source, whence it was my intention to cross over to the Omuramba Ua' Matako, where my men had instructions to rejoin me with the wagon. It was *viâ* Omuramba Ua' Matako that I hoped finally to penetrate to the Cunenè.

My object in remaining "in the field" was twofold—exploring and hunting. A small strip of country still remained unmapped, and I felt confident that I should meet with elephants in the neighborhood of the Omatako Mountains. The natives, however, tried to deter me from going, representing the country in that direction as impassable by reason of a severe drought. Scarcely a drop of rain, they said, had fallen there during the last twelve months; but I refused to credit their statement.

After a few days devoted to rest and recreation the wagon started for Otjimbingué. I accompanied it as far as Omapjie, where I bade the men farewell. On regaining my now much-diminished party on the Omaruru River a striking incident occurred, which, under date of the 8th of July, I find thus noted in my journal:

"About eight o'clock last night, while 'observing,' I heard the growl of two lions at a short distance down the river: the brutes approached rapidly. The dogs did not appear to like the sound.

but still went off barking toward the river. While waiting for the meridian height of a star I walked back to the tent; on seeing me, Kamapjie remarked, 'I don't know what is the matter with "Gipsy." She started along with the other dogs, but soon came back, and, staggering, fell into the fire.' I found the poor beast violently convulsed, froth flowing freely from her mouth. I ran a lancet into one of her ears, drawing off some blood, which seemed slightly to relieve her. Scarcely had I done so, and returned to my instrument, when there was a sudden *backward* rush by the dogs, accompanied by cries from the men, 'The lions! the lions!' Gathering up my sextant, horizon, etc., I retreated precipitately to the fire, where I found all the dogs, except one called 'Chips,' crouched in fear, and trembling. 'Where is "Chips?"' I exclaimed. 'Killed by the lions,' was the immediate reply. 'Did you hear him cry out?' 'Yes, yes,' answered Kamapjie, 'I heard him utter a faint howl or two.' Seizing a firebrand, the bull's-eye lantern, and my gun, I thereupon proceeded in the direction whence the dogs were seen to retreat so hurriedly, and within a dozen paces of one of the men's fires there were, sure enough, the marks of a gigantic lion's paw. A little farther on we discovered the spot where poor 'Chips' had evidently been seized, but could see nothing of his destroyer. I set fire to the grass, but it did not burn well, and after a farther unsuccessful search we retreated back to the bivouac. I took it for granted that the lions had carried away the dog to be devoured at their leisure; but in this I was mistaken, for this morning he was discovered dead near the spot where he had been seized, and—if I except some gashes about his head, neck, and shoulder, as also the disappearance of his left ear—almost untouched.

"We had scarcely regained and stirred up our bivouac fires before the lions once more began to roar and growl most furiously, within less, I should say, than two hundred yards from our camp, but from opposite quarters. Snatching up my double-barreled smooth-bore, I leveled in the direction of one of the brutes, and, estimating the elevation as well as I could, fired. The bullet must have passed pretty close to the animal, for it instantly silenced him, and, moreover, compelled him to beat a precipitate retreat. On the other lion, still exerting his musical powers, another hissing bullet had a similar effect. However, we did not go to sleep, but kept watch during the remainder of the night; the Damaras all the while making a most hideous noise, cursing and vilifying the lions most lustily—a custom of which I was not before aware; it is one also prevalent among the North African Arabs."

While this was going on poor "Gipsy" expired. She died very quietly, evidently in her senses—if I may use the expression—for to the last she acknowledged my attentions. I never could make out what caused her sudden death. She was a great favorite with us all, and so likewise was "Chips"—a very brave dog. Both were buried in one grave. Their loss at that time was a very serious one to me, for I had now only two dogs left, who had become so scared and cowed by the late event as to be utterly useless—indeed, they refused to stir from our heels.

Wild beasts of every description abounded in these parts, and we found them daring to temerity. The Omuramba was, besides, haunted by lion man-eaters. In the previous year these monsters had succeeded in carrying off two men from Mr. Green's camp, when on his return from the disastrous Ovambo expedition, already alluded to in these pages. The particulars of this horrid story will be related in the sequel of this narrative.

I have no particular dread of lions, nor am I, generally speaking, a particularly nervous man; but I do fear and dread such a monster as a man-eater. Set me face to face with an enemy, be he white or black, beast or man, in the broad light of day, and I will take some odds against him; but a skulking, sneaking, poaching night-prowler, whose cat-like motions and approach no ear can detect—whose muscular strength exceeds that of the strongest ruminating animal—who will pass through your cattle and leave them untouched in order to feast on human flesh—is, I think, a creature which may reasonably inspire terror. There is something hidcous in the thought of lying down nightly in expectation of such a visitor. I remember having been once very much frightened, partly by my own imagination and partly by a reality. This occurred shortly after the receipt of a letter from Mr. Green relating the unfortunate result of his Ovambo expedition, and the attack of lion man-eaters on his party. I was then returning from a journey to Walwich Bay, accompanied by a native youth, and was traveling late at night in order to reach my destination on the following day. I had been sixteen hours in the saddle, felt rather tired, and, finding my steeds in the same humor as myself, I dismounted. Having tied the beasts to a small tree and gathered some grass for them, I threw myself at length on the ground, making neither fire nor bed. I was soon dozing away, my mind busy among old familiar hunting scenes, when suddenly I fancied I saw a grim old lion, his mane tattered, and clogged with human blood and gore, stand before me. I tried to close my eyes against the horrid vision, but in vain; there seemed a secret power of fascination in the brute's dreadful stare. My looks were no sooner averted than my eyes opened wide to stare again at the monster. *His* eyes glistened, *his* mouth watered, while his every motion seemed to say, "Ay, I am a veritable man-eater; I love the flesh of your species above that of all other animals." My anguish became at last intense. My heart seemed to grow so big with terror that I thought it would burst. After several fruitless efforts, I finally tore myself out of this frightful trance, and, springing to my feet, looked around in amazed bewilderment. "Where was I? Had I been dreaming, or was it a reality?" At that moment a sound struck my ear which at once restored me to the full possession of my faculties. "Surely that growl was a lion's," I muttered to myself; and my suspicion was instantly corroborated by a fresh roar, leaving no doubt as to whence it came. I tried then to distinguish the form of the brute, and did so, I believe. I felt agitated, and waking the boy, and hurriedly placing the saddles on the backs of the horses, rode off. But, though thus in some degree relieved, I did not feel quite at ease until the day broke, when my nervousness was at once gone.

Before I dismiss altogether the subject of my doings in Western Damara Land, it may perhaps not be out of place to say a few words of its physical features, as this whole region is a *terra incognita* to Englishmen.

Kaoko Proper, *i. e.*, Western Damara Land, differs from the rest of this country (excepting, perhaps, the immediate vicinity of the sea) only by the absence of extensive plains; in other respects all parts of Western Africa resemble each other closely. This particular district forms a high plateau, rising from 2000 to 4000 feet above the low lands. It possesses comparatively few natural springs;

yet water is not scarce, for the ground is deeply scored and indented all over by numerous periodical water-courses, which intersect the whole region from east to west. In some parts it is densely wooded, or rather bushed; in others rugged. The pasturages are, nevertheless, excellent—in short, the Kaoko is well adapted for the occupation of a pastoral people.

Granite, limestone, and sandstone are the characteristics of the soil of this entire tract, that is, of all Western Damara Land. The first of these formations runs parallel with the coast, or about north and south, shooting out occasionally to some distance inland. Excepting in the immediate neighborhood of the sea-coast (where it is found in one continuous range for nearly 400 geographical miles), it rises in isolated and detached masses, varying in height from 1000 to 3000 feet and upward, sometimes in the form of huge boulder heads, but more frequently in peaks. Granite, indeed, constitutes the chief and most interesting features in the mountain scenery of this country. Some of the finest specimens of this rock are to be seen in the beautiful cones of Okonyenya, Omatako, and in the grand boulders and bluffs of Erongo, Dounsia, Otjonkoama, etc.

The limestone and sandstone formations run, on the contrary, eastward, flanking the granite, but generally with an east and west bearing; in fact, abutting nearly at right angles on the igneous rock.

The limestone predominates toward the north of the Omaruru River, while the sandstone flanks it (the limestone) on the east, running nearly parallel with the Omuramba Ua' Matako.

The three different kinds of limestone, so characteristic of England, viz., the chalk, the carboniferous, and the oolite, are all to be found here considerably developed, and may be duly recognized by their distinguishing peculiarities. The carboniferous formations, escarped ridges and ranges on parallel lines to each other, are bold, stern, and rugged in aspect, clothed with a scanty and dwarfish vegetation, and, on the whole, forbidding and repulsive in appearance. They improve, however, as one proceeds northward and eastward. In the former direction these formations assume a softer outline, and are covered with a rank vegetation, consisting chiefly of scented and aromatic plants, shrubs, and trees. The eastern ranges, which often rise into lofty mountains, are also adorned with a luxuriant vegetation, and are very picturesque. Those seen from Omanbondè, for instance, the nearest point being about twenty English miles, are especially striking and grand. They can only, however, be seen to advantage during the rainy season, when the breadth of light and shadow, ever varying with the now brilliantly illuminated, the now fantastically and gorgeously clouded sky, gives them a thousand varied and beautiful aspects.

The sandstone, again, consists chiefly of table-shaped hills with vertical sides, usually very grotesque and imposing. The finest specimens of the formation are to be met with in the elevated tables of Etjo, Konyali, Ombororoko, and Omuveroo. These rival the granite in point of picturesqueness. On the shores of Omanbondè, the limestone and the sandstone form a junction, as it were, but the latter rock is from that point lost to view, the limestone overlapping it continuously eastward round by the south; yet this range rarely rises conspicuously above the level of the surrounding country.

The granite and sandstone are strongly impregnated with oxide of iron (in some instances, too, the limestone), which gives a reddish tint to most of the formations. I never, however, observed any indications of regular mineral deposits in the Kaoko, or, indeed, in the whole of Western Damara Land, excepting always portions of the Otjirokaku and the Otjomokojo mountain systems; but to the south of the Omaruru River both iron and copper ore exist in considerable quantities. Several mines of the latter mineral have been opened and worked, but have been all lately abandoned. The ore has been generally very rich, but the carriage, both by land and water, is so expensive, that as yet every mining speculation in this country has turned out a failure. Specks of gold have occasionally been found in this ore. As to iron, it is, as I have said, very plentiful. It occurs either as iron-stone, or pure in a crystallized state. The rocks about the lower course of the Swakop abound in both forms. which are generally found imbedded in granite and quartz. But the copper ore thrives best in mica-schist and sandstone. It is, nevertheless, largely disseminated through quartz, though that formation is evidently not congenial to its growth, as no body of ore has ever been found in this species of rock.

CHAPTER VI.

My traveling Stud.—Game plentiful.—Giraffes, Zebras, Gnus, and Koodoos.—Two Giraffes killed.—Lions, Hyenas, Jackals, and other Beasts of Prey.—Great Numbers of Natives.—Honey in great Quantities.—Visitors from the civilized World.—A Night Watch for Game.—Elephants descried.—An Elephant Hunt.—Two Elephants killed.—The Rejoicings of the Damaras on the Prospect of a Gorge.—A Breakfast on an Elephant Foot and a Dish of Honey.

On the third day after the departure of the wagon I set out for the Omuramba Ua' Matako. My "traveling stud" consisted of eight or nine carriage and draught oxen, four donkeys, the old horse, and a few sheep and goats for slaughter and milk. My "personal," again, was composed of Kamapjie, one youth, and three Damaras. I besides expected shortly to be joined by the Bechuana lad Tom, whom I had sent to Otjimbingué to bring on any letters or papers that might chance to be waiting for me at that place.

The Persian monarch who so ungallantly said that women were at the bottom of all mischief, was, I take it, not very far wrong. Through the wiles of a woman I temporarily lost the services of Kamapjie, the most useful of my native attendants. He had married a young girl before he left Otjimbingué, and, on the wagon starting for that place, asked whether his wife should accompany Mortar or remain with us. I told him to please himself. The woman remained; but just as we were setting out she slipped away secretly. Kamapjie requested permission to pursue the fugitive; on being refused, he took himself off too. This loss, just then, was most severely felt, as my party was already very small—in short, insufficient to meet the requirements of the expedition. Moreover, this desertion had a very injurious effect on my other servants, who supposed, and with much apparent reason, that Kamapjie and his amiable spouse had absented themselves from fear of the dangers to be encountered in my service. I kept my eyes on their movements, and succeeded in preventing any farther elopements.

Game now became more plentiful. At the fountain Ombolo (situated on the Omaruru River), which I reached on the third day, I found the country pretty well stocked with giraffes, zebras, gnus, koodoos, etc., and had some very decent shooting. One morning I bagged a fine stag koodoo and two giraffes. The circumstances attending the death of the latter are worth recording.

I was proceeding leisurely along, and had nearly reached the summit of a rising ground, when suddenly a noble giraffe stood before me. Snatching the gun from my native attendant, I ran forward a few paces, leveled, and fired. The bullet told loud-

A WELL-STOCKED SHOOTING-GROUND.

ly on the shoulder of the animal, and, staggering (or apparently so) over the brow of the hill, it was lost to view. I took it for granted that he was killed, or, at all events, mortally wounded; but, before I proceeded to ascertain whether this was the case or not, I reloaded my empty barrel. Reaching the spot where I had first espied the brute, I observed him a short way off, not only alive, but fleeing away at full speed—at least so I thought at the time. I at once fired again right and left, but, to my extreme annoyance, missed with both barrels. A few minutes afterward I once more came up with him, and this time my aim proved more correct, for with a single bullet I laid him prostrate, and with another behind the ear caused his instant death.

I tried now to ascertain where my first bullet had taken effect, but nowhere could I discover any marks except the last two wounds just mentioned. I felt sure, nevertheless, that it had sped true. Suddenly a thought struck me, and I exclaimed almost involuntarily, "By heavens! there must be another giraffe; yes, surely there must. Besides, this is a smaller animal than the one I first fired at." And, turning to my henchman, I asked, "Was there not a larger giraffe?" "Yes, yes," he promptly replied; "the one you fired at when you first took the gun from me was much larger." And, sure enough, so it proved; for, quickly retracing our steps, we discovered a beautiful cow giraffe dead within less than twenty paces from the spot where she had received the fatal wound. I made a similar mistake at a subsequent period while hunting elephants, with this difference, that I was not at all aware of having killed my quarry until two days afterward; in short, I had brought down two very large elephants in two successive shots, thinking all the time that I was firing at one and the same animal.

Game being thus abundant, lions, hyenas, jackals, and other beasts of prey did not fail to attend upon their victims. Indeed, they kept up a terrible hubbub of dissonant noises during the night, causing us much annoyance and disturbance. One evening, before night had yet set in, two lions made their appearance, and destroyed within sight of our camp a sheep that had accidentally been left outside the kraal.

A few elephants had visited the Ombolo fountain about four or five days previous to our arrival, but had not since been heard of. I concluded, therefore, that they had treked on to Omuramba Ua' Matako.

If we had hitherto met but few natives, we now saw more of them than was desirable. Indeed, the Omaruru River, as in their better days, was evidently one of the favorite resorts of the Damaras. From time to time they brought us large supplies of honey, for which I readily gave them a few beads, tobacco, fat, etc. Honey was unusually abundant this season; any quantity of it might have been obtained from the Damaras on very advantageous terms. A trader might do a good business in this article and the wax, which must, of course, be sold with it.

I had appointed Ombolo as the rendezvous where my messengers to Otjimbingué were directed to join me. Accordingly, after somewhat more than a week's absence, they returned, accompanied by a few friends, who had kindly come to pay a visit to the lonely traveler. This unexpected and agreeable surprise, with a goodly supply of newspapers, letters, etc., enabled me to form a pretty good notion of what was going on both at home and abroad, as also to inform other friends, in turn, how I was progressing. I verily believe the value of a letter is never fully appreciated until one becomes, as in my case, shut out for long periods from all communication with the civilized world.

On the 20th of July I reached a place called Hokahanja, situated on the Omuramba Ua' Matako, and commanding a full view of the noble mountains of the same name. I had by this time, in some degree, accomplished one of the objects of this excursion, viz., I had surveyed and mapped a region hitherto unfrequented by the white man, and but rudely represented on the charts.

Geographical research was indeed the prime purpose of the present expedition; hunting and sporting but secondary considerations. But, now that subjects for the compass and ruler were temporarily exhausted, I determined to enjoy my gun. I cared but little, however, for any game except elephants. Accordingly, making many inquiries about these animals from some Ovatjimba whom I found encamped at Hokahanja, I had the satisfaction of learning that they roamed about the neighborhood in considerable numbers. I lost, therefore, no time in setting out in quest of the noble prey; but, after several days' fruitless search, though there was abundant evidence of their late visit to the place, we could discover the beasts themselves nowhere, and returned to camp in any thing but a pleasant temper.

Success was, however, nearer than we suspected. I had scarcely dismounted when a stranger Damara stepped up to inform me that three male elephants had drunk at some pits a short way off on the preceding night. This was good news, and revived our drooping spirits amazingly. Having then enjoyed the luxury of a good wash, and partaken of Desert John's humble fare, I was once more jogging along on my faithful steed, the ox Seeland.

After a short but smart ride we reached the spot indicated, and at once made preparations to attack the elephants should they again honor the place with a visit. Two nights elapsed without our seeing any thing of them. On the morning of the third day, however, and while refreshing the inner man after a long night's dreary watch, unbroken by any thing save the howl of the hyena, the mocking laughs of the jackals, and the growlings of a naughty lion, a native, whose duty it was to report on the appearance of wild animals, suddenly "dropped in," and silently deposited at my feet a small branch of a thorn-tree. Any explanation on the man's part was unnecessary; for, after having carefully examined the twig, which was much jagged and cut by the marks of teeth, I at once came to the conclusion that it had been torn from its stem only a few hours previously by elephants, and merely inquired, "Where are they? and how many in number?" To the first of my queries he replied by pointing to some low broken hills in the neighborhood; to the second he could give no precise answer. He had left some of his companions, however, to watch the movements of the elephants.

In ten minutes I was *en route*, duly equipped. After a rapid and hot march of rather less than two hours' duration, we saw the three natives left as sentinels running toward us in fiery haste, exclaiming, out of breath, "We have seen them! we have seen them! there are three of them!" adding, "But there"—pointing to a small eminence on which was stuck up another "Blackey," looking very much like a huge baboon—"you can see for yourself." I did not wait to be told this twice, and had soon the satisfaction of verifying with my own eyes the statements of the natives. The elephants were then distant about three quarters of a mile apparently, slowly browsing among some brushwood at the foot of a low ridge. A few seconds enabled me to make my arrangements. Leaving a couple of men on the rock to watch the movements of the animals, I proceeded with the rest to the attack, making a considerable circuit in order to get to the leeward of our game, the wind being at first exceedingly unfavorable.

Having gained the foot of the hill where the brutes were last seen, I sent two natives ahead and up the hill to reconnoitre. A low whistle—the signal to advance—was soon heard, which quickly brought me alongside of the scouts. The elephants were still almost on the spot where they had been first seen, but I could only make out two. Putting fresh priming and caps to my rifle, and ramming the bullet well home, I dropped noiselessly down the rock, accompanied by one of my own Damaras, who carried a spare gun. The rest of the party were instructed to remain quietly in their safe hiding-place. A couple of minutes' walk brought me within range of one of the elephants, and, the cover being admirable, I advanced to within about twenty-five paces of the spot where he stood. He was then somewhat aslant from me, but soon turned to me his broadside. Some minutes, however, elapsed before I could make out the exact position of his shoulder. I once attempted to get a little ahead of him, but soon found my situation less favorable than before, and therefore stuck to my first post. With my heavy rifle (carrying steel-pointed conical bullets three to the pound) ready poised in my hand, and a double-barreled smooth-bore, ready cocked, on the ground beside me, I anxiously waited for a chance to fire. I wanted him to move a step or two forward, when I knew his shoulder must be fully exposed. Suddenly he did so, and as quickly I covered his heart, the jungle re-echoing the next instant with an explosion of twelve drachms of Hall's best rifle powder. The effect was deadly. With a frightful rush forward (it was the most tremendous plunge I have ever witnessed by any wild animal), he fell prostrate within about 150 yards of my place of ambush.

Another elephant was evidently following the stricken animal (I did not see him, but judged as much by the noise occasioned by his flight), and having quickly reloaded, I pursued the fugitive. Suddenly, when within less than 200 yards of my intended victim, I found myself in his presence. He was partially facing me, his huge ears spread like a pair of studding-sails, giving a defiant and threatening air to his whole attitude. I did not, however, hesitate, but fired at once at his shoulder, when he instantly betook himself to flight. My henchman, at this moment becoming frightened at the close proximity of the gigantic creature, instead of handing me the spare gun, also ran away. Reloading the rifle, I was soon once more in pursuit, and had shortly the satisfaction of getting again within sight of the poor beast, who, from the quantity of blood on his spoor, was evidently seriously wounded. My attendant now rejoined me. I managed this time to fire all my three barrels; but, though every bullet sped true, they had not the effect of bringing the brute down. To my surprise and satisfaction, I soon discovered, nevertheless, that instead of trying to make his escape (perhaps he felt unequal to the task), he gradually began retracing his steps.

Hearing just at this moment a peculiar hammering noise close under the hill, I turned aside to ascertain its cause. It arose, I found, from a party of Ovatjimba who were busily possessing themselves of a nest of honeycombs. In their company was a number of noisy curs, who, on our approach, began to give tongue in a most alarming manner. For a moment I really feared my quarry would escape me; my misgivings fortunately proved unfounded, for I soon overtook the poor creature resting under a small tree. I crept quite close up to him, and poured once more the contents of all my barrels into his body. Unfortunately, in pulling the trigger of the smooth-bore, both barrels went off together, and the gun being light, and charged with twenty drachms of powder, its rapid recoil struck me violently in the face, one of the cocks burying itself deep in my upper lip and loosening some of my teeth. The shock almost stunned me; it was enough to have prostrated a horse; yet I almost instantly recovered myself. As to the elephant, he did not seem to have been hurt at all, for he remained quite motionless. Large bullets and powder now failed me; I therefore sent my attendant for the spare supply left with the men on the rock. While waiting for his return, I rammed down a couple of small bullets in the rifle and fired again. The result was the same as before, i. e., *nil*. Having at last been rejoined by my men, I gave the wretched animal a couple of additional five-ouncers as a *coup de grace*, when he sunk slowly on his haunches, once more righted himself, and then fell with a crash, a corpse!

While thus engaged a third elephant had been espied by the men on the look-out, and on being informed that he was seen to walk in the direction of his first prostrated companion, I hurried off at once in search of him, but had not gone far before I found myself surrounded with numerous Ovatjimba, or poor Damaras, making the most terrific hubbub in celebration of my success, or rather at the prospect of a gorge on six tons of elephant flesh. I can not describe my annoyance on finding myself thus unexpectedly baffled in my object; for of course the surviving elephant, scared by the noise, had precipitately left the spot where he had been seen. Had it not been for this annoying incident, I should, in all probability, have come up with, and perhaps have killed him too, which would, indeed, have made a glorious day's sport. As it was, I had done pretty well. I had bagged, to use the sportsman's phrase, two fine young males, measuring respectively from the shoulder 11 feet and 11½ feet. The tusks, however, were not on a par with the size of the animals, the largest not much exceeding 50 lbs.

By this time more than fifty Damaras were on the spot, while others were flocking in on all sides, including even Bushmen and Berg Damaras from the neighboring mountain Etjo. The sudden, and to me perfectly astonishing and inexplicable appearance of these carnivorants strongly reminded me of a flight of vultures. The next morning I breakfasted on an elephant's foot, done under the ashes, and a dish of honey—a meal fit for a king.

CHAPTER VII.

Night Watches and Day Trackings.—A great English Sportsman and a great English Traveler's Opinion of Dr. Livingstone.—A Moonlight Ambush.—Living Pictures of Animal Life.—Nature's Menagerie.—Two more Elephants killed.—A Night Assemblage of a large Herd of one hundred and fifty Elephants at a drinking Tank.—The furious Trumpetings of the Herd when fired at.—Female Elephants particularly vicious.—A Cow Elephant-hunt.—The Hunter hunted.—Narrow Escape.—Following the Spoors of a Herd.—The Emigration of Elephants.—Paterfamilias, or General of Division.—An unsatisfactory Shot.—A Tree torn up.—A Picture of Rage and Grandeur.

AFTER the event narrated in the preceding chapter, I worked hard, watching by night for elephants at the water, and following on their spoors in the daytime, but met with no success proportionate to my exertions, which were really severe. I do not mean, however, to task the reader's patience by requesting him to follow me through all my vicissitudes of good and ill luck, through my weary marches and countermarches, through the cold, cheerless nights, and the days of scorching heat, which painfully diversified this exciting quest, but will content myself with selecting a few incidents attending it most worthy of note, which will exhibit under different aspects, and in striking circumstances, the character of the most antediluvian, perhaps, from size, as well as of the most interesting of animals.

I had arrived one day, a few minutes before sunset, at a large vley of water called Okavaoa, of which I had previously heard nothing; for the Damaras, as often mentioned in my former work, are most tardy informants. I only discovered the existence of this reservoir, or tank, by mere accident. From the number of footprints in the sand at the place, it was evident, nevertheless, that it was at times much resorted to by elephants. There was, however, some danger in facing them, as the locality was, with the exception of three or four ant-hills, destitute of adequate shelter. Time, moreover, did not admit of constructing a "skarm," or place of concealment; yet, not relishing the idea of losing a chance, I determined at all hazards to take up my position for a few shots on one of these ant-hills, and carried this resolution into effect on a night when the moon was at its full, a circumstance much in my favor.

A great sportsman and a great traveler[*] once told me—prefacing his pleasant remark with a "saving your presence"—that he considered ambushing for game at night nothing better than

---

[*] On asking the same gentleman what he thought of Dr. Livingstone, he returned me the following characteristic reply: "Well, to look at the man, you would think nothing of him; but he is a plucky little devil."

"dirty poaching." But I must beg leave to differ from my friend, to whose superior judgment in sporting matters I otherwise respectfully bow, for I am quite sure he has had little or no experience in this matter, and probably for this simple reason, that he is always richly furnished with well-trained hunters, and thus has at command the easiest and surest means of enjoying his gun without the fatigues attendant on night watching. During my peregrinations, however, in South Africa, I have seen something of every sort of sport—whether at night by the side of the mirrored water or the "salt-lick," or by day on foot or on horseback—and I must conscientiously declare that, in my opinion, a moonlight ambush by a pool well frequented by wild animals is worth all the other modes of enjoying a gun put together. In the first place, there is something mysterious and thrilling in finding one's self the secret and unsuspected spectator of the wild movements, habits, and propensities of the denizens of nature's varied and wonderful menagerie—no high feeding, no barred gates, no harsh and cruel keeper's voice having yet enervated, damped, or destroyed the elasticity, buoyancy, frolicsomeness of animal life. And then the intense excitement between each expected arrival! The distant footstep, now heard distinctly rattling over a rugged surface, now gently vibrating on the strained ear, as it treads over softer ground—it may be that of a small antelope or an elephant, of a wild boar or a rhinoceros, of a gnu or a giraffe, of a jackal or a lion! And then what opportunities present themselves of observing the habits and peculiarities of each species, and even of individuals, to say nothing of the terrible battles that sometimes take place at these encounters, which can so rarely be witnessed in the daytime. I have certainly learned more of the untamed life of savage beasts in a single night's *tableau vivant* than during months of toilsome wanderings in the broad light of the sun.

Nevertheless, under even the disadvantage of daylight, what can be more picturesque or exciting than the groups of strange wild creatures which constantly cross the path of the traveler, who, plunging into wilds and saharas, finds himself at once in the midst of their quadruped tenants, in their very haunts and homes? or, in the words of Pringle, perhaps the only poet who has derived inspiration from Africa,

> "Away, away from the dwellings of men,
> By the wild deer's haunt, by the buffalo's glen;
> By valleys remote where the oribi plays,
> Where the gnu, the gazelle, and the hartebeeste graze;
> And the kudor and eland unhunted recline
> By the skirts of gray forests o'erhung with wild vine:
> Where the elephant browses at peace in his wood,
> And the river-horse gambols unscared in the flood;
> And the mighty rhinoceros wallows at will
> In the fen where the wild ass is drinking his fill.
>   .   .   .   .   .   .
> O'er the brown Karroo, where the bleating cry
> Of the springbok's fawn sounds plaintively,

And the timorous quagga's shrill whistling neigh
Is heard by the fountain at twilight gray:
Where the zebra wantonly tosses his mane,
With wild hoof scouring the desolate plain;
And the fleet-footed ostrich over the waste
Speeds like a horseman who travels in haste,
Hieing away to the home of her rest,
Where she and her mate have scooped their nest,
Far hid from the pitiless plunderer's view
In the pathless depths of the parched Karroo."

To return to my story. I had not been long perched on my post of observation, *i. e.*, the ant-hill, before a crashing and cracking among the trees and bushes in the neighboring thicket announced the approach of elephants; in a few moments afterward the looming of a dozen huge unwieldy figures in the distance told of their arrival. They appeared to be young males. I was too far to fire with any certainty of success, and therefore left my ambush in order to stalk within range; but the beasts were on their guard, and soon began to retreat, a shot at the nearest hastening their exit. The lead sped true, but not fatally, and the troop disappeared immediately. I had scarcely withdrawn to my ant-hill when another herd, consisting of full-grown bulls, rapidly approached the water, with a steady, heedful step. I ran to a small tree to intercept them, and just as the foremost of them had fairly passed me, in rather dangerous proximity, I pulled the trigger. Receiving the bullet, the brute uttered a faint cry, and with ears erect, and

H

proboscis swaying to and fro, turned and fled, passing within a few paces of the spot where I stood. One of his companions took the same course on the opposite side of the tree, thus placing me between two tremendous foes. I felt frightened, but fortunately they did not attempt to molest me. The elephant I had hit also, to my no small surprise, made his escape in safety. I felt annoyed at my bad success, and was asking myself how it was that my last shot had not proved fatal, when I observed two other elephants cautiously approaching, halting in their approach at some little distance from the water. After a while, however, the leader, more courageous than his associate, pushed forward, stopping, nevertheless, now and then to listen. I was at this moment well covered by an ant-hill, and had my rifle in rest at my side. Having arrived within less than a dozen paces of this spot, just opposite my temporary ambush, the animal stopped short. That pause proved his death, for the next instant a well-directed bullet pierced his heart. Turning sharply round, and staggering forward about fifty paces, he came heavily to the ground, a lifeless mass. He proved a very fine elephant. After a while his companion, who had hurriedly retreated on hearing the report of the gun, again appeared. Of course I was at once in attendance, and was flattering myself that he would give me a fine chance of a broadside, when just at that moment a puff of wind in the wrong direction sent him away in double-quick time. As he was thus retreating I suddenly pulled the trigger, and with good effect, for the beast was found dead next morning at no great distance from the place where he received the wound. On discharging this last shot I was in a sitting posture, and the recoil of the rifle fairly knocked me head over heels, disabling at the same time—which was far more disagreeable—my right shoulder, generally on my hunting excursions protected with a pad, that had been accidentally, on this occasion, left behind at the bivouac. The rifle which did this mischief was charged with twelve drachms of powder. I never afterward exceeded nine and a half, and I have found by experience that quantity to be more than sufficient.

Besides the excruciating pain I suffered in my shoulder, I was also hurt in the chest; nevertheless, I stuck to my post of observation for a while, and was well rewarded for my patience, for the best part of the night's entertainment was yet to come. I had returned but a short time to my ambush, when a large herd of female elephants, with their calves, came on, perfectly heedless of the firing which had previously taken place. With a rush they gained the water, exactly opposite to where I was perched on my ant-hill. Soon afterward they were joined by several other troops pouring in from different directions, consisting of cows and bulls intermixed. It was quite remarkable to observe how they ranged themselves closely side by side, like a line of infantry. They drew themselves up in single file, occupying the entire width of the water (which at that point was 300 yards broad). I estimated their numbers at between 100 and 150. The moon was just then nearly at its zenith, and shed a glorious and dazzling light on the huge creatures below. I felt no inclination to disturb so striking a picture, and, indeed, if I had been so disposed it would little have availed me, as the vley in the direction occupied by the elephants was totally destitute of cover. So all I could do, and did, was to look on, sigh, and admire.

When the elephants had ceased drinking and were about moving away, I hurried forward to intercept their retreat, and, as the very last of them was disappearing, succeeded, with some difficulty, in shouldering my rifle and firing. The rush and the trumpeting which followed this discharge was truly appalling. The herds actually seemed to yell with rage. They were, indeed, an unusually savage lot, as I shortly afterward discovered in an encounter which very nearly cost me my life. My last shot, though a hurried and uncertain one, took effect; a fine cow was killed by it, but her carcass was not discovered till two days afterward. I thus brought down three elephants that night, besides wounding two others.

Some little time after the incident just related, I found myself one morning at a place called Oromboto, a favorite drinking rendezvous of elephants.

A RIGHT ROYAL FROST.

There was no visible water, but the animals could generally procure a sufficiency by digging a few feet below the surface of the earth with their trunks, a mode of quenching their thirst to which they are very partial. There were, however, several other and similar watering-places in the neighborhood; in order, consequently, to have more than one string to my bow, I sent parties in various directions to search out fresh spoors. One of these parties returned almost immediately with the news that they had suddenly come upon two young male elephants. I was soon in pursuit of them; but, alas! on reaching the spot where they had been seen, we found, instead of two bulls, a herd of cows and calves—some of my old acquaintances. I felt at first very loth to attack them, and for two reasons: first, because she-elephants are infinitely more dangerous than males; and, secondly, because they yield but little ivory, to say nothing of the mischief done to the species, who are slow breeders, producing, moreover, only one calf at a time. As I was, however, on the spot, and, besides, really in want of meat—hundreds of starving Ovatjimba following in my train begging for food—I, after due hesitation, resolved on the assault.

I had crept up to within less than thirty paces of a noble cow, and was only waiting for the brute to present some eligible point to fire at, when, while thus watching her movements, two others had unperceived approached me from behind, and, before

I became aware of their nearness to me, were actually only about fifteen yards from where I sat. Indeed, they would probably have been upon me in a second or two had I not chanced to cast my eyes on my native attendant, who was crouched alongside of me in fear and trembling, with his teeth chattering quite audibly. He had discovered the danger, but had either not the sense to warn me, or had become too frightened to speak. It was by following the man's fixed and frightened gaze that I first became conscious of our unpleasant situation. To rise to my feet—to clear, with a tremendous leap, the first bush that obstructed my flight, was but the work of a moment. The brutes pursued me instantly, and I was obliged to abandon precipitately a second ambush I had taken up. The troop at last stopped, and, following their example, I dropped flat behind a bush.

The whole herd was now facing me, distant only a hundred yards. What with their small, peering, restless, mischievous-looking eyes, huge flapping ears, elevated trunks, etc., their appearance was altogether most fierce and threatening. I was more than once in the act of pulling the trigger at the foremost cow, but was afraid, feeling certain that if she received the shot, even should it prove fatal, the entire body of them would once more be at my heels. While in this dilemma, they suddenly wheeled right about. This was my time, and I instantly fired at the original leader. The act proved a rash one. With a shrill and heart-piercing trumpeting, the beasts charged down upon me furiously. Those who know what it is to run for one's life can easily imagine that I did my best to outstrip my pursuers. The rifle, a heavy one, considerably impeded my progress; but the shorter the distance became between me and my foes, the tighter I grasped my weapon. For some seconds my escape seemed more than doubtful; but, providentially, just as I was almost out of breath, the elephants stopped short in their chase. Had they but followed for another fifty yards, destruction would have been inevitable, for I had to cross a considerable *open* space.

At last, feeling myself in tolerable security, I halted, and ascended a conspicuous ant-hill to ascertain what my enemies were about; but I could only perceive, as I thought, a solitary elephant standing under a tree, just on the edge of the open space alluded to. Thinking it might possibly be the one I had fired at, and that she might be more or less disabled, I ventured to approach, but had not proceeded far before I found out my mistake. Instead of a single elephant, it turned out to be about one half of the whole herd; and they looked so exasperated and so on their guard, to say nothing of the exposed nature of the ground, that I at once withdrew, thinking discretion in this case the better part of valor. But, seeing me, they soon renewed their charge, now and then stopping as if to reconnoitre. I managed, nevertheless, to stow myself away in a place of security, whence I watched their movements with great curiosity.

Coming to a certain spot, probably where we had been standing, they would suddenly halt and examine the ground, apparently with great care. They would then as suddenly move off at full speed, with trunks erect, ears flapping most audibly against their rugged sides, switching at the same time their stumpy and almost hairless tails rapidly to and fro. After a while they were lost to view, and I was not sorry at their departure, while I secretly vowed never to molest cows, more especially when accompanied with calves, unless I could get adequate cover.

My bad luck on the present occasion was compensated for in some degree on the ensuing night, when a fine male elephant dropped dead to my shot.

One more story, and I shall have done with elephants, for the present at least.

At an early hour on the day previous to the one I had fixed on for my departure from Oromboto, I took up the spoors of an immense herd of female elephants; and the reason why I so soon broke the resolution so lately formed was, that in the spoors just mentioned there were tracks of first-rate bulls among those of the cows. Now I hoped to find the bulls by themselves, or perhaps lingering behind the rest of the troop. The direction these elephants at first pursued led me to suppose they were about to visit their usual haunts, but subsequent circumstances soon convinced me that, far from this being the case, they were evidently taking their leave of this neighborhood altogether. Indeed, I came to the conclusion that they were returning to their homes in the Kaoko, having found that country, on my return journey through that part of Damara Land, every where quite void of elephants, though celebrated as their habitual abode. Hour after hour elapsed, miles after miles of weary walking were passed, without the least indication that the herds would come to a halt. The zeal of the trackers began to flag, and I felt inclined to give up the pursuit, when suddenly, at about two o'clock one afternoon, we espied the rear-guard of the stupendous game slowly wending their way across some rising ground a short distance ahead. At this sight every face brightened, the step became once more elastic, and hunger, thirst, and fatigue were all forgotten at the exciting prospect before us.

Leaving all my people behind with the exception of one of my own native boys, I started in pursuit of the quarry. The cover unfortunately was scanty and unfavorable in the extreme; but, in the hope of finding better, I followed leisurely and cautiously in the immediate track of the elephants, keeping a sharp look-out on every side for fear of leaving any behind. Suddenly my henchman pulled me by the sleeve, and at the same time pointing to a small break on our left (above which appeared the backs of some suspicious-looking animals), whispered, "Bull elephants." "Capital," I responded, in the same subdued tone; and at once leaving the herd immediately before me, I made for the spot indicated. In a very short time I found myself within easy range, but, to my dismay, discovered that almost all the animals were females with their young. There were two or three fine males, however, one of whom evidently acted as the *paterfamilias* to this portion of the emigrants, or, militarily speaking, as a general of division. This particular elephant was standing in a position outskirting the rest, but his shoulder, unfortunately, was partially hidden by two large calves, which the jolly old patriarch was busily caressing. A very slight change of attitude was all I required to enable me to send him to the land of shades, and I waited in breathless anxiety for this opportunity. To my intense disappointment, however, the huge brute all at once tossed his trunk on high, and giving his sides two or three smart slaps with his monster ears, turned abruptly round and made off, instantly followed by the whole herd. But it would never do to allow them to escape thus. Springing, therefore, to my feet, and advancing a few steps, I leveled and fired at the second in size of the males just as he was disappearing from view. The bullet struck him, but very unsatisfactorily, for it glanced off and went

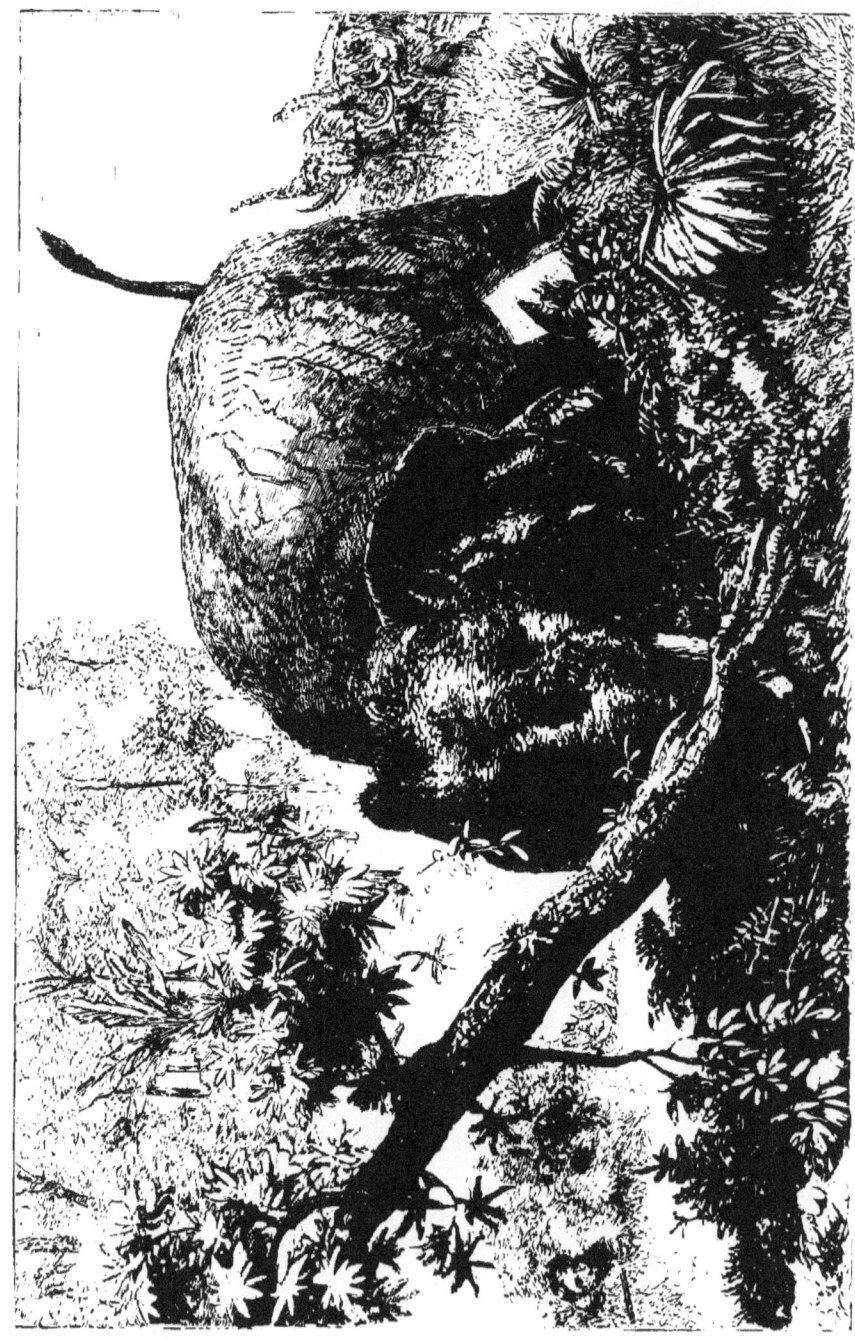

FURIOUS CHARGE OF A PATERFAMILIAS.

hissing through the air. In a moment the retreating column turned right about, and made a furious and headlong charge all but over me. I had thrown myself flat on the ground, sheltered only by an insignificant little shrub. A false move would have been death. After looking about him inquiringly, the *paterfamilias* made a second random dash at the supposed foe, in which charge the enraged brute actually tore up by the roots and carried off a whole tree. He looked the very picture of rage and grandeur as, for a few seconds, he stood exposed to full view, part of the shattered tree still clinging to his tusks. I was thoroughly scared, and held my breath in dreadful and agonizing suspense. Not being able to discover any thing, he once more, accompanied by the rest of the troop, faced right about, and was soon lost to view in the jungle. I hailed their departure with rapture; for, though I had failed in my object, I felt heartily thankful that my life was saved.

CHAPTER VIII.

A Herd of Camelopards or Giraffes.—One Shot.—A comic Scene.—A Lion wounded.—The Antelope.—The Eland.—The Numerousness of this ruminant Tribe.—The Springbok, its extraordinary Agility.—A Damara trading Caravan destined for Ovambo Land.—Retainers of Afrikander.—I refuse to join the Caravan.—Dearth of Water.—Rejoined by the Wagon.—Start again to the Eastward.—Lion Maneaters, a Native carried off by one of them.—Mr. Green's Narrative.—Lion Chase.—Fragments and Bones of the Native discovered.—Another Visit from a Lion.—Dismay in the Encampment.—Wild Boars.—Dogs no Match for them.—I overtake the Caravan, and determine to accompany it for a while.

Besides elephant-hunting I had also some other sport, for the country was fairly besprinkled with a variety of game. Indeed, had I killed for the mere sake of killing, I might easily have destroyed great numbers of the *feræ naturæ;* but I abstained from the temptation, first, because I am averse to wanton slaughter, and, secondly, because I made it a point seldom or never to fire at any other game while in the pursuit of elephants—a rule I strongly recommend to such of my readers as may hereafter engage in this spirit-stirring chase. The reason of this recommendation will be obvious when I state that, the moment the natives get the prospect of a feast, they care not a straw for any thing else; and as the sportsman is more or less dependent on them as trackers, carriers, etc., this consideration is really to him an important one. The keener the appetite of his followers is kept, the more effectual will be their efforts to aid him.

One morning I met with an adventure of a somewhat novel kind. I was accompanied by nearly one hundred starving Ovatjimba, and having come unperceived upon a herd of camelopards, I succeeded, after a short stalk, in bringing down a good-sized bull. While the poor brute was still in his death-struggles, the natives, in their usual wild, careless manner, came running up to surround him, joyfully uproarious in the anticipation of an unexpected banquet; for a gorge on animal flesh is to savages the height of happiness. I kept aloof from the motley group, being aware, from previous experience, that a wounded giraffe in his expiring agonies is a most dangerous foe. And it was well I took this precaution; for suddenly the prostrate beast made a violent effort to rise, and heaving his branchy neck on high, describing with it a kind of semicircle through the air, falling at the same time again, while using his heels most effectually, heavily to the ground, he sent all the by-standers in an instant sprawling in the dust. At first, dreading some mischief, I ran forward to assist any who might be hurt; but seeing that, beyond a heavy fall, a few scratches, and the loss of sundry pieces

I

of skin, no serious injury had been sustained, I burst into a hearty laugh, for the appearance of the discomfited crew, with their crestfallen looks, stupefied aspects, and dust-covered figures, was highly ludicrous.

Lions were not uncommon in these parts; but, except at night, when they occasionally exerted their odious musical powers, we neither saw nor heard much of them. One day, however, about three o'clock in the afternoon, we came unexpectedly upon a huge male lion, walking at kingly leisure about two hundred yards in advance of us. Unfortunately, my double-barreled rifle, which I had discharged in the early part of the day, was unloaded. I had intended to clean it out at the first halting-place, much resorted to by elephants, which I hoped to reach on the ensuing evening. Thus it happened that as I rode along I could, merely out of curiosity, keep the brute in view. We gained, however, rapidly on our royal attendant, and my henchman having come up with the "smasher," I felt the temptation to become nearer acquainted with his majesty irresistible. Accordingly, when he was about one hundred paces distant I suddenly dismounted, and, raising the heavy elephant rifle to my shoulder, quickly drew the trigger just as the lazy animal was about to disappear under a small tree. We could distinctly see the bullet (a 5-ounce) enter his hind quarters, apparently traversing the entire length of his body, for it took its egress through one of his shoulders. Uttering a growl, down came his majesty instantly on his haunches; yet, strange to say, although the whole party was in full view of him, and making, besides, a considerable noise, he continued quite unaware of our presence, and kept staring intensely ahead. I had soon loaded another rifle (the double-barrel this time), and was just putting the caps on, when the brute slowly rose and limped forward. He did not proceed far before he lay down; and I was already within less than twenty yards of him, and about to emerge from behind a tree that had afforded us mutual concealment, in order to give him the *coup de grace*, when suddenly, and for the first time, he perceived me, and, rising on his feet, disappeared before I could get a shot at him in a thick brake immediately at his back. There, being pressed for time, we left him. There was not much blood on his track, but splinters of bone strewed the ground in more than one spot. The ultimate fate of this lion is unknown to me, though it is scarcely possible he could survive the terrible wound he had received.

In the course of my rambles in this district I met with numerous traces of elands, but only once caught a glimpse of the animals themselves. I had never before seen this fine antelope so far to the southward in Damara Land, but had once been informed that a herd had descended as far as Otjimbingué.

I was, however, very particular in my inquiries about this numerous tribe, for the great peculiarity of the zoology of South Africa is the predominance of that particular form of the ruminant order of Mammalia called Antelope. The horns of these ruminants marking their species, as most of my readers may know, are of two kinds in respect of substance. One consists of almost solid bone. Such horns, or, more properly, antlers, are peculiar to the deer class; they are usually branched, and are shed and renewed annually. The other kind of horn consists of a cone or core of bone, covered by a sheath of true horny matter; such horns are never shed, but are increased by annual growths; the ruminants possessing them are called "hollow horned;" they comprise the ox, the sheep, the goat, and the antelope, and, save the anomalously horned giraffe, no other kind of ruminants but these exist in South Africa. The antelopes, however, have been there created in unusual numbers, and in a great variety of specific forms, constituting a series that fills up the wide hiatus between the goat and the ox, and on which the ingenuity of the splitting naturalist has been, and still is exercised in the manufacture of *Sub-genera*, and the imposition thereon of long and hard names, such as *Catoblepas, Aigoceros, Acronitus, Cephalopas,* etc.

The gemsbok (antelope oryx) is remarkable for its long and straight horns, with which it sometimes transfixes the lion, whom it has been known to beat off, and even to kill. A larger species of antelope is that which is called the "roan," or bastard gemsbok. But the blesbok is the most peculiar of them all. It is of a beautiful violet color, and is found in company with black wildebeestes, and springboks in countless thousands, on the vast green plains of short, crisp sour grass, occupying a central position in South Africa. Cattle and horses refuse to pasture on the grassy products of these plains, which afford sustenance to myriads of this antelope, whose skin emits a most delicious and powerful perfume of flowers and sweet-smelling herbs. A secretion issues from between the hoofs of the animal which has likewise a pleasing odor. The giant antelope of the tribe is that species which the Dutch Boers call eland, that is, elk. It stands often six feet high.

The power of these ruminating animals to endure thirst or to abstain from water varies greatly in different species, and depends upon the organization of the second cavity of their complex stomach, called by anatomists the reticulum, and by agriculturists the "honeycomb bag." In some the cells are extremely shallow, and form a mere pattern of hexagons by raised lines on the surface; in the other species these lines rise into walls, and the cells are deep; in others the deep cells are divided into smaller ones; in the camel tribe they are expanded into bags; and in proportion to their capacity of retaining fluid is the ruminant's power of abstaining from drinking. It is doubtful, however, whether the long-abstaining kinds of antelopes never drink; this is certainly not the case with the eland, though the dew-drops collected in the morning's grazing may suffice, when stored up in the cells of the reticulum, for the day.

All these graceful and agile creatures exist in countless numbers on the fertile flats of South Africa. One of them, the springbok, has earned its name from the extraordinary and almost perpendicular leaps it makes when hunted. This animal bounds without an effort to a height of ten or twelve feet at one spring, clearing from twelve to fourteen feet of ground. It appears to soar—to be suspended for a moment in the air; then, touching the ground, to make another dart, or rather flight, aloft, without the aid of wings, by the elastic springiness of its legs.

To resume my narrative. After roaming about the country to my heart's content, finding that the elephants had temporarily absented themselves, I determined to give up shooting for the present, and to devote some time to rest and rational recreation. Accordingly, I repaired to Otutundu, situated on the Omuramba Ua' Matako, where there was abundance of water and pasturage for my cattle. I had appointed no particular locality as a rendezvous for my people, now daily expected with the wagon from Otjimbingué. I had left it to their own discretion to strike the Omuramba wherever they might find water abundant. But Otutundu was as likely a place to find them as any other, being one of the chief halting-points for wagons from the southward toward the river in question. My party, however, had not, on my reaching that place, yet arrived; and having waited some time without receiving any news of their proceedings and whereabout, moreover thinking it just possible they might pass me unnoticed, I deemed it advisable to dispatch a couple of men to inform them where I was, and to bring on the wagon. Having succeeded at the same time in engaging some native carriers, I profited by the opportunity to forward my ivory to Barmen.

While awaiting the arrival of the wagon, I was unexpectedly joined by a Damara trading-caravan destined for Ovambo Land. It consisted of upward of 400 persons—of men and women in about equal numbers. These traders brought with them a few cattle and sheep, but their chief articles of barter were strings and corselets, with beads and buttons made from the shells of ostrich eggs. For this female gear, which was much in demand among the Ovambo women, they received in exchange assegais, hatchets, dagger-knives, iron and copper beads, iron anklets, iron bracelets, etc. But in the present instance I very much suspected that trade was a mere pretense—a cloak, in short, to veil their real object, which I had no doubt was to spy out the country. A portion of the Damaras constituting the caravan were retainers of J. Afrikander, who had long contemplated, as I well knew, a descent on the Ovambo, and was only waiting for a plausible pretext so to do. The other members of this traveling community claimed (under one of Katjiamoha's sons) a sort of independence, though they acknowledged Afrikander as their head. The leaders of the expedition were very anxious to secure my company, but, dreading the companionship of such a number of importunate and unscrupulous beggars, I declined the honor. In order, in fact, the more effectually to shake them off, I started on a short excursion round the neighborhood, and, on my return to camp, was pleased to find that the nuisance had disappeared. I now flattered myself that I was quit of their company forever; but in this hope I was deceived, for it was not long before I overtook them.

The country in which we were traveling had been represented by various informants as excessively dry to the eastward; but having hitherto found abundance of water at all the points I had visited along the Omuramba, I reasonably doubted the correctness of this description, and determined to ascertain the fact for myself. A couple of days' exploration proved, alas! that the natives had in this instance spoken the truth. The disappointment was great, as it had now become evident that I could not, with any certainty of success, travel much farther until the rains fell, a period still far distant. I determined, however, in the mean time, to make what progress I could. If I could but get as far as Otjituo (one of the most easterly points reached by Mr. Green in the preceding year), something would be gained. I only awaited the arrival of the absent men to begin the operation.

On the 29th of August the wagon at last appeared. It was now about seven weeks since I had last seen it. The repairs it required, being much more extensive than was at first anticipated, had occasioned the long delay in its reappearance. I now lost as little time as possible in setting out on my excursion eastward. Just before starting, Pereira asked permission to return to Otjimbingué, to make some arrangements for his wife, who was residing at that station; and, as my progress could be but slow, and he would have time to overtake me, I granted his request. I profited by this opportunity to write to a few friends and acquaintances, as also to obtain an additional stock of stores, etc., which I expected to arrive by the first vessel at Walwich Bay. Pereira was likewise to bring on such letters and papers as might chance to be at Otjimbingué for me. We both left Otutundu on the same day in opposite directions.

In the afternoon of the second day from our departure we reached water, *i. e.*, a small collection of dilapidated pits composed of quicksand, on the banks of the Omuramba. It was with the utmost difficulty we could obtain from this scanty source sufficient drink for our cattle, sheep, etc.—

a foretaste of the troubles henceforth to be encountered.

A fine old bull-elephant had lately, as we gathered from his footprints, been on this spot to quench his thirst; thinking he might return, or that some of his associates might visit the place, I took up an ambush close by on the following night; but my watch was in vain. Toward morning, two lions hard by began to roar most lustily. It is strange how the sound affected me. I could scarcely believe I was the same being who, a few years before, would bivouac single-handed in the very midst of these animals, scarcely noticing their presence, while now their mere growl made me nervous. In this instance, however, it was perhaps not so much to be wondered at, as it was in this very neighborhood that two man-eaters had, in the previous autumn, attacked Green's party in the most daring manner, carrying off one of his native servants from the very midst of his camp.

My friend having kindly placed parts of his journals at my disposal, I avail myself of his permission to introduce here, with a few trifling alterations, the particulars of this tragical event.

"*Oct. 21st*, 1858. Last night a terrible tragedy was enacted in my cattle-fold by two daring lions. The night was intensely dark, with occasional rain; and fearing lions might select such a night to surprise their prey, I sat up watching until a late hour. I had just lain down, remarking to my friend that in case of a visit from these brutes the oxen would give the alarm, when on a sudden there arose an awful scream, followed by a death-like groan, such as I shall never forget; the very recollection of it chills my blood. Two lions had entered the inclosures, and succeeded in carrying away a poor fellow, whom they tore to pieces and devoured within a short distance of our camp. We neither could nor dared attempt a rescue. The unfortunate man was lying in his hut with his wife and two little children, when one of the monsters forced his way through from the back, and seized him, at the same time inflicting two wounds upon the woman. The poor wretch, in his hurried exit, had evidently, in endeavoring to save himself, laid hold of the poles of the hovel, for the whole back part of the tenement was carried away.

"On making the terrible discovery, a scene ensued which defies description, and which must have been seen to be fully realized. Of course, sleep was out of the question; and in order to guard as far as possible against a similar occurrence, we kept up a constant discharge of fire-arms during the remainder of this woeful night.

"This morning, as soon as it was light enough to see, we took up the spoor of the lions, and within about two hundred yards of the kraal discovered the spot where it was evident the poor man had been destroyed and devoured. The cincture he had worn round his waist was alone left to tell of his dreadful fate, though in following up the trail some parts of his leg bones were afterward found. We chased the brutes for about twelve miles, when we were compelled to relinquish the pursuit without having obtained a shot at them—without, indeed, having caught more than one glimpse of them in the distance. I much regretted having started without my horse, which, though useless as a hunter, would undoubtedly have taken me sufficiently near to get a shot, and to lead the pack of dogs up to the enemy."

On the second day after the fatal accident Mr. Green bid farewell to the dreadful place, thinking thereby to get rid of his terrible foes; but they followed on his spoor, and on the evening of the third day one of the man-eaters once more entered his inclosures. On this occasion the horrid monster passed by the oxen without molesting them, but, entering the sheep-kraal, carried off one of its inmates, putting the remainder to flight. "What with the screechings of the terrified women and children," writes my friend, "the hallooings of the men, the rush of the cattle and the sheep, firebrands whizzing through the air, the discharge of fire-arms, the growls of the lions, and other discordant noises, the scene was one which baffles description. I leveled my rifle at the marauder as he was passing the wagon, not above five paces distant, but unfortunately missed fire, and when I again pulled the trigger he had disappeared in the

CHASE OF THE WILD BOAR.

darkness. This lion was almost immediately joined by his companion, when they set up a roaring duet that lasted, with very little intermission, until break of day. Continual discharges of fire-arms kept them from doing farther mischief."

Wild boars were rather numerous along the Omuramba, and frequently afforded us excellent coursing. The speed of these animals is surprisingly great. On open ground, when fairly afoot, I found the dogs no match for them, and yet some of my curs were rather swift of foot. The dogs, nevertheless, dodged them at times successfully; at others they came willingly to bay. They fight desperately. I have seen wild boars individually keep off most effectually half a dozen fierce assailants. I have also seen them, when hotly pursued, attack and severely wound their pursuers. We killed occasionally two, and even three of them, in the course of a day. When young and fat they proved capital eating, and from their novelty were quite a treat. Other game was also almost daily secured, and my party gorged to their hearts' content on animal food. Indeed, we had plenty to spare for our new friends, the Damaras of the trading caravan, whom we had overtaken in the neighborhood of Omborombonga. The animals we usually killed were koodoos, pallahs, and other wild creatures, who can abstain long from drinking, for water is exceedingly scarce in this country—so much so that it was only with very great difficulty we could obtain a sufficiency for our cattle, etc.

I had hoped to find elephants along the Omuramba, as during the previous summer they had been very numerous in these parts. The late great drought, however, had made them abandon this favorite haunt, to muster, it was reported, in great force at Omanbondè—Galton's magnificent imaginary lake, which, on our visit to it in 1850, turned out to be but a large dried-up vley. The Damaras destined for Ovambo Land proposed taking this place *en route;* and, having previously ascertained that the Omuramba was impracticable for traveling beyond a certain point, I determined, as I had just then plenty of leisure time, to accompany them. I left the wagon and the greater portion of my people at a place called Othumbu Yakausha, and on the morning of the 16th of September arrived at Omanbondè, or Saresab, as it is called in the Hottentot language.

CHAPTER IX.

A Retrospect.—Omanbondè a Sheet of Water.—Rhinoceroses, Hippopotami, and other large Game in Abundance.—A beautiful Landscape.—Elephants numerous.—Fatigues and Dangers of Elephant-hunting.—Hints to Elephant-hunters.—Extreme Thirst.—Extreme Exhaustion.—A Man killed by a Rhinoceros.—A Creeping Stalk of a Rhinoceros.—Attack of a Rhinoceros.—An adventurous Chase.—Discovery of the Man killed.—Accidental Death.—Damara Grave, and Rites of Sepulture.—The Feast after the Funeral.—Lions attack a crippled Rhinoceros.

It was now close upon eight years and a half since I first visited Omanbondè. Eight years and a half! the fifth part of man's life in its full vigor. What was I at the beginning of this period, and what am I now? Where are the once ruddy cheeks? Where is that elasticity of foot and spirit that once made me laugh at hardships and dangers? Where that giant health and strength that enabled me to vie with the natives in enduring the extremes of heat and cold, of hunger, thirst, and fatigue? Gone, gone—ay, forever! The spirit still exists unsubdued, but, what with constant care, anxiety, and exposure, the power of performance has fled, leaving but the shadow of my former self. What have I accomplished during these long years? What is the result of all this toil, this incessant wear and

K

tear of body and mind! The answer, if candid, must be apparently very little. This is a sad retrospect of the fifth part of a man's life, while still in the pride of manhood. And yet I feel that I have not been idle—that I have done as much as any man under similar circumstances could have done; and so, with this poor consolation, I must rest content.

On my first visit to this place in company with Mr. Galton, Omanbondè was, as I have already mentioned, nothing more than a large dried-up vley, and this being again a year of severe drought—at least to judge from the state of the Omuramba—I had expected to see it in a similar condition. Most agreeably was I then surprised to find a sheet of water four and a half miles in extent, abounding with water-fowl, and largely resorted to by a great variety of game and wild animals, such as elephants, rhinoceroses, elands, koodoos, gemsboks, zebras, pallahs, lions, etc. There were no hippopotami, however, though plenty of "sea-room" for a dozen or two. Besides this vley, I discovered another in the immediate neighborhood almost rivaling Omanbondè in size; several Bushmen villages besprinkled its borders or banks, which were very high, but sloping, not steep, and richly covered with a luxuriant vegetation, consisting chiefly of very fine groves of acacias, and the giraffe thorn-tree, just bursting forth into spring life. In the background, and to the northward, were the broken and picturesque limestone ranges of Otjirokaku, Otjomokojo, etc. Altogether the scene, very pleasing, was rendered perhaps more so by the contrast it afforded to the dry and parched state of the country immediately surrounding it. To me it was a real oasis in the desert, and I at once determined to send for my wagon, and settle down quietly until Pereira's return from Otjimbingué.

Elephants being rather numerous in this locality, I lost no time in beginning operations against them. I took advantage of the moonlight to watch for them at night, and followed on their spoor in the daytime. At first I was unfortunate, but at last met with considerable success. Some of my prizes proved splendid specimens of the giant race, with tusks that a Gordon Cumming would have beheld with rapture. I had several very interesting, and sometimes dangerous encounters with my huge game; but having already, and so lately, given a series of adventures with these animals, I will not at present enter into details, but merely confine myself to a few general remarks.

Elephant-hunting on foot and in the hot season is most laborious and harassing work. Indeed, a long experience of this pursuit has brought me to the conviction that, under such circumstances, it is far more trying and distressing to the constitution than the most severe manual labor. It was rarely or never that I could track, stalk, and kill my elephant, and return to camp in less than ten hours;

more frequently it occupied twelve, fourteen, or sixteen—nay, I have been as much as two days and a night on one hunt. My attendants (native) were at times so completely done up—and I generally nearly as much so—that on their return home they would fall asleep where they stood, alike indifferent to hunger, to the chilling night air, or to the scorching sun, as the case might be. I found it at last necessary to divide on these occasions my men into two parties, each party taking its regular turn of duty. It was not hunger or fatigue, however, that was so trying as the heat. The sun "blazing in a sky of brass," heating the atmosphere to a state of suffocation, and the loose sandy soil to a blistering intensity, made "Water! water!" the incessant cry; but water—frequently half boiling—even when we could carry a decent supply, did rarely allay our burning thirst. Indeed, every fresh draught seemed sometimes merely to augment our ardent craving for more, which often almost bordered on madness. A giddiness, a languor, a sense of oppression throughout the whole system, a choking sensation in the throat, difficulty of speech, a fearful palpitation of the heart, and a nightmare feeling about the chest, were the frequent consequences of our excessive fatigues. For my own part, when once fairly done up, nothing could restore me to myself but quiet, a plentiful supply of cool water, and, above all, a good wash. I remember, on one particular occasion, when, after a long running chase, I had come up within 150 yards of an elephant I had seriously wounded, being so thoroughly exhausted as to be actually unable to advance a few paces to give him the necessary *coup de grâce*. I was obliged to rest a few minutes, and before I could recover myself the brute had moved off, and was lost to me forever. Words, indeed, can convey no adequate idea of the hardships and sufferings of the elephant-hunter on foot, at the dry time of the year, in regions where water is scarce. Experience alone can enable one fully to understand the severity of the sport in which he takes so much delight.

There were also a good many rhinoceroses at Omanbondè, but it was difficult so to guard so large a sheet of water as to obtain a shot at them when they came to drink at night. I managed, however, to knock over a few; and knowing the general predilection of readers for adventures ending in a tragical result, I give them the following story, or rather narrative of an event witnessed by myself, which will show the great ferocity of these animals, and the dangers attendant on attacking them without extreme precaution.

On the night of the 19th of September, favored by a beautiful moon, I had taken up my position alone, as usual, in a shallow nullah, or natural ditch, whence I could command an extensive view. At about eleven o'clock a herd of elephants approached, and just as the leader was about to cross the nullah where I was stationed, I fired. The bullet struck the beast in the forepart of the shoulder, and I thought I had certainly killed him, when, with a loud shriek, he wheeled abruptly about, and, dashing furiously into a neighboring cover, effected his escape.

All was now again silent; and after waiting patiently a long time in the hope of some other game, and getting tired at last of the useless watch, I made for my camp. I had not, however, proceeded many steps before I perceived, to my delight, two black rhinoceroses sauntering leisurely along at the farthest westerly extremity of the marsh. At once dropping my spare gun and my blanket, I threw myself flat on the ground, and began creeping toward my unexpected quarry. The locality, unfortunately, did not afford me the slightest cover—not even a tuft of grass—and the "stalk" consequently became one of difficulty and danger. I had proceeded perhaps about twenty paces, when, to my annoyance and dismay, I saw the rhinoceroses turn abruptly away from the water and make straight for my person. On making the discovery, I am free to confess that my first impulse was to run away; but, on second thoughts, I resolved to abide their approach. Having advanced to within about sixty yards of me they abruptly halted, eying suspiciously the black mass before them. Their survey evidently gave them but little satisfaction; for, uttering a snort, and tossing their unwieldy heads on high, they retreated a step or two backward, as if preparing for a charge. Seeing this, I determined to be beforehand with my antagonists; and, notwithstanding their unfavorable position, I knelt down, leveled full at the breast of the foremost, and pulled the trigger. The bullet took effect. On receiving the shot the brute swerved somewhat to the right, and then dashed wildly forward, followed by his companion. I at once felt convinced that one of them was seriously, if not mortally wounded, and, having reloaded, I followed quickly in the direction indicated by their noisy progress. After a few minutes' walk I came up with both; they were standing quite still, evidently listening. But on my attempting to creep up to them, the one in the rear made a furious charge toward me, and I was heartily glad to save myself by a precipitate flight. I had nevertheless ascertained, beyond doubt, that the wounded beast was a complete cripple, and anticipated no difficulty in finishing him on the following morning.

Accordingly, as soon as it was light enough to continue the search with something like safety, I started in pursuit of my game, accompanied by the very best of my Damara attendants (Kozengo), and the lad Chookoroo, to carry a spare rifle. A short walk brought us to the spot where I had left the rhinoceroses on the preceding night. Pools of blood marked the progress of the one whose right fore-leg was evidently smashed. Knowing the great ferocity of the black rhinoceros when wounded, I repeatedly warned my attendants to be on their guard. I had done so for the last time, and we had just emerged from some low brushwood, purposing to enter a small thorn brake, when, lo! the monster lying on his side, to all appearances quite dead. On making this discovery, Kozengo turned smilingly to me, and ejaculated "Jacocca"—dead. "Well," I rejoined; "but take care, for there was another rhinoceros in company with him last night."

I had taken a step or two forward, and was in some measure hidden from the animal by a small tree, when suddenly I observed my attendants wheel about and retreat precipitately. Not seeing the cause of their sudden flight (though of course suspecting it), I stood my ground, when all at once I caught sight of the brute protruding his ugly head within a few paces of my person. As he was coming right at me, I deemed it, under the circumstances, imprudent to fire, and quickly took to my heels. He followed at his best pace, which was really very rapid, considering his crippled condition. In my hurried flight my wide-awake blew off my head, and fell right in the path of the pursuing beast, who pulled up abruptly at the sight of it. Swift as thought, I turned on my heels and fired, but fairly, I believe, missed, for the monster at once dashed forward again, snorting violently. After running for a short distance he again halted, but kept looking about him in a very restless manner. I then crept cautiously up to within about 100 yards of him, and just as for a moment he exposed his broadside full toward me, I fired. He dropped dead to the shot.

Having ascertained that his life was quite extinct, I hallooed for my runaway men, but receiving no answer, concluded they had returned to camp. Quieted by this thought, I was gazing at the prostrate animal, when all at once my attention was drawn to a confused noise hard by, as of a number of human beings discussing some exciting event; and in a few moments I saw several natives, headed by Chookoroo and "Paadmaker"—the last of whom I had sent on the spoor of the wounded elephant—emerge from the bushes. The lad was crying bitterly, while Paadmaker had his hands tightly clasped to his sides, just like a man seized with sudden pain. My first impression was that the man had been hurt by the elephant; but, alas! his grief arose from a far more serious cause. A dreadful suspicion then took possession of me, and I hastily exclaimed, "Where's Kozengo?" "Dead, sir!" was the solemn and startling reply. "Dead?" I repeated; "impossible! how? why, the rhinoceros has never been out of my sight. Besides," addressing myself, "I have heard no scream, no groan, nor any other cry of distress." "Oh yes," sobbed poor Chookoroo, "Kozengo is dead; he is killed by the rhinoceros." "Show me the man and the spot," I said, as I mechanically turned to follow the men. We had not far to go. Within a stone's throw I found the unfortunate man lying under a bush, stiff and motionless! His forehead was split in two, apparently by a single thrust of the horn of the infuriated animal, and part of the dislocated brains was mingling with the dust. His face, which was slightly turned upward, wore the same calm, placid, though somewhat heavy expression as in life. For a moment or so I could scarcely realize the terrible event, and, involuntarily addressing the corpse, I muttered, "Are you really dead, Kozengo? Why did you not run farther off; you had plenty of time to save yourself?"

"So as I gazed on him, I thought or said,
 'Can this be death? then what is life or death?
 Speak!' but he spoke not: 'Wake!' but still he slept."

We found this poor fellow, as I have said, lying under a bush with his head close upon the ground. Had he throughout kept this position—and probably he did so—it seems impossible that the rhinoceros should have seen or smelt him, especially as the wind was in the man's favor. It is my belief, therefore, that the beast was accidentally passing the spot, and finding his victim in his path, had accidentally, as it were, destroyed him. The animal, from the moment I fired at him the first time until his death from the second shot, had never stopped running. The accuracy with which he had hit upon the unfortunate man was consequently the more remarkable. If the man had willfully placed himself before him, and said, "Now try to do your best to hit me here in the head," he could not have succeeded better. There was one poor consolation in Kozengo's untimely end, viz., he had died instantaneously. He had not had time even to utter a cry, and the agony of death was over the instant it was felt.

I staid to see the poor man interred. A hole for this purpose was scooped in the ground between four and five feet deep, about as long, and two feet wide. Under this again, and on one side, a smaller hole was hollowed out, just sufficiently large to admit of the corpse in a reclining position. This was the grave, and was carefully lined with fine soft grass. The body was then doubled up, the head being forced between the legs, and there secured by means of part of the enormous coil of bandages which encircled the man's waist, in the usual Damara fashion. His face, and as much of the body as was practicable, was afterward covered over with a sheep-skin, forming part of the dress of the wife of the deceased man. Thus "shrouded," his remains were deposited in the grave, which was bedecked in the same way as its cavity had been lined. Sand was then shoveled over the whole, and every particle of the soil removed in digging the sepulchre was scrupulously replaced, or rather heaped up in a mound over it. Even the sticks, pieces of bark, etc., made use of in the operation, were left on the spot. And, lastly, a quantity of thorn-bushes were stuck in a circle round the tomb, in order to prevent wild animals from disinterring the corpse. The ceremony being concluded, a particular kind of root was dug up, and, being divided into small pieces, each of the chief by-standers tasted it—a charm, I presumed, against death or injury from the departed.

A singular and affecting incident occurred just as the last shovelful of earth was thrown upon the grave. A small dog belonging to the deceased made at this moment his appearance; he smelt first all round the mound beneath which rested the remains of his late master, then, wagging his tail, looked wistfully up into my face with an expression which said, "What have you done with him?"

Kozengo's wife, who had been informed of her sad bereavement, attended the funeral, and exhibited the most heart-rending sorrow—at least outwardly. The wailing was of a most melancholy description—a sort of chanting, with a peculiar (almost hysterical) ejaculation after each intonation. Poor woman! I heartily sympathized with her, and I am sure I was the only person present of all the numerous assembly (by this time all the Damaras had reached the spot) who at all felt for her lonely condition. Many a laugh was heard, but no one looked sad. No one asked or cared about the man, but each and all made anxious inquiries after the rhinoceros—such is the life of barbarians!

DISAPPOINTED LIONS.

Oh, ye sentimentalists of the Rousseau school—for some such still remain—witness what I have witnessed, and do witness daily, and you will soon cease to envy and praise the life of savages!

I have omitted to notice a rather remarkable circumstance connected with this rhinoceros hunt. While following up the trail of the animal we came to a spot where one or two lions, probably taking advantage of his crippled condition, had evidently attacked him, and, after a desperate scuffle, had been compelled to beat a precipitate retreat—perhaps chiefly through the assistance of his companion, who had evidently only left him when he could walk no farther. This is the sole instance I know of lions daring to attack rhinoceroses; though I have seen it stated in print that not only will they assail, but can master the horned monster.

CHAPTER X.

A Troop of Lions.—A Watch by Night.—Wild Animals at a Vley.—A Duel between a Lion and Lion-hunter.—Dogs and Damaras.—An exciting hunting Scene.—One hundred Damaras in the Field.—Another wounded Lion.—Dinner on Beefsteak *au Lion* and Hump *de Rhinocéros*.—Lion's Flesh very palatable.—The Ovambo Caravan still in the Neighborhood.—The Feeding-time of the Ovambos after a Day's successful Sport.—A disgusting Spectacle.—Change of Route.—A Bevy of black Damsels.—Advice about Marriage.—A Road practicable for the Wagon.—News from Europe.—How I dispose of my Ivory.—A Collection of Insects and Birds.—Swifts and Swallows.—Tremendous Storms of Thunder and Lightning.—The peculiar Beauty of the Sunsets.

A FEW nights after the tragical event above recorded I was again at my post of observation at the water, when I encountered a troop of lions under circumstances which exhibited these royal beasts in a somewhat new light.

In the early part of the night I had observed several animals gliding noiselessly to the water, but considerably out of range. Not being able to make out what they were, I slipped quietly out of the skarm, and approached the spot where they were drinking. I got, from the nature of the ground, pretty close to them unperceived, yet was still unable to name them. From the sound of lapping at the water, I concluded that I had hyenas before me, and as one of three animals was leaving the vley I fired. The bullet took effect, and, uttering a growl, the beast disappeared. Whereupon, "Surely not lions!" I muttered to myself. The remaining two had in the mean time also ceased drinking, and were moving lazily away, when a low shrill whistle from me at once arrested their steps. I leveled and pulled the trigger; in vain this time, the ball went too high—in short, right over the object aimed at. The animal did not, however, budge an inch, and I now clearly saw a lion. Rising to my feet, I shouted, in order to drive him off; but he remained stationary. I did not at all like his appearance, and hastened at once back to my ambush to reload. When again quite ready and on the look-out for him, he was gone; but almost immediately afterward two others resembling the first approached the water. Having drunk their fill, they were about to retrace their steps, when suddenly—my person being purposely exposed to view—they seemed to espy me, and eying me for a few seconds, one—the largest—made straight for my skarm. This seemed strange; but, to make quite sure of his intentions, I stood up, and when the brute was within about forty yards of me, shouted. To my utter surprise, instead of moving off he came quickly on, till at a distance of twenty-five paces or thereabouts he suddenly squatted, evidently intend-

L

ing to spring on me. "Nay, old fellow," I muttered to myself, "if that's the ticket, I will be even with you;" and, dropping the double-barreled gun which I held in my hands at the moment, I seized the elephant rifle, leveled, took a very steady aim at his chest, and fired. The bullet sped true, and I thought I had killed him outright; but not so, for after rolling over two or three times, he scrambled up and decamped. However, I had no doubt in my own mind that the wound would prove fatal. On receiving the shot he gave a startling growl, and in making his escape was joined by his associate, who had, while the duel was pending, remained a passive spectator.

At break of day, taking up the spoor of the wounded animal, I had only proceeded about two hundred yards when the dogs gave tongue at a small bush, where immediately afterward I saw a stately lion rise to his feet and limp forward two or three paces. But the exertion was too much for him; he halted, and, turning half round, looked fiercely at his assailants. Not being myself in a favorable position, I shouted to my men to fire. Kamapjie responded to the call, and the lion dropped to rise no more. In an instant the dogs were clinging to his ears, throat, head, etc. The brute, still alive, grappled bravely with his assailants. The next moment half a dozen assegais were quivering in his body, and a hundred more or so would soon have been similarly sheathed had I not prompt-

DEATH OF A LION.

ly ridden up and stopped the Damaras, who were rushing in upon the prostrate foe like maniacs. I wished the dogs to finish him, and they did so; but three of the best were wounded in the scuffle, only one, however, at all seriously. The aim which had killed this lion had been most perfect. The bullet had entered exactly the centre of his chest, and, traversing the entire length of his body, had taken its egress through the right hind quarter. It was really, therefore, to me a matter of great surprise that the beast had survived the wound so long.

This was decidedly the most exciting hunting scene I have ever witnessed. Besides my own people, more than one hundred Damaras were in the field, vociferating frightfully, and waving and darting their ox-tail plumaged assegais with a ferocity and earnestness that would have made a stranger think they were preparing for some dreadful battle. Nearly as many more—to say nothing of a host of women and children—were seen hastening toward us from the camp, which was in full view. Indeed, before the lion had breathed his last, more than three hundred human beings were on the spot.

The lion, a male, proved a first-rate prize, in excellent condition, and of giant proportions, but possessing scarcely any mane. His head was very beautiful—a perfect picture. Having given orders about the disposal of him, we took up the trail of the other lion, who, to judge from the quantity of blood lost, must have been seriously wounded.

Tracking him for about half a mile, we came up with him in a dense brake; but the Damaras kept up such a riotous noise that the few dogs left with us—the greater portion having returned home—were insufficient to bring him to bay, so he managed to escape. Once, indeed, we caught sight of him as he was crossing a small opening, but here, the bushes becoming thicker than ever, we left him. The chase was a short one, but exceedingly exciting. Had I been alone, *i. e.*, with merely my own people about me, it is very likely I should have succeeded in dispatching this brute too, apparently a she-lion of huge stature.

That day I dined on beefsteak *au lion* and hump *de rhinocéros*, done under the ashes. On sitting down to this singular meal, I could not help remarking, partly addressing the cook and partly myself, "I wonder what her majesty the Queen of England would say to such fare?" "Oh, what a beast the man must be!" I had never before partaken of lion's flesh, but found it very palatable and juicy, not unlike veal, and very white. Rhinoceros hump was also a frequent and favorite dish of mine.

The Ovambo caravan alluded to in the preceding pages were still sojourning in my neighborhood. At first they behaved themselves with due decorum, but, on a closer acquaintance, proved a perfect nuisance, more especially when feeding (not dining) time came. Very often, on killing game, I had to fight for morsels of it; nay, I was at times necessitated to threaten my black friends with the gun before I could obtain needful food. The scenes that sometimes presented themselves on these occasions were truly disgusting. To say nothing of the screams, vociferations, curses, etc., which were deafening, assegai stabs and knobkierie blows were administered indiscriminately and remorselessly, all for the sake of a lump of meat. Just endeavor, reader, to imagine from one to two hundred starving and ferocious dogs laying hold of a carcass, each tearing it away in his own particular direction, at the same time biting and snarling incessantly at his neighbor, and you will have a faint notion of the beastly scrambles I allude to. I have seen human blood flow as freely at these feeds as had that of the animal we were devouring. The sacred ties of kindred and friendship were totally lost sight of in the all-absorbing anticipation of a gorge. All the revolting qualities of man in a barbarous condition were brought on these occasions out into startling relief. Human nature seemed lower than that of the brute creation, while at the same time almost diabolical.

In order finally to accomplish the object of the expedition, it had been my intention to follow up the Omuramba Ua' Matako as far as Otjituo, thence across to the Omuramba U'Ovambo, by which means I trusted to reach the Cunenè. But, on looking at the map one day, it became evident to me that the more direct route would be to go straight from Omanbondè to Okamabuti (Galton's most easterly point), and thence on to the last-named water-course. By keeping at first to the westward of Galton's route, moreover — merely crossing it at Okamabuti — new ground would be explored, and thus two objects gained.

The Damara caravan (whose leaders I had some difficulty in persuading that I had no intention of visiting those scoundrels the Ovambo) at last determined to move ahead; and having learned that they purposed crossing the eastern extremity of the Otjirokaku Mountains, I determined to accompany them part of the way, thinking I might thereby learn something to my advantage. Accordingly, packing a few necessaries on my donkeys, I set out on the 25th of September, accompanied by a few native attendants.

Though the caravan had started an hour or two before me, I overtook it just as its inmates were emerging from dense thickets on the banks of Opondongaula, the name of the water situated in the neighborhood of Omanbondè. The motley ranks of this grotesque company, winding leisurely along the sinuosities of the reed and rush-covered shores of the tank, furnished a scene exceedingly pleasing and picturesque.

I had, moreover, an excellent opportunity of inspecting and appreciating the charms of an immense and varied bevy of black damsels, who were tripping along the greensward—for here *was* a veritable sward—either in single files or in little knots, some carrying immense bundles on their heads, Grecian fashion, while others (the aristocracy of the caravan) sauntered forward with an air of indolent and swaggering superiority. As I rode slowly through their yielding and attractive ranks, I did my best to win a smile here and an affectionate glance there; but, sad to relate, I made but a slight impression on the "fair" assemblage, who declared with great simplicity that, had my person only been *black*, *I might* have passed muster; hinting also delicately—of course, ladies, whether black or white, are always delicate—that a little less *dress*, and a slight varnish of fat and ochre—pointing to their own perfumed and greasy—oh pardon, ye fair, the obsolete term—bodies, would greatly improve my appearance. Charming flatterers! For once in my life I regretted having a Caucasian origin and a clean shirt.

"Charles ——," once wrote Sir Thomas —— to my father, "should marry by all means; and if he has not a white wife in view, who would be sick one half the year and a burden to him the other, let him take to himself a black princess with property of her own." Sir Thomas —— was evidently a practical man, and doubtless a philanthropist. "His suggestion, he might think, would not only be good for Charles, but an infusion of fresh blood into the sluggish veins of the African would," the baronet probably argued, "be a great improvement on the negro type—might lay, indeed, the foundation of an Anglo-Saxon African negro-colony in the interior of a benighted continent, and possibly do more toward civilizing its barbarian natives than all the influence exerted by zealous missionaries, enterprising travelers, adventurous traders, or daring Nimrods." I am free to confess that from this point of view there is much in Sir Thomas ——'s recommendation to tempt and tickle the fancy. Yet I thought, in the words of Clapperton—that prince of the middle or romantic travelers' age—"it would be a pretty end of my travels to set up with a tunbutt for a queen."

On the second day after leaving Omanbondè I reached a fine fountain called Otjomokojo, situated at the foot of the mountains of the same name. Two days later found me at a small collection of wells, to which the Damaras gave the name Otjihejnenne. These wells were scooped out of the limestone, the prevailing rock of the surrounding country. From Otjihejnenne, the Damara caravan proceeded too much to the westward to suit my purpose; finding, therefore, that a longer stay in their company would only be waste of time, I bade them farewell, and forthwith retraced my steps to Omanbondè, which place I reached in safety, after an absence of five days, having ascertained during that time that the country, so far as I went, was in every respect practicable for wagons, which being precisely what I wanted to know, the object of this excursion was now fully attained.

Elephants having, at least in a great measure, abandoned Omanbondè, I gave up hunting, and devoted my spare time to exploring the marsh, in search of specimens chiefly, but also to obtain occasional supplies of game for the larder. Snipes and ducks were rather plentiful. The former I had never before met with in any part of the wide tracts I had explored. There were likewise several species of water-hens, rails, plovers, etc., and I occasionally bagged a hawk or a marsh-hamer.

On the 30th of October Pereira joined me. He brought me a parcel of European letters, together with other news, which I need scarcely say were highly welcome.

I had by this time collected a considerable quantity of valuable ivory, and being anxious to deposit it in some place of security, I tried to induce several of the numerous travelers at Ovatjimba, who had, from time to time, flocked to Omanbondè in search of elephants, to take this treasure to Barmen. They seemed at first willing to accept the charge, but at the eleventh hour left me in the lurch. I therefore, deeming it unsafe to leave property of so much value concealed at Omanbondè, found it necessary to turn Pereira's face once more toward Otjimbingué. I was perfectly well aware that no rain in any considerable quantity would fall for at least two months, and as the journey to and from the place in question could easily be accomplished within that period, nothing would be lost, but much might be gained by the mission.

As I was now probably on my last exploring excursion in Southwestern Africa, I was anxious, in addition to birds, etc., to make a good collection of insects; hitherto my success in this respect had been on a very limited scale. A sprinkling of rain, however, having fallen in the month of November, the young grass, plants, bushes, etc., sprouted rapidly out, affording appropriate food to insects, which, the instant they are so provided for, spring into existence as if by magic. More of the miniature creation may be seen in an hour's time, after a shower of rain, than during months of dry weather; and nothing, I imagine, conveys to the mind so forcible a conviction of the stupendous power and unfathomable wisdom of the Creator as an insight into the myriad forms of insect life. What completeness, what diminutiveness! what shapes, what beauty! what elegance, what solidity! He who can rightly read, appreciate, and interpret Nature's small print, will find therein an inexhaustible source of enjoyment and recreation; but he may find himself also almost pinned down to the microscope, and by magnifying the little may become incapable of contemplating the great.

I saw much during my stay at Omanbondè to amuse and instruct me. "A short time before sunset, myriads of *winged* termites are there seen issuing every where out of the ground, and after frisking about for a few minutes in the pleasant evening breeze, dropping helplessly to the earth again, to become instantly a prey to their enemies —a species of large brown ant, who in this locality also appear contemporary with their congeners."

Toward the end of November immense flocks of swifts and swallows appeared. For several consecutive days they passed over our camp just before sunset in such numbers as literally to darken the sky. Sometimes these "flights" would extend in one direct line for about one and a half to two miles, covering, at the same time, a space several hundred feet broad, and apparently as many deep.

December set in rainy, with thunder and lightning at times truly appalling; and as part of our camp was formed under a wide-spreading kamel thorn-tree, I was kept in constant alarm, as this kind of tree is a powerful conductor of the electric fluid. Any anxiety I might suffer on this account was, however, richly compensated by the beautiful and striking skyscapes and atmospheric coruscations attendant on these storms.

"*Dec. 3d.* Showery day. What a wonderful effect the accidents of light and shade have on a landscape! The Otjirokaku Mountains look quite grand at times, indeed almost Alpine, and yet their average height above the plain can not exceed 1000 feet. Although twenty miles off, their rugged and smooth surfaces can occasionally be clearly distinguished, nay, the very slopes of the rock ledges may be sometimes discerned. The wonderful transparency of the atmosphere at certain periods of the year in this country, now for instance, admits of landscapes being seen at an immense distance, while in the hot season, objects comparatively near look dim and indistinct, and at times are altogether indiscernible.

"The sunsets generally very lovely, sometimes of a very peculiar beauty. Once I remember, just after the sun had disappeared, the whole region of the sky near and on the verge of the horizon assuming exactly the resemblance of a rainbow; there were all the colors composing the glorious arch, but the "stripes" were three times as broad as those seen in the bow of promise, and ran in horizontal instead of vertical lines, or rather layers. It was a strangely beautiful pageant."—*Author's Journal.*

CHAPTER XI.

The Damara Caravan forbidden by Chipanga, the successor of Nangoro, to enter Ondonga.—The Ovambo's superstitious Dread of Fire-arms.—The Party belonging to the Caravan steal the Cattle and Property of the Ovambo.—A Descent made upon the Ovambuenge by the Makololo.—A Guide with a Harem of Wives.—A Battle between two Bushmen Werfts.—Dr. Livingstone's Opinion that Bushmen never quarrel about Women.—A Native Woman wounded by poisoned Arrows.—I endeavor to capture the Offenders.—Two of their Party made Prisoners.—Not guilty.—Effect their Escape.

The Damara caravan, alluded to in the last chapter, returned suddenly and unexpectedly to Omanbondè. To my surprise, I learned that they had not succeeded in getting farther than to the neighborhood of Etosha. Here they had encountered one of the Ovambo outposts, the occupants of which had peremptorily forbidden them to proceed farther. To remove this unforeseen hinderance, messengers were dispatched to the paramount chief of the tribe, Chipanga, the successor of Nangoro. The answer they received was a decided negative. To their repeated entreaties to be allowed to enter Ondonga, he invariably replied, "On no condition whatever."

In the interchange of messages that ensued, much

was also said about white men. Indeed, ever since Messrs. Green and Hahn's engagement with the Ovambo, Chipanga had lived in constant trepidation. On the mere report of my being at Omanbondè, he fled precipitately to a distant Bushman village, there to hide himself, it was said, till assured of my absence from the neighborhood. This barbarian not only believed that white men's guns were invincible, but also entertained the notion that, without any weapons, by merely looking at a person, a white man could cause his death. "If not," the brave chief was heard to exclaim, "how was it that Nangoro was killed by the mere report of fire-arms?"

The Ovambo never seemed thoroughly to understand the dreadful efficacy of these weapons until their disastrous defeat by Green and his party. It would appear that their previous fearlessness arose in a great measure from merely seeing, when fired, the flash of the discharged gun, and *not the missile*. "When we throw an assegai or shoot an arrow, we SEE it going through the air," said they, "but with your rifles nothing but a harmless fire is perceived." From a supreme contempt of our arms, they had now, however, gone to the other extreme, and had a most exaggerated notion of their fearful destructiveness.

To avenge themselves on the Ovambo for their refusal to let the travelers pass through their country, a party belonging to the caravan, under one of

Katjamaha's sons, attacked and carried off all the cattle from the obnoxious post. The pretended traders more immediately attached to the service of Jonker Afrikander did not, however, participate in this outrage. On their arrival at Omanbondè, the thieves followed up this *coup* by robbing a small Bushman werft, and beating the women nearly to death. One of the unfortunate sufferers came to me with tears in his eyes to complain, and as the Bushmen in this neighborhood had always shown themselves friendly both toward me and the Damaras, the conduct of the latter was the more disgraceful and brutal. I felt exasperated at the lawlessness of their acts, but it was no easy matter, single-handed, to compel 150 cut-throats to do justice to a poor Bushman. However, my blood was up, and, seizing a double-barreled rifle, I placed the muzzle of the weapon within a few inches of the head of the chief of the party in question, who happened to be sitting by my fire at the time, and threatened him with instant destruction unless restitution was made forthwith to the complainant. My threat had the desired effect, for in the course of a couple of hours all the purloined articles were forthcoming, to the no small satisfaction of myself, and to the great joy of the poor man.

The Damaras brought with them a report that a party of white men (alluding probably to the Portuguese) had attacked, and to a great extent destroyed, a nation called Ovambuenge, living to the east

M

of the Ovampo. This gave me some anxiety, as, in case there should be any truth in the story, it might throw serious obstacles in my way, the nation in question being the first with whom I should, in all probability, come in contact. At a later period I discovered that there was some ground for the report, but that the aggressors were not white men, but the Makololo, who had made a descent upon the Ovambuenge, and carried off almost all their cattle, besides many captives of both sexes. But more of this hereafter.

The leader or head man of Jonker's Damaras, Koroinene by name, had in former years lived much in the neighborhood of Omanbondè, and was supposed to possess an intimate knowledge not only of the country between this point and the Ovampo, but also of that to the north and east. He was, moreover, a very shrewd and intelligent Damara—an unusual phenomenon among this people; and as I had no guide of any description, I deemed it of importance to secure the services of this man for my intended journey. On being sounded on the subject, he at once expressed his readiness to accompany me in the capacity of guide. There was, however, a serious objection to this engagement, for the man was encumbered with numerous wives and a host of servants, most of whom refused to return to their homes, declaring that they would go with their master. There was no alternative. Either I must set out "guideless," or bear with the nuisance. I chose the latter, but gave Koroinene expressly to understand that he only, with one or two more, would be fed at my expense.

On the night of the 23d of December a battle took place between two Bushmen werfts situated in the neighborhood of Omanbondè, when several men were slain on both sides. A party of mine, who had been sent in search of elephants, surprised groups of these natives of the bush in a state of great excitement and agitation, but of the details of the fray they learned nothing.

Dr. Livingstone, in his missionary travels, says he never knew but one instance of a fight originating in a quarrel about women. It is to be presumed, therefore, that the great traveler alludes to such nations as possess *cattle*; for among the Bushmen and others who have no herds, woman is too frequently the *belli teterrima causa*.

The day after receiving news of the fight a lamentable incident occurred which greatly provoked me. A woman belonging to my guide's party had gone into the veldt, as was her daily custom, in search of edible roots, etc., when she was surprised and attacked by three Bushmen, who discharged several arrows at her. One of these missiles sped true, burying itself several inches deep in her left buttock. The poor creature shouted for assistance, but our camp was too distant for her weak voice to reach us; it had the effect, however, of frightening the villains away. The woman, it seems, did not arrive at her temporary home until after dusk, and, unfortunately, her friends left the tale untold until the following morning, when they informed me of it. The poison had then already spread to such an extent as to make all my little skill unavailing. And, indeed, I very much doubt whether any surgery in the world could have saved her. In order to satisfy her husband and friends, I did, nevertheless, all that I thought could be done under the circumstances.

Strongly suspecting that the men who had committed this outrage belonged to the identical werft to whose inmates, as just related, I had at considerable personal risk restored some stolen property, I felt greatly exasperated, and vowed revenge could I but catch the miscreants. It was of the utmost importance, it is true, to be on good terms with the Bushmen; but, at the same time, it was equally necessary to inspire them with a wholesome fear of us. Kindness, without a due mixture of sternness, is thrown away upon savages. Accordingly, all available hands, well armed, were quickly dispatched in pursuit of the murderers, though I entertained little hope that they would be overtaken and captured. Contrary, however, as it seemed, to my expectation, late at night on the same day the party returned, bringing with them an elderly Bushman and a very fine young female. But the former, according to the wounded woman's own testimony, was not the real culprit, and the other prisoner, though the wife of the man who had fired the fatal arrow, I neither could nor would touch. I determined, nevertheless, to keep both for a short time as hostages, thinking it possible that the husband of the woman might be induced to come to her rescue.

The guilty horde did not, as I had imagined, belong to the werft alluded to; they lived farther off, near the Otjomokojo Mountains, and had only accidentally, on this occasion, extended their wanderings to my neighborhood in quest of game. My surprise and anger, therefore, were somewhat abated, for these poor people had from time immemorial been at deadly feud with the Damaras, and both parties were in the habit of butchering each other indiscriminately (men, women, and children) whenever an opportunity occurred for gratifying their mutual hatred.

After thirty-six hours of intense sufferings the wounded woman breathed her last. In the confusion that ensued—every one running to have a look at the corpse—the captive Bushman, whose fetters had been somewhat slackened, managed to make his escape. This was rather annoying, but there was no remedy. The woman was shortly afterward allowed to walk off, thus leaving us no farther chance of catching the real culprit. Our determined proceedings had, however, so thoroughly scared the Bushmen that they precipitately fled our neighborhood.

CHAPTER XII.

The Rate of Absorption and Evaporation of Moisture in the dry Season.—The Return of the Party sent to Otjimbingué.—Preparations for a fresh Start.—We make for the Omuramba U'Ovambo.—Reasons for this Choice.—Bid Farewell to Omanbondè.—Description of my Suite.—The Guide ignorant of the Route.—A Passage through a Forest.—The Guide allowed to depart.—Difficulty of finding Water.—Indications of Bushmen Villages.—A small Well discovered.—Bushmen make their Appearance.—Their contradictory Descriptions of the Omuramba, supposed by Travelers to be a Branch of the Cunenè.

The rains had by this time fallen in considerable quantities; yet so great is the rate of absorption and evaporation at this season, that pools of from forty to fifty feet long, and several feet deep, would dry up in the course of a week. Still, I hoped to find sufficient rain-water to serve our purpose, and only waited for the return of the party sent to Otjimbingué to commence operations. Fortunately I had not long to wait, for on the morning of the first day of 1859 we had the satisfaction of greeting our comrades, safe and sound, in our camp at Omanbondè. A few days more sufficed to make the necessary and final arrangements.

My guide (Koroinene) had proposed to follow up (or rather down) the course of the Omuramba

Ua' Matako as the most eligible way to reach the Ovambuenge (also called Ovapangari). But, though it was advisable to give the Ovambo a wide berth (and their outposts extended to the neighborhood of the nation in question), I did not adopt his proposal. Mr. Green had already tried to penetrate northward by the very route that Koroinene suggested; he had found it impracticable, and it was not likely that I should succeed where he had failed. My friend had, moreover, supplied me with a chart of his explorations in these parts, in which he points out another river-course, Omuramba U'Ovambo. This river had, where he first struck it, a northeast current, which, together with the statements of the Bushmen, and other circumstances, led both Mr. Green and the Rev. Mr. Hahn to the conclusion that it was identical with the Cunenè, *i. e.*, a branch of that mysterious stream. Supposing their surmises to be correct, it was of the utmost importance to me to gain this point; for, though only periodical in its flow, the river would, no doubt, by following it up toward its source, supply a sufficiency of water. After due deliberation, I determined, therefore, to make for the Omuramba U'Ovambo with all convenient speed.

Accordingly, every thing being in readiness, we bade farewell to Omanbondè on the afternoon of the 5th of January. We moved in the following order: I myself, attended by a henchman to carry the rifle, proceeded ahead; then came the road-party, consisting of the guide Tom, and three to four Damaras, armed with powerful American axes; next followed the wagon, attended by Mortar and two or three native lads; while Pereira and the remainder of the Damaras brought up the rear with the cattle, the sheep, the women, the hangers-on, etc. We looked quite a respectable and picturesque procession.

On the fourth day after leaving Omanbondè we reached Okamabuti by a totally different route to that followed by Mr. Galton in 1850.

Clusters of small limestone hills surround this place, and, in order to learn something of the country before us, I took my guide to one of these hills, which commanded a good and extensive view; but, to my extreme annoyance and surprise, I found that, beyond the immediate neighborhood, the man was totally ignorant of the tract in the direction of our proposed route. This discovery was as unexpected as it was disappointing. I consequently found myself precisely in the same condition as when at Omanbondè. I had now to trust entirely to my own instinct and previous experience in conducting the expedition with safety and success.

Mr. Green's route was still to the eastward of us, and I calculated that in about two days' journey we might easily reach it. After some little delay at Okamabuti we set out for a small fountain hard by. Here we bivouacked, and on the following day continued to journey on, keeping the beautifully-wooded hill of Otijtijka to our right. We had not proceeded far before we entered a very dense brake, which ere long became a forest. Finding that all our efforts to cut our way through this wood of noble timber made but slow progress, I deemed it best at once to unyoke the oxen and send them back to the fountain we had just left. Pereira was ordered to accompany the cattle, and, after seeing them duly fed and watered, to rejoin us on the following afternoon, when I hoped to have opened a clear passage for our advance.

Just at this rather critical moment our *soi disant* guide requested permission to return home, urging as a reason that one of his wives was suffering from bad health. That the woman was really ill I had no doubt; but the real cause of Koroinene's desire to leave me was, I felt sure, quite different from the alleged one. However, as the man was at present not only useless, but a positive nuisance, I gladly acceded to his request; and having liberally furnished him with "grub," tobacco, etc., for the road, he took his departure.

Pereira returned with the cattle at the appointed time, and having succeeded in making a tolerably good path through the forest, we continued our journey. Since leaving Omanbondè we had not found a drop of rain-water. Several small vleys that we passed had evidently been full at no distant day, but were now quite dry. This was a great disappointment, for without guides it is an exceedingly difficult and laborious task to find water in these drouthy districts. Next morning we were early stirring, and the country being tolerably free from bush we made good progress. But there was no sign of water, though the sun had nearly reached its meridian. We came, however, upon fresh Bushmen tracks, which, together with the appearance of numerous Guinea-fowls, doves, etc., led us to conclude that water was not far off. It was, neverthless, despite these unmistakable signs, less easy to find than might be supposed, for the locality was intersected in every direction by numerous small footpaths, which greatly puzzled our search. At last, being in advance of my party, I struck a path evidently more frequented than the rest, and by following it up for a short time had the satisfaction of finding a small well. There were, besides, two or three other pits partially filled up with rubbish. From the nature of the rock, however (calcareous tufa), I doubted not that by digging a sufficiency of water might be obtained for both man and beast.

While busily engaged clearing out the pits several Bushmen made their appearance. They did not seem in the least afraid or suspicious, which I very justly attributed to the good treatment they had experienced at the hands of Messrs. Green and Hahn on their journey to the Ovambo in the year preceding my visit. At this place we found the spoors of their wagons; but their route inclining after a while too much to the westward to suit my purpose, I determined to pursue my own course in a direction nearly due north. Two of the Bushmen we had fallen in with agreed to guide me to the next water, which we reached at an early hour on the following day.

I lost no opportunity of questioning my present guides about the country and the people, etc., we were about to visit, but found the task so difficult, and their accounts so conflicting, that after a while I ceased my inquiries. One party represented the Omuramba as a permanent stream; said that the sun was on the *right* cheek, eastward along its course; that both Bushmen and black people lived on its banks; that both nations possessed cattle; that hippopotami and alligators inhabited its waters; that the distance to the said Omuramba was five days' journey, and thence three days' on to the black people—particulars, all of them, in total disagreement with the account of Messrs. Green and Hahn.

On the afternoon of the 16th of January I crossed a *dry*, narrow, but somewhat deeply depressed river bed, having at this point a nearly due north and south course. From its insignificant appearance I paid no particular attention to it, and continued to journey on. At an after period, however, I ascertained that this was the veritable Omuramba U'Ovambo, spoken of by the travelers just mentioned, and identical with their supposed branch of the Cunenè. Yet being still under the impression that the river in question was to the north of us, and had a northeast course, I thought that, by pursuing our present direction, we could not fail to strike it sooner or later.

CHAPTER XIII.

Comparatively good Road.—Pretty Scenery.—Fruit and Forest Trees.—A sandy Soil.—Thorn Jungles.—Scarcity of Water.—Vleys dried up.—The Heat intense.—Guides declare there is no Possibility of proceeding farther.—Delight on finding Water.—An Accident happens to the Wagon.—The Axle-tree renewed six Times.—The Acacia Giraffe and the White Ant.—Monotony of Toil, Anxiety, and Hardship.

HITHERTO, with few exceptions, the country had proved tolerably favorable for wagon traveling, and afforded besides, at times, very pretty scenery. The forest and fruit trees we met with were remarkably fine. Of the former there was one of a kind which particularly struck me, for it seemed to be at once tree, creeper, and parasite. Parts of its roots might occasionally be seen loosening their holds on the ground, through a powerful attraction toward another tree of a totally distinct species, twining and spreading around the latter till the two growths became one. This plant has a smooth, light-colored stem—or rather stems—with an oblong leaf, and shoots up to a very considerable height. Of the fruit trees I noticed the "almond" (I call it thus from want of a better name) ranked foremost. Large in bulk and handsome in foliage, its fruit in look resembles a plum, but has an acid flavor, and a stone inside, which contains a soft kernel, in taste and appearance not unlike the almond. I have already spoken of this tree in the pages of "Lake Ngami."

We had till now, as I have just hinted, found our progress much easier and more pleasant than it had been heretofore, by the comparative openness and smiling aspect of the country. Of short duration, however, was this agreeable traveling; for two days after we had left the Omuramba the scene changed totally, and in every respect for the worse. Instead of a fine champagne region of limestone tufa, finely dotted over with groups of handsome trees and bushwood, we now entered on a loose, sandy, undulating soil, frequently covered with odious, embarrassing thorn jungles, in places so dense as to require hours to clear a path through them. The oxen, moreover, unaccustomed to the heavy sand, dragged the wagon very unwillingly along. About the same time, too, another serious difficulty —the frequently recurring one, want of water— presented itself. The rains had evidently fallen but very sparingly, or not at all, in these parts. As long as we kept on the limestone we had found a sufficiency of fountains and old dilapidated wells to quench our thirst; but here, though there were many fine vleys, they were almost all dry, and, finally, they failed us altogether.

On the 19th of January we had been nearly two

days without a drop of water for the cattle. The heat was intense; the sun scorched us like a great blazing fire. Our guide, a sensible old fellow, looked misery itself, declaring repeatedly that any attempt to penetrate farther in this direction would prove fatal to us all, as there was not a single well or natural spring for a hundred miles. This he spoke from hearsay, acknowledging that he was personally totally unacquainted with the country. This was disheartening tidings; but I had made up my mind to go through with my adventure at all hazards. Accordingly, saddling my old horse and packing a little drinking-water on the donkeys, I set out, accompanied by two or three of my native attendants, in quest of a new supply of the precious liquid, giving orders to the remainder to retrace their steps with the wagon should I not make my appearance in the course of the next day.

Leaving the men to follow with the donkeys as well as they could, I put my Rosinante to his utmost speed, and, as good luck would have it, after nearly three hours' hard riding, discovered, to my great relief, a vley, which, though of no great capacity, would still afford us a supply for a few days. I thereupon rejoined my wagon and men on the same night, by whom, I need hardly say, my success was hailed with rapture. On the following day we moved on to the water. Reader, if you have not personally experienced such a deliverance in extreme need, you can not understand the delight and thankfulness it imparts.

Our guide now earnestly requested to be allowed to return home, urging his incompetency to be of any farther service to us. On condition of his procuring a substitute I acceded to his demand; though, to say the truth, I did not at present much care for guides, especially as our progress, owing to the uncouthness of the veldt, was so slow that I well knew no Bushmen would remain with us. There was one consideration, however, which rendered a guide from place to place very advantageous to us: it was this—he would be able to tell his countrymen who we were, whence we came, and the object of our journey, etc. Him they would believe, or at least to him they would listen, while our own account of ourselves would probably be laughed at, and all the more suspected, as we were coming from an enemy's country. Scarcely any thing, indeed, is more dangerous to a traveler than suddenly, without an introduction, to present himself before a strange and uncivilized people.

The old man did not wait to be told twice that he might depart. Contrary to my expectation, however, he, after an absence of about thirty hours, returned, bringing with him several young men to serve as our future guides. I did not like their appearance; they seemed much too young, and very ignorant. Nevertheless, I accepted their services, chiefly for the reason just mentioned, being at the same time somewhat indifferent as to whether they might choose to decamp or to fulfill their engagement.

While awaiting the return of the old guide I had explored the country a little ahead of us, and had fortunately discovered a group of small vleys. The water, it is true, was of the very worst description. It had evidently been frequented for some length of time by troops of elephants, whose wallowings and excrements had converted it into something like a cesspool. Nevertheless, I hailed the filthy puddle with joy, as affording at least an escape from parching drought.

Having got every thing in readiness for a start, we were able, shortly after our new acquaintances had joined us, to continue our journey, and on the following day I had the good fortune to discover a fine vley of clear water. I say discover, for our guides had, as I previously suspected they would do, decamped that morning. A few minutes' walk from this vley a serious accident occurred to the wagon. By the carelessness of the driver, the hind axle had come in contact with a prostrate kamel thorn-tree, and the shock had broken one of its arms. To break an axle-tree is, under all circumstances, a serious mishap; but when it occurs in a wild, inhospitable region like the one we were traversing, destitute of suitable wood for repairing the damage, the mischief is incalculable. In the course of about 150 miles I had to renew this axle more or less six different times, neither a pleasant nor an easy task, especially as only one sort of tree to be found in this country, namely, the *Acacia giraffe*, indigenous to Damara Land and the adjacent tracts, is suitable to this piece of wheelwright work. I must mention, too, as a singular fact, that not one of these trees in a hundred—nay, I might safely say, not one in a thousand, is sound! Almost all of them are either decayed in the heart, or so perforated by worms and ants as to be quite useless. They look fair enough as they stand in the field or forest, but attempt to employ them in any species of carpentry or building, and they will generally be found, from the causes I have named, totally unserviceable.

One evening, while pursuing our route, we were nearly poisoned by some wild beans which the cook had picked up along the road. Seeing him about to put them into the saucepan, I remarked, "Mortar, I was once made very ill by eating those beans in a raw state," adding that I thought they might prove harmless if properly prepared by fire. Finding the vegetable somewhat palatable, I partook of it rather freely, as did also the cook and Pereira. But scarcely had we finished our meal when we were seized with sudden nausea, violent headache, and throbbing of the heart. Finally, however, and providentially, the poisonous stuff was entirely ejected by a violent retching. No serious result ensued; the only effect being a nauseous taste in the mouth throughout that night and the following day, accompanied by much bodily prostration, a good deal like that produced by swallowing a large dose of castor-oil.

This "bean," so hurtful to man, proved quite wholesome to the cattle, sheep, and goats, who ate it, both leaves and fruit, greedily.

But I will not task the reader's patience by a recital of each day's proceedings. They were generally days of much toil, anxiety, and hardship. Sometimes we found abundance of water, while at others we suffered all the tortures of Tantalus; and when not employed in mending the wagon, I was always afoot or on horseback in search either of game, vleys, or a passage, and sometimes of all three.

CHAPTER XIV.

Gadflies.—Another Elephant Hunt: interrupted by a Storm of Rain.—A very jeopardous Position.—An arduous Chase.—An Elephant charges his Pursuer.—Wounded severely.—Brought down after a long Hunt.—Another Elephant bagged.—Plenty of Provision.—The Natives flock together to devour the Carcasses.—Jerking and Drying.—Slow Progress.—The Number of Bushes and Trees cut down to clear a Passage.—One hundred and seventy Bushes felled every three hundred Yards.—The incredible amount of Labor to advance one Mile.—Description of the Country.—Variation of the Compass.—Some Alteration in my Course.

I HAD calculated largely on game for the support of my party, but in this respect was sadly disappointed. One of the causes of this scarcity of wild animals was to be found in the swarms of gadflies, of the most venomous description, which infest this region. This fly attacks alike man and beast, and at every sting draws large drops of blood. My native attendants suffered agonies from their assaults, and the state of the cattle was scarcely less pitiable. The bellies of the poor brutes were sometimes—and I speak without exaggeration—literally one mass of coagulated blood. The Bushmen assured me—and I could well believe their statement—that cattle and beasts of prey often died from the poisonous stings of these bloodthirsty insects. They followed us for days, settling at night in clusters underneath the wagon.

Formidable, however, as they were, they could not drive away the mighty elephant, though he, no doubt, was not exempt from their torments. As we proceeded, we met daily with fresh indications of this animal's propinquity; and as our slender stock of cattle for slaughter was fast decreasing, I determined to go in search of my old enemies at my earliest convenience. Accordingly, having, at a pretty early hour one morning, come across the recent trail of a fine bull, I at once started in pursuit of him. After several hours tracking, we found that he had joined a group of she-elephants with calves. This was any thing but a pleasant discovery. However, we persevered, and after a couple of hours farther "spooring" sighted the herd, when, to my no small satisfaction, I saw the old gentleman straying a little apart from the rest of the company. I made instant arrangements for attacking him, but could not; for at that moment the rain came down in such torrents, and with so much violence, as completely to darken the atmosphere, entirely obscuring objects but a very short distance off. Under these circumstances, all I could do (and that was not done without some difficulty and danger) was to keep the brute in view till the weather should clear up. Being too, at the time, very slightly clad, having on me only a pair of trowsers and a flannel jacket, I doubted much whether I should be able to keep my rifle dry, a matter of the utmost consequence; for, if the piece should miss fire at the critical moment, it might cost me my life. The storm having at last abated, I set a couple of men to watch the movements of my intended prey, while I retired behind a small brake to light a fire and dry my rifle. I found my poor followers, on joining them, half dead from the long, cold, soaking shower-bath they had been exposed to.

At the beginning of the rain, I must here notice, we had lost sight of the other elephants, but were still aware of their nearness to us by hearing at short intervals the trumpeting of one of the herd—most probably of the leading cow—and no doubt for the purpose of keeping the troop together.

The bull was, meanwhile, sauntering leisurely to and fro in an open and very exposed place, where I dared not attack him. At last he moved into some low scattered bush, and, as the sun was fast declining toward the west, I determined, having no time to lose, at once to approach him, which I did with a stout heart. I stalked up unperceived to within about sixty paces of where the animal stood, and fired. The bullet sped true, for he uttered a loud shriek, ran forward a short distance, then stopped and remained motionless. Turning sharply round, he in a few minutes passed me within one hundred paces, at full speed, whereupon he received another shot, which also appeared to have taken effect. He was then making straight for the cows, but, fortunately, the second wound made him swerve from that direction, and gave me a third shot at him. The distance, however, of my mark this time, fully 200 yards, was too great; my bullet nevertheless, as subsequently found, struck the beast in the left fore leg. He was almost immediately afterward hidden among the bushes, but we, that is, myself and henchman, following quickly on his traces, soon sighted him again. He was losing, we perceived, much blood; yet, whenever we tried to get within range of him, he turned round and charged us with great fury. The brute was evidently seriously wounded, but of so savage a disposition that we were obliged to approach him very cautiously. Following patiently on his spoor for about half an hour, we espied him standing behind a small bush nearly facing us. The cover was rather poor, and I waited long in the hopes of seeing him move on. He did not, however, stir. I had therefore no alternative; so, making the best I could of his position, I at last, with great precaution, succeeded in stalking up unperceived to within a reasonable distance of my mark. The bush, unfortunately, behind which he had stationed himself completely hid his shoulder. Guessing at it, nevertheless, as well as I could, I fired, and with deadly effect, for the poor brute, after rushing forward a few paces, fell to the ground a corpse. This elephant proved a very noble prize. His tusks were excellent, and alone well rewarded my trouble and perseverance.

The very next morning, having gone out to reconnoitre, I fell in with the fresh trail of another bull elephant, which I tracked, stalked, and killed, without any assistance from my man; and this elephant was an enormous beast, measuring nearly twelve feet in height at the shoulder; yet he was quite a young animal, with comparatively small tusks.

We had now meat in abundance—indeed, more than we well knew what to do with, and I was anxiously looking out for Bushmen to eat it up, for I hate waste, when a werft of these people, attracted to the spot by the report of the rifle, made their appearance just as the carcass of the last-killed animal was about to be served up. The Bushmen of these regions are as stout, well fed, and good-looking fellows as one would wish to see.

Heavy rains, and the process of jerking and drying our meat, delayed us at this point fully a week. On the 7th of February we were, however, able to move forward, but made little progress on that and on the following two days. Indeed, the whole distance we advanced might have been accomplished in a single hour under favorable circumstances. The late exceeding wetness of the weather and the denseness of the bush, or rather forests, before us were the causes of this delay. Instead of low sandy ridges overgrown with low thorn coppices, we had now to traverse lofty ranges, covered with splendid trees, some of which were entirely new to me, while underwood or jungle too was so thick that it was difficult even for a man on foot to pick his way through it. The labor and time, therefore, required for clearing a passage for wagons was very great —the reader may judge how great when I tell him that we were, more than once, as much as three days in crossing ridges not above a mile wide. Three or four axes were incessantly plied by me from early dawn till dusk, and seven or eight men were constantly engaged in the same work. Another fact will perhaps give a better notion of the difficulties we had to overcome. I take it from my journal as jotted down at the time.

"Had the curiosity to count the number of bushes (and trees) cut down in order to open out a path to a certain distance. In this calculation I invariably found in 300 yards 170 bushes felled; that is, about 1000 bushes a mile. I reckoned, besides, four stalks to each bush, a very low computation, which gave 4000 distinct branches, every stalk or branch (varying from the size of a finger to that of a man's leg) usually requiring from three to four strokes of the axe; thus *one* axe must actually have descended 12,000 *times in the course of a single mile*. Conceive the incredible amount of labor the passage of one such mile supposes—indeed, we are just now proceeding something short of a snail's pace." We have, however, about 200 miles of this sort of country to traverse before we reach our journey's end, so that, in round numbers, there must be 2,400,000 strokes of one axe, or 1,200,000 to each of two axes (the number usually employed), delivered, and no less than 200,000 bushes and trees cut down before we can get over this space. And this work *was* successfully performed.

Between every two ridges of this uncouth tract there was an open gully, a kind of Omuramba, varying from 100 to 400 feet in width. These Omurambas usually afforded liberal supplies of rain-water, were pretty free from bush, and, presenting a hard, smooth surface, were very favorable to wagon traveling. Unfortunately, however, they extended (with a regularity quite surprising) in a due western and eastern direction, or nearly so.

The variation of the compass in these parts is rather more than a score of degrees to the northwest. By a western course, therefore, I must necessarily have lost ground rapidly, while an attempt to proceed on a contrary slant would have proved nearly equally misleading. Having thus scarcely an alternative, I determined on the following plan, the only one that struck me as ultimately likely to issue in a satisfactory result: I resolved to follow the bed of the gullies in a westerly direction until I should light upon a point where the ridges might be crossed with less difficulty. This route would enable me, at least, to keep up my "northing;" and, in the mean time, the country might improve, possibly become more practicable.

My rather jeopardous and difficult position strongly reminded me of seafarers in the close neighborhood of a coral-reef or an iceberg, anxiously examining every aperture and break in the obstruction opposing them in the hope of finding a safe passage for their frail skiff.

On the well-wooded ridges just spoken of I discovered *moss*, a species of vegetation I had not observed before during my travels north of the Orange River.

CHAPTER XV.

All Hope of finding the Omuramba described by Travelers renounced.—Doubts about its being a Branch of the Cunenè.—The River pointed out by the Bushmen quite distinct from the Cunenè.—A sandy Country, a continuous Forest.—An unexpected Visit from a Bushman, an old Acquaintance of Messrs. Green and Hahn.—He consents to be our Guide for some Distance.—I promise to kill an Elephant for him and his People.—Encampment by a fine Vley of Water.—A benevolent Bushman.—An Elephant struck dead by Lightning.—Fruit-trees and Forest-trees.—Their Description.—A Forest-tree of huge Dimensions and spreading Foliage.—Another Elephant-hunt.—Elephants in Herds as numerous as Cattle, like a large Army.—Their shrill Trumpetings at Night.

I HAD now given up all hope of finding the Omuramba U'Ovambo, unless the small river-course crossed on the 16th of January, as already mentioned, should turn out to be identical with that stream. That this was really the case I began to entertain strong suspicions; for if Messrs. Green and Hahn's statements and surmises were in any measure correct, I must necessarily, long ere this, have struck the river. As to the supposition of those travelers that the Omuramba U'Ovambo is a branch of the Cunenè, I had my doubts; I moreover thought that, instead of flowing toward Onondova, it was merely a current from that lake, the source of which must be looked for elsewhere—another riddle—and that, like the Dzouga, lost for a while in the sand, it might possibly join the minor Omuramba Otjituo farther on.

The river to which the Bushmen now pointed was evidently quite distinct from the Cunenè and the Omuramba U'Ovambo. It was in all probability the Mukuru Mukovanja, so well described to Mr. Galton and myself by the Ovambo, who declared that it was *the* great river.

On the 18th of February we found ourselves scarce of water, and, at the same time, lost all traces of those gullies which had hitherto befriended us. Instead of traversing parallel wooded ranges, we now entered on a comparatively level country covered with one continuous forest. The soil was composed of a fine white sand, so loose and yielding that both man and beast sank into it ankle deep; and as we had no choice at present with regard to routes, all I could do was to keep due north, the course pointed to by the Bushmen as the directest one to the river.

At about this time, just as I had returned one day from a hard ride in search of water, and, having been successful, was refreshing the inner man, a fine-looking Bushman chief stood suddenly before us. He had accidentally come across my horse's spoor, and thinking the rider might belong to some white man's party (he had seen Messrs. Green and Hahn when on their journey to the Ovambo), he unhesitatingly followed it up till he reached the wagon. I felt much gratified at this encounter, first, because the man could speak well of us to his countrymen, and, secondly, because he would be of the utmost service in guiding us to springs, wells, and vleys, now very difficult to find. He (Kanganda was his name) agreed at once to accompany us for some distance, and I, on my part, promised to kill an elephant for him and his people at the earliest opportunity.

In the afternoon of the second day after our new guide had joined us we arrived at several wells scooped out of the sand, having in the mean time obtained water for our cattle at a small vley. Another day's travel brought us to a large one of good clear water. Both this place and that which we had just left (*i. e.*, the wells) were resorted to regularly every dry season by certain Ovambo with their cattle.

I was suffering at this time excessively from rheumatic pains in my back, so much so that neither standing, sitting, nor reclining brought me any relief—indeed, the pain was at times so excruciating as almost to drive me frantic. Nevertheless, in order to fulfill my promise to the Bushmen (who were now anxious to return home), and with a view to the replenishment of our own exhausted larder, I made up my mind for an elephant hunt as soon as we could find fresh and fair-sized spoors. This happened the very next morning after our arrival at the vley, when the trail of a large male elephant was discovered hard by our camp. Saddling the

PURSUIT OF AN ELEPHANT.

ox "Seeland," I was soon in pursuit, and, notwithstanding the early hour, had the good fortune to come up with the brute after about an hour and a half tracking. I brought him down at the second shot, and with a third killed him outright. The beast was unusually savage, which I attributed to his having several assegai wounds, one of them evidently of recent date, on his body. He was a large elephant, with excellent tusks. The Bushmen were of course in ecstasy at my success, and their chief returned forthwith to his werft to fetch the remainder of his people to feast on the carcass.

There was a fine vley of water in the immediate neighborhood of the spot where the elephant fell. Here, then, we pitched our camp; and the jerking and drying of the meat, the heavy rains, with the repairs required by the wagon, occupied so much time that we were long delayed at this place. Our guide would go no farther; he promised, however, to find a substitute, and was as good as his word. At the expiration of a very few hours he brought to take his place a fine elderly Bushman, who had the most benevolent countenance I ever saw. This man conducted us to another werft, distant about a day's journey and a half. Indications of elephants, which had lately been scarce, now became numerous; so, in order to keep the natives in good-humor, as also, if possible, to divert their thoughts from what they might deem the motives of my journey, I started on another hunt, which gave me no satisfaction, for, though I once succeeded in coming up with a good-sized bull, and even got a shot at him, the chase proved a failure.

While a party of Bushmen were following up the spoor of this wounded beast, they came upon the carcass of a she-elephant who had been struck dead by lightning. This was the first instance I had known of these huge creatures being destroyed by the electric fluid, though it often occasions the death of the smaller kind of game. The natives, however, assured me that the occurrence was not at all an infrequent one during the rainy season. They had once stumbled, they told me, upon the remains of a full-grown male, whose head had been completely severed from his body by a thunder-stroke, and all his bones completely smashed.

As we traveled along, we observed, from time to time, several trees quite new to us, some fruit-bearing, others simply forest-trees. Of the former, one bore a dark green fruit as large as an orange, and nearly, when ripe, of the same color. Its shell or rind is of moderate thickness, the whole of the inside consisting of a kind of pulp, in which a great number of fleshy seeds or kernels are imbedded, which the natives roast in hot ashes and eat with their meat. When unripe these kernels are bitter and unpalatable, but in their mature state they are good food, and their scent is delicious. Essential oil might probably be expressed from them; indeed, the Bushmen extract from this fruit a fattish kind of matter which they use as an ointment for their bodies.

Of the forest-trees I noticed, there was one in particular that attracted attention from its handsome foliage and huge dimensions. We encamped one day under the wide-spreading branches of one of them, which was, as we found by measurement, fifteen feet three inches in circumference. Its leaves look at a little distance like those of a species of birch, indigenous to northern Europe, called "hanging" birch; its masses of foliage are, however, differently disposed. Many of these trees have large natural hollows in their trunks, which, during several months of the year, serve as reservoirs for rain-water. This peculiarity greatly benefits the natives, and I myself have frequently quenched my thirst from these singular cavities. The water thus obtained is sucked up through reeds or long hollow grass-stalks. Few and far between, however, was aught to excite curiosity. On the whole, the landscape was monotonous in the extreme. Indeed, nothing can be conceived more dreary and desolate than traveling through interminable forests, where, whether one ascends the highest hill or mounts the loftiest tree, he can see but a few hundred yards before him. We could not, like the outlaws of the forest of Ardennes, recline

"Under an oak, whose antique roots peep out
Upon the brook that brawls along the wood."

It had rained abundantly; pools of rain-water,

some of considerable capacity, were numerous; and having bivouacked one night by one of them, we were surprised on the ensuing morning to find the trail of a good-sized male elephant. Strange to say, neither dogs nor men had been aware of his presence, though he had quenched his thirst within easy gunshot of the wagon. I determined, therefore, our new guides being a very suspicious and discontented set, to put these grumbling fellows into a better humor by killing, if possible, this animal, which might induce them to conduct us to some Bushman werft in advance. Fortunately my efforts were crowned with success, for, after a tedious and intricate tracking, we sighted the brute, and not long afterward he received my first shot. At the second discharge he fell, but, though unable to move from the spot, he rose to his feet, and before life was quite extinct seven more bullets were lodged in his body. This fact was not remarkable, for it frequently happens that an elephant seriously wounded will patiently receive broadside upon broadside without exhibiting the least symptom of distress beyond that occasioned by the first wound. One might, therefore, leave the moribund brute to die a lingering death; but I could never endure the sight of an animal in pain. There is, besides, some danger in such case of losing one's game, for it sometimes happens that he will temporarily recover and walk off.

A very remarkable instance of this fell within my own experience. One night I had brought down a very large elephant, who, after lying on his side above half an hour apparently quite dead, suddenly rose to his feet and made off. I killed this animal ten days afterward on almost the same spot where he had first fallen, and identified him by his wounds, and more especially by a piece of ivory that had been broken off from one of his tusks on the first encounter.

I had often heard the natives say, on being questioned about the haunts of elephants, that in such or such a locality "they walked about as thick as cattle," but never till now had I been able to verify this apparently exaggerated statement. I did so at present, for the whole country in the neighborhood of the vley lately referred to, with the adjacent plains, was literally one net-work of elephants' footprints. The trees and bushes, moreover, were so broken down and trampled by their inroads, that one might fairly suppose a large army had just traversed the veldt. During the daytime the animals were not visible, but at night their shrill trumpetings would frequently startle us from our sleep. If, instead of exploring, I had turned my attention exclusively to elephant-hunting, I might have had magnificent sport and profit too. The temptation to do so was strong, but I considered it ignoble, however great the allurements I had to resist, to swerve from a predetermined purpose for the sake of gain and personal gratification.

CHAPTER XVI.

The Difficulty of finding Way and Water increased.—Guides decamp.—Conflicting Opinions about the Road to the River.—I leave the Wagon to explore the Country.—The Capture of a whole Werft of Bushmen.—Two of them compelled to be Guides.—Tied together as Prisoners.—A Native Woman captured.—A Werft of twenty or thirty Huts.—Conversation with the Chief of the Hamlet.—Reach Ombongo.—A periodical Water-course.—Great Anxiety as I approach the Water, Bushmen have often so contradictorily described.—Was it merely a Valley periodically filled with Water, or a mighty River?—Our Guides hide their Arrows in the Trees from fear of Robbery by the Ovaquangari.—I perceive on the far-away Horizon a distinct dark blue Line.—I recognize at once a great River.—This River called by the Natives the OKAVANGO.—Reflections, Description, Conjectures.

AFTER the necessary delays occasioned by cutting up and drying our meat, etc., we continued to journey on, the bush becoming, if possible, more and more dense, harassing, and retarding to our march. It would be wearisome to dwell on our wretched progress; while, to add to our embarrassment, our discontented and suspicious guides threatened to leave us. It was, however, to us of the utmost importance at present to retain their services, as the difficulty of finding both way and water increased daily. I therefore earnestly requested them to stay with us, at least till other Bushmen could be found.

But no persuasions or offers of handsome rewards could induce them to remain; and one day they unexpectedly decamped, leaving us to grope out our way as best we could.

Elephant paths now became exceedingly numerous, crossing and recrossing the country in every possible direction. Sometimes half a dozen or more of these paths might be seen converging toward some particular point, *i. e.*, a vley; it was impossible, therefore, to know how to select the proper one. Yet we dared not neglect them altogether, as by following them on we could alone find water. At one time one of these tracks actually led us back toward Damara Land. This, however, would have mattered little had I known the exact course to pursue; but the Bushmen had so contradicted each other's statements that I felt completely puzzled. At times these perplexing conductors would point to the north, at others to the N.E., and some even said that due east was our proper route for finding the river. In this uncertainty, cruising about day after day in the intricate bush with our cumbersome vehicle was distressing in the extreme; I therefore, after a while, determined on leaving the wagon at some vley, and proceeding with a few draught and carriage oxen ahead, to explore the country, and, if possible, discover the river.

To dispatch this business quickly, with some chance of success, I packed up the smallest quantity of necessaries possible, and, selecting a few of the most light-footed and enduring of my native attendants, started on the expedition. That same day, at about sunset, we perceived a small column of smoke issuing from a cluster of trees, and by sending part of my people in a roundabout way in advance, we succeeded in capturing all the inmates of a small Bushman werft. The whole party captured consisted but of a few women and children and two or three grown-up men. The poor people were of course desperately frightened, but I soon pacified them by presents of meat and tobacco. Thinking it unadvisable at the time to make any mention of my need of guides, I merely gave them to understand that I was *en route* for the river. I was determined, however, should they not decamp during the night, to secure a couple of the men on the following morning. My mode of proceeding answered well, for at an early hour the next day, on going to their werft (we bivouacked at a pool of water hard by), we found them enjoying themselves, in all security, by a roaring fire. Without a moment's delay I ordered two of them to rise and to accompany us. They were extremely loth to comply, but I soon gave them to understand that obey they must—that they had no alternative.

After several hours' smart traveling we halted at a fine vley of water and partook of some refreshment. Before we had quite finished our humble meal the Bushmen rose, saying they were returning to their home, at the same time pointing to an elephant path as our route. But this would never do; so, springing at once to my feet, I seized and secured one of the fellows, who then reluctantly consented to accompany us. Now the office of guide is naturally to lead the way, but it is an extremely difficult thing to induce an African aboriginal to proceed ahead of a party; he takes always every possible occasion to loiter behind; therefore, dreading the consequence of allowing the man his liberty, I hit upon the following expedient to prevent his absconding. I fastened his right hand to the wrist of the left hand of one of my attendants, leaving rather more than three feet of thong between them, so as not to embarrass their movements. The Bushman was then ordered to proceed, and, in order to prevent all chance of escape, I followed close at his heels. The man was in a desperate fright, and stopped repeatedly, begging hard to be let loose, but I turned, of course, a deaf ear to all his entreaties.

Late in the afternoon of this day we came upon several pretty fresh tracks of Bushmen, and, following them steadily up, espied after a while a woman digging for roots. She was soon secured, but until addressed by our guide (whom I had now set at liberty) she was in great trepidation. Five minutes' farther walk brought us to a werft consisting of between twenty and thirty huts.

While my men were here making every thing snug for the night, I had some conversation with the chief of the place, a fine, intelligent young fellow. He told us that by smart traveling we might reach the river in a day and a half. This was cheerful news, the more so as he promised to conduct us thither personally. I lay down to rest consequently that night more contented than I had been for many a day, and in much better spirits.

On the next morning we were stirring early. About noon we reached an omuramba called Ombongo, the first real periodical water-course we had met with for a distance of more than 150 miles. At this point this course ran in a nearly northern direction. In its bed we found several fine vleys of water, and even some natural springs, the first we had seen since leaving the calcareous tufa spoken of in the preceding pages. We halted here for about an hour and a half, and then continued our journey till sunset, when we pitched our camp for the night.

The following day was to solve the problem that had so long engaged all my thoughts, and which was to mark a momentous crisis, not only in my present travels, but also in my entire life. I felt, therefore, considerable anxiety about the description of river I was on the eve of discovering. Some Bushmen we had encountered in our wanderings had positively spoken of it as a mere omuramba, *i. e.*, a kind of deeply depressed valley, with a succession of vleys periodically filled with water, while others had asserted that it was a permanent stream, traversed by the natives in canoes, and abounding in hippopotami, fish, and alligators. I dreaded lest the first of these accounts should turn out correct, for in that case all the great expense incurred, and the immense amount of labor lavished on its discovery, would prove valueless and abortive.

At break of day we were afoot, but, the morning air being raw and sharp, I had at first some difficulty in getting the guides along. After about six hours' journeying at a rapid rate, these Bushmen suddenly stopped short, and each of them, drawing from his quiver two or three arrows, carefully concealed them among the trees. On demanding an explanation of this singular proceeding, I was simply told that the Ovaquangari were a very unscrupulous set of men, who, whenever they thought themselves strong enough, would take forcible possession of any thing that struck their fancy; and as the concealed missiles were new, and of some value to the Bushmen, they were, they said, loth to lose them. They also warned me to be on my guard, as the natives, whose villages we were now fast approaching, were fierce and savage. This was an old tale, and, though I did not despise the warning, I conjectured that our sudden and unannounced arrival among them would cause rather fright and consternation than any demonstration of hostility on their part.

After this little delay we again proceeded, but had not gone far before I perceived on the far-away horizon a distinct dark blue line. "Ah ha!" I exclaimed to myself, "in the valley of which that line evidently forms the border, there is surely something more than a mere periodical water-course." A few minutes afterward, catching a glimpse of an immense sheet of water in the distance, my anticipation was realized to its utmost. A cry of joy and satisfaction escaped me at this glorious sight. Twenty minutes more brought us to the banks of a truly noble river, at this point at least 200 yards wide. This was, then, in all probability, the Mukuru Mukovanja of the Ovambo, which these people had given us to understand flowed westward. Taking it for granted that their statement was in this respect correct, I had stood some time by the water before I became aware of my mistake. "By heavens!" I suddenly exclaimed, "the water flows toward the heart of the continent instead of emptying itself into the Atlantic!" For a moment I felt amazed at the discovery. "East!" I continued to soliloquize; "why, what stream *can* this then be, in this latitude and longitude? Tioughe? No; that channel alone is much too insignificant to form the outlet for such a mighty flow of water. Well, then, it must be one of the chief branches of that magnificent river, the Chobe." This was my first impression, which was to some extent corroborated by the natives, who described this river, called by the Ovaquangari "Okavango," as forking off in two directions in the neighborhood of Libèbè, one branch forming the said Tioughe, the other finding its way to the Chobe. But, on more mature consideration, I strongly question the correctness both of my own impression and of the account of the natives.

It is true Dr. Livingstone, in one of his early maps, lays down a river as coming from Libèbè toward Sekeletu's town; and I myself, when at Lake Ngami, heard of a water communication existing between these two places. But as the Tioughe is known to send out a branch toward Chobe considerably below Libèbè, *i. e.*, south of it, called Dzo, it is just possible that this is the stream alluded to by the natives. Furthermore, the country for a great distance about Libèbè, is known to abound in immense marshes; it is probable, therefore, that the Okavango, though of such large dimensions, is more or less swallowed up in these extensive swamps, leaving merely sufficient water for the formation of the Tioughe and its inundations. Unquestionably Dr. Livingstone, if he succeeds in revisiting Sekeletu's town, will be able to settle this question.

CHAPTER XVII.

The Terror of the Ovaquangari on our Approach.—The Natives cross the River in several Canoes, armed to the Teeth.—Ordered to lay aside their Weapons and talk peaceably.—The Difficulty of communicating with them in the Ovambo Language.—They are made to understand the Object of our Visit.—The Chief sends us Food.—I make known my Intention to visit the paramount Chief, Chikongo by name.—Dispatch a Messenger to him.—He intimates a Wish to see me.—A suitable Conveyance refused.—Procured at last by threatening to leave the Country.—A Sail on the Okavango.—The Boatman a great Blackguard.—Shows the white Man as a wild Beast to crowds of Natives.—The Women exceedingly ugly.—The River described.—Hippopotami and Alligators.—Picturesque Landscape.—Modes of catching Fish.—Bivouac under a Tree, with the Wind for a Bedfellow.—Description of a Werft.—All the Chiefs of the Nation assemble to meet me.—Portrait of Chikongo.—His Hospitality.—The Makololo.—Dr. Livingstone's Attempts to civilize this People unsuccessful.

ALL the villages and cultivated lands of the Ovaquangari being situated on the north bank of the river, there was no access to them except by means of canoes. For these we had to wait, and, while doing so, the natives perceived our approach, upon which, as I had anticipated, a general panic ensued. The children and women set up a most piteous howl, and the men ran about shouting like maniacs. Each village, or rather homestead, was invariably within easy hail of its neighbor; our sudden arrival, therefore, was announced throughout the country with almost the same speed as a telegram would convey a message.

A number of men were soon seen collecting on the opposite bank, and, many questions and answers having been interchanged with the Bushmen, a canoe was put out, and shortly afterward we saw our friends transferred to the opposite shore, where no doubt they were closely questioned about the strangers.

After about two hours' conversation with our guides, the Ovaquangari seemed to be in some degree satisfied; for, at the expiration of that time, several canoes full of men were observed issuing from the reeds and advancing toward us. Having landed at some little distance below our camp, these men, armed to the teeth, came on with great circumspection. And as my party was small and no match for such numbers, I, after exchanging a few words with them, ordered our new acquaintances to lay aside their weapons, when, I said, we could talk peaceably together. The head man of the surrounding homesteads was among them—a remarkably fine-looking savage, with a countenance stamped with good sense and intelligence. But, indeed, all the men were tall, well-built fellows, richly bedaubed with grease and ochre, the wealthier being also profusely covered over with iron and bead ornaments.

The Bushmen had given us to understand that these people spoke a dialect of the Ovaherero; I had therefore flattered myself that our interview would prove both easy and profitable, but soon discovered that it might not be so satisfactory as I had anticipated. Indeed, though many of the natives understood a little of the Damara language, it was evident that their tongue was identical with that of the Ovambo. Notwithstanding, however, this disadvantage, we quickly made them understand that the object of our visit was simply to see and explore the country, and that, above all, toward themselves we entertained no sentiments but those of peace and good-will.

Our broken conversation having lasted for some time, the chief rose, saying that, as we might be hungry, he would return to his werft and get us some food. I felt thankful for this proffered supply, as our own scanty stock was all but exhausted. The promised fare, however, was not forthcoming till the following day, when we were presented with four or five small baskets of meal, some fresh ripe mealies, several pumpkins, and a cow. The vegetables especially were very acceptable, for, to speak the truth, dry elephant flesh had been for the last two months our principal nutriment.

The great chief of the nation we were now among, Chikongo by name, resided at a considerable distance to the southward of the point where I first struck the river. To him a messenger was dispatched on the day we reached the Ovango, to apprise him of our arrival in his dominions, which expressed, at the same time, my desire to have an interview with his highness. To this message an answer was received in the afternoon of the third day. The chief intimated a wish to see and speak with me at his werft, as he was not able, he said, to make me a visit in person. Being, therefore, really anxious to see the man, I at once acceded to his request. On demanding, however, whether suitable conveyances had been provided for myself and party, I was unceremoniously informed that I must go on foot. But that I was not at all disposed to do, and told the messengers that I would not visit their chief in so beggarly a way. "Well, there are no canoes for you," was the reply. "Very good," I rejoined; "if you do not choose to convey me to my destination in a proper manner, I shall at once retrace my steps;" adding, "that no doubt Chikongo would be much displeased at such a result of my visit to his country." At this remark they laughed outright, telling me, in plain terms, that though Chikongo was the head of the nation, every man was captain of his own homestead and master of his own property. This independence was no doubt very fine, but showed but little respect for their chief, whose influence over the tribe I naturally concluded to be very limited. Such, indeed, was the case, and is almost universally so with respect to the great heads of tribes throughout Africa.

P

One hears of such and such a chief being very powerful; from certain established customs, and, above all, by the support of the principal men of his nation, he may be so; if, however, he neglects them, he is left to his fate, which is too frequently assassination.

To return to my story. My determined language had ultimately the effect of procuring me the promise of two canoes; these were to be placed at my disposal at an early hour on the following morning. At break of day, therefore, I was stirring, but neither men nor canoes appeared. Patience is a virtue that should be especially cultivated by the African traveler; but that desirable quality failed me in the present instance, and I angrily dispatched one of my servants to hasten the men on, with a threat that in case they disappointed me I should decidedly, as I had already declared, leave the country without farther delay. Suiting my actions to my words, I thereupon ordered up the oxen, and began to make preparations for a start "homeward." This, as all our operations could be seen from the opposite bank, had the desired effect. In double-quick time one of the promised canoes made its appearance—only one; and it was a dirty, narrow little dingy, not capable of holding more than my few "traps," myself, and the paddle-man. I felt annoyed at the bad faith of the natives, yet, as any altercation would only have caused additional delay, I put the best face I could on the matter,

THE WHITE MAN A SHOW.

and at once embarked. The Bechuana lad, Tom, was my only attendant, and he, together with the chief's men, took an overland route, a place of rendezvous having been previously fixed upon between us.

My boatman was a stout, sturdy fellow, but a great blackguard. The stream on which we had embarked has rather a rapid flow, estimated at from two and a half to three miles per hour; by keeping within its current, great progress might consequently have been made. But this did not suit the views of my boatman, who, in order, he said, to avoid hippopotami, kept poking the canoe among reeds and shallows, stopping at every spot where he had a friend or acquaintance, and calling out, at the top of his voice, to the inhabitants far and near to come and have a look at the white man. Thus very frequently twenty or thirty people might be seen issuing from a single homestead to have a stare at me. The whole scene reminded me of visitors to a menagerie stopping outside some wild beast's den curiously to examine the monster. On these occasions I had favorable opportunities of surveying the fair sex. I found them an exceedingly ugly-looking lot—thick-set, square, with clumsy figures, bull-dog lips, and broad, flat faces. Even without the grease and ochre, so delicious and ornamental to the body in the opinion of all savages, some of the females would have been perfectly hideous. With their crisp woolly hair standing erect in little tangled knots, they might, had their countenances been more animated and intelligent, have been reckoned good models for the Furies.

Notwithstanding the little annoyances I have mentioned, I enjoyed the trip very much. After traversing for so many years the eternal "deserts" of Damara and Namaqua Land, the sight of so much water was naturally very welcome; besides, as in my native country I had from infancy been accustomed to navigating rivers and lakes of the first magnitude, a row on this truly fine stream could not but be delightful. It had at this point a remarkably straight course, winding nevertheless in short curves, here and there, in many places, while its width did not fall short of three hundred yards. Occasionally little islands—the favorite resort of hippopotami and alligators—were seen emerging from its bosom, a clear channel of deep water, at least one hundred yards broad, being always on the one side or the other of them. The surrounding landscape was not particularly striking, but, on the whole, pretty and effective; indeed, many parts afforded a positively picturesque scenery. The higher parts of the valley were luxuriantly covered with tall, handsome, dark-foliaged forest-trees, beautifully set off by the lighter vegetation of the lower grounds, where vast corn-fields, interspersed with occasional huge wild fruit-trees, groups of acacias, etc., spread pleasantly before the eye. The north bank of the river, with very few exceptions, was alone cultivated; yet I do not think this inferred inferiority in the productive qualities of the other bank, but simply fear of foreign invasions. The soil was composed of fine sand and clay thoroughly intermixed, the underlying rock of the country, consisting of calcareous tufa, being strongly impregnated with iron. The rocks, however, were rarely visible, never except in the immediate neighborhood of the river, where the strength of the current had probably removed the overlying strata of sand. These rock-ledges were invariably luxuriantly overgrown with rank and varied growths of sea-weeds gracefully overhanging the stream, which washed and sprinkled them as it swept by the rocks' base with a purling and meandering murmur. Additional attractions were given to many parts of the river by great numbers of water-fowl, especially of ducks and geese. One species of the latter struck us from its gigantic size, the goose standing when erect, as far as I could judge, at least four feet high, while its body certainly looked as large as that of a good-sized terrier dog.

Fish abounded, and the natives employed various means for capturing them. I was much struck by the resemblance of their toils to those used by the fishermen of the north of Europe. But more of this hereafter.

Late in the afternoon we landed, and encamped for the night under a noble sycamore, measuring (five feet from off the ground) twenty-five feet in circumference. We could not possibly have selected (though, to be sure, we had no choice in the present instance) a worse spot for bivouacking; for, though the trunk afforded some protection, the wind, on this cold, blowy night, swept round the sides of the tree in eddies, one current of air passing down our backs and another up our legs. To add to our discomfort, not a stick of fuel was to be had, and that villain, the boatman, would not budge an inch to help us until compelled by force. Some coarse meal and hot porridge, presented to us by the inmates of a neighboring village, constituted our supper. This meal finished, we at once resigned ourselves to sleep.

On the following morning we were early stirring, but were unexpectedly informed that we must have the permission of Chikongo before we could proceed farther. Now, as this gentleman's residence was still far off, I remonstrated strongly against this hinderance; and fortunately, after a delay of about an hour and a half, we were allowed to resume our onward course.

Between ten and eleven o'clock A.M. we reached our destination. We were not, however, permitted to land at the village; so, while waiting for instructions, Tom and I set about preparing a light breakfast, which we had hardly time to dispatch when orders arrived for us to present ourselves before the chief. Five minutes' walk brought us to a werft— a most filthy, poverty-stricken, miserable-looking burrow. It consisted of a great number of low huts, constructed in the bee-hive fashion, crowded into a very limited space, each hut being partitioned off from its neighbor, and surrounded by vertically placed mattings, made of thin split wood, precisely similar to those manufactured by the peasantry of the north of Sweden for the purpose of being converted into panniers. Places set apart for palavers or consultation, and friendly chat, dancing-rooms, etc., were also environed, and separated from each other in the same way. The whole hamlet was besides encompassed by a stout palisading. Weeds and rank grasses grew and thrived amazingly every where all over the place. A spot had just been cleared of this waste vegetation for my reception; it was thronged by the élite of the nation, who had assembled there in great numbers.

Having waited a few minutes, a tall, rather spare-made, middle-aged, and not unprepossessing-looking man made his appearance. This was the chief, Chikongo. His person was less decorated than that of most of his followers, but round his neck he wore an immense coil of fine beads—a common ornament with the well-to-do class of his countrymen. By being constantly bedaubed and plastered over with grease and ochre, these decorations had become one solid and compact mass. The upper parts of his arms were encircled by bracelets formed entirely of the white valuable shell so often alluded to by travelers, while from his waist depended several handsome dagger-knives of native workmanship. The whole of his body was moreover shining and dripping with ochre and butter.

One of the men sent me by the chief spoke the Sichuana language fluently, and as my attendant was a native Bechuana, I had now considerable facility in explaining to Chikongo the object of my journey, my wants and my wishes. He listened patiently, but made few or no remarks; and the interview having lasted a short time, broke it suddenly off, saying, "Now you are probably hungry and must eat. It grieves me from my heart that I can not entertain you as I should wish. Till the Makololo came and robbed me of my cattle I was rich, and lived well; at present I can only bid you welcome as a Bushman." This was but too true.

The reader will probably recollect allusions having been made in the preceding pages to a report, which had reached me at Omanbondè, viz., that a party of white men had, the year previous to my visit, attacked the Ovaquangari nation, and carried off much cattle, besides making captives of men, women, and children. The aggressors, however, were not white men, but that scourge of central South Africa, the *Makololo*.

This was, then, the result of all Dr. Livingstone's earnest endeavors to dissuade these people from committing depredations on their neighbors! All their fine promises to that noble explorer, with their professions of peaceful dispositions, were, as we here see, mere delusions, to use the lightest word, on both sides. I very much fear that this tribe have two faces for Dr. Livingstone. There is no doubt that he possesses very great influence over them, a fact which has been abundantly proved by the very handsome manner in which they have treated and assisted him; and when that admirable man is on the spot, unquestionably every thing goes on well and smoothly; but no sooner, I suspect, is his back turned, than the old Swedish saw—"*När katten är borta, dansa råttorna på bordet*"—literally, when the cat is away, the rats dance on the table—is at once fully verified. After all, a missionary, be he ever so practical a man, or ever so much esteemed, is never likely to know the secrets of a savage community. That such is the case has been abundantly proved in almost all countries where missions have been established. My own experience tells the same tale. Human nature is loth to confess its frailties (for the knowledge of good and evil is inherent in every human bosom) where in these frailties there is no participation, and where they find but a sentimental sympathy. "Men," as a certain historian finely says, "may praise, but they seldom love those who elevate themselves above the ordinary passions and prejudices of their race."

CHAPTER XVIII.

The Mambari.—Traders from the Confines of the Kingdom of Benguela.—Visit the Ovaquangari every Year.—Peddler Expeditions as far as Libèbè.—Much valuable Information, especially respecting the North and its Natives, to be derived from these Traders.—They convey a Letter for me to the Governor of Benguela.—They also forward one to the R. G. S. of London.—I think of returning to my Men left with the Wagon.—Chikongo objects to this Proposal, as his People have not yet "had time to stare at me."—The Savages quite on a Par, in Point of Intelligence, with the Ovambos.—Agricultural Pursuits.—Trades of the Ovaquangari.—Various Tribes to the Northeast of this People.—No permanently settled Nations.—Only Bushmen.—Rejoin my Wagon.—Tremendous Penalty for my successful Enterprise.—Attacked by a malignant Fever.—Five of my Men prostrated by the same Disease.—Anticipate a like Fate for the Remainder of my Party.—I hesitate about incurring the Responsibility of persisting in my Enterprise.—Determine, on Reflection, to do so.

At Chikongo's werft I encountered several Mambari, *i. e.*, black traders from the confines of the kingdom of Benguela. If these were true representatives of their tribe, little could be said in their favor either physically or mentally. They were below the average stature of men, very slenderly built, with low foreheads, and generally unimpressive and unintelligent features. They brought with them slaves and ivory, for which they received in exchange the usual African commodities, beads, guns, ammunition, etc. I was grieved to find that they had also introduced into the country ardent spirits, which appeared to be extravagantly in demand among the Ovaquangari.

The Mambari visit this people regularly once a year, and afterward push their excursions as far eastward as Libèbè. But, though their route lies in these peddler expeditions for many days along the Okavango River, they never make use of canoes for transporting their merchandise. The ivory is always carried on men's shoulders.

It was clear, however, despite their uninviting appearance, that these men, having frequent commercial communications with people inhabiting the North imperfectly or not at all known to Europeans, could furnish me with much and valuable information respecting that country and its natives. Unfortunately, my interpreter flatly refused to interrogate the traders—for reasons no doubt best known to his chief Chikongo. I managed, nevertheless, to get from them a promise to convey to the Governor of Benguela, or to some other officer in authority in his majesty's dominions, a letter, in which I informed his excellency that I purposed, in the course of the year, paying a visit to the district under his government, and requested his kind assistance toward the accomplishment of this design. I also profited by the same opportunity to write to

Dr. Shaw, secretary to the Royal Geographical Society of London. These epistles duly, I believe, reached their destination.

As my absence had been already sufficiently prolonged to create uneasiness in the minds of the men left behind with the wagon, I naturally felt anxious to retrace my steps; I accordingly acquainted the chief with my intention. But he would hear of no such abrupt departure, saying, with great simplicity, that it would not even allow him or his people time to stare at me. "Moreover," added he, "who knows that you will ever return to us?" Anxious as I was to regain my wagon without farther delay, I was no less anxious to stand so well with my new friends as to insure to future visitors a safe and hearty welcome among them. Demurring, therefore, no longer to yield to the chief's request, I passed that and the following day beneath his hospitable roof.

The people, though, like all savages, somewhat rude, behaved, on the whole, with propriety. They were exceedingly merry, but evinced much curiosity, and made many clever inquiries as to the uses, fabrication, etc., of various utensils we had brought with us. It was evident I was once again among an intelligent race of men—quite on a par, in this respect, with their western neighbors, the Ovambo, whom they so closely resemble in language, habits, costume, and domestic customs, that any separate description of them would be superfluous. A reference to "Lake Ngami" will satisfy the curious on this head.

Like the Ovambo, the Ovaquangari engage in agricultural pursuits, and ply many trades, that of blacksmiths more especially. They manufacture all the ornaments, household utensils, farming implements, arms, etc., in use among their own people; they also export these articles largely. Their principal traffic is, however, confined to iron and copper, both ores being indigenous to their country —at least that part of it which lies north of the Okavango River.

This tribe are also very much addicted to barter, and keep up thereby a constant intercourse with their numerous neighbors—an intercourse greatly facilitated by their fine navigable stream.

East of the Ovaquangari are the Ovabundija, the Ozomboo, and the Bavickos, of which the capital is the well-known Libèbè. To the southward only Bushmen and impoverished Ovaherero exist, while to the west we find the Ovambo, as also a powerful nation called Ovakuenyama. North and northwest again, a great number of small tribes flourish. The following are those best known: the Datiekombo, Morodi, Papero, Masaka, Chirongo, Majambi, etc. These live along the river in the order here enumerated. West of these, and north of the Ovakuenyama, we find Kazima, Evari, Ehandá, Vasipongo, etc. To the northeast there are no permanently settled nations; the only inhabitants of these regions are Bushmen, and the scattered remnants of black tribes, once rich in corn-land and cattle, but now impoverished—the Bakalahari, in short, of this desolate part of the world.

On the third day from my arrival at Chikongo's I departed, and next morning joined that portion of my party left where we first struck the river. Three days more, and I regained my wagon in safety. But, alas! had I then been aware of the tremendous penalty my successful enterprise had imposed, and was farther to impose upon myself and party, it is very doubtful whether I should not have returned homeward at once, instead of revisiting, as I had determined to do, Chikongo; for, on the night after my return, I was attacked by a malignant fever, from the effects of which I have never to this day recovered, which brought me speedily to the verge of the grave. It is impossible to describe the terrible agony that seized me when I felt the first symptoms of this malady. It was but a slight quivering of the body, but I knew it too well to entertain any doubt about what it betokened. Of course it was not a coward anticipation of pain, however severe and lasting, that so much distressed me. Ah! no: it was the certain knowledge that all my energies, bodily and mental, would be prostrated, and that, too, at a time when they were most needed, that so shocked and unnerved me. My first impulse was, as I have said, to hasten home; but then there rose before me the promise I had made to the chief, and the prospect of future success should I recover, which, with many other equally cogent reasons, urged me to persevere in the course I had decided upon from the moment I caught sight of the Okavango River, which was to prosecute my discoveries to the very utmost as long as there remained the smallest and most remote chance of their being crowned with success.

After a day or two devoted to rest, we therefore pushed forward, but had not proceeded far before five out of the six men who had accompanied me to the river were seized with the same malignant disease as myself. Of these, after an illness of only two or three days, one died. This sudden death seriously alarmed the others; and feeling certain that their ignorant and superstitious fears would greatly retard, if not altogether hinder their recovery, I once more paused. I felt convinced, too, that on reaching the river again the remainder of my party would also be seized with fever. The reader need not therefore be surprised that I once more hesitated to jeopardize so many lives. My uncertainty, however, did not last long; after carefully weighing all the *pros* and *cons*, I determined to continue the journey. Thus I argued: "Let us suppose the worst, viz., that my whole party is laid prostrate; well, with care and good nursing, most of them, including myself, may, in the course of two or three months, be sufficiently restored to health to go forward. The invalids, if any remain, I can, should he continue friendly to my plans, and I have no reason to think otherwise, leave with the chief. My stock of provisions, dead or alive, is, it is true, not very great, yet there is sufficient to support life for at least seven or eight months. Moreover, I am amply provided with articles of exchange, for which I can always command corn and other vegetables for an almost unlimited period." These considerations encouraged me to persevere. But, alas! how true the proverb, "Man proposes, and God disposes," the sequel will show.

Here, however, to vary the monotony of my narrative, let me pause for a while, while I invite my readers to accompany me on a sporting excursion, wherein occurred an incident or two of sufficient interest, I think, to be chronicled in a chapter apart.

CHAPTER XIX.

A Leopard hunted by Dogs.—An extraordinary Leap.—Leopards and Panthers.—Their stealthy, fawning Mode of attacking their Prey.—The Chetah.—An Antelope Hunt.—Among the Elephants again.—A Presentiment and a Prophecy.—An exciting Chase.—A Night Hunt.—A pastoral Picture of Elephants enjoying themselves.—A dangerous Position.—A Mistake.—Two Elephants shot instead of one.—A glorious Day's Sport.—Three Elephants bagged.—A new Attack of Fever.

ONE evening, a little before sunset, while I was still suffering from the effects of fever, all my dogs suddenly began to give chase to some animal, which the distance did not enable us to distinguish. To judge, however, from the rapid alternating attacks of the pursuers, they evidently had a formidable antagonist before them. I was too weak to keep quite up with them, but my curiosity was so strong that I almost did so. They were, I conjectured from their steady, unbroken, deep bay, close upon the haunches of their enemy, yet I could not distinctly see either the dogs or the object of their pursuit, when all at once a magnificent leopard sprang right before me, from the topmost branches of a tall acacia, clearing, with a single bound, all his fierce assailants. I was so astounded at the magnitude of the leap—without having witnessed it one can hardly form a notion of the distance oversprung—that, looking first at the tree, and then at the spot on which the beautiful beast had alighted, I could not withdraw my eyes from the scene of it. Had the dogs followed my example—that is, had they been equally fascinated with the fine muscular action of the comely creature, they would certainly have lost their prey; but rage alone animated them, and before the panther had proceeded a hundred yards they had overtaken and torn him with such force and ferocity to the ground, that by the time I reached him the poor brute gave no other signs of life than the quivering of his panting limbs. Pereira put him out of his pain by firing a rifle into his heart.

Before I proceed farther, I must add a few words about the leopard and panther. These creatures are most remarkable for the perseverance and patience with which they watch their prey. They lurk in ambush among bushes or verdure on the borders of forests, and spring with a sudden and tremendous leap on such animals as may pass by. So prompt, so rapid, and well-timed are their movements, that few whom they attack escape. They resemble the cat in their mode of seizing their prey. They approach by drawing themselves along on their bellies, by gliding softly through shrubs and bushes, by concealing themselves in ditches, or, if showing themselves, by assuming a mild and fawn-

THE LEOPARD AND HIS PREY.

ing appearance, and watching the favorable moment for darting on their victims. At one leap they fasten on the back of any poor brute they may be lying in wait for, which they seize with the left paw and teeth in a way that it is impossible for it to escape, while with the right paw they in a few minutes tear it in pieces. They then suck the blood, devour a part of the flesh, and carry the carcass into the nearest wood for a future meal. The chetah, or hunting leopard, is frequently tamed in India, and used in the chase of antelopes. It is carried in a kind of small wagon, chained and hooded, lest, on approaching the herd, it should be too precipitate, and not make choice of a proper animal. When first unchained, it does not immediately spring toward its prey, but winds, with the utmost caution, along the ground, stopping at intervals, and carefully concealing itself till a favorable opportunity offers; it then darts on the herd with astonishing swiftness, and overtakes them by the rapidity of its bounds. If, however, in its first attempt, which consists in five or six amazing leaps, it does not succeed, it loses breath, and, giving up the point, at once returns sulkily to its cart.

On one occasion I saw three chetahs in the field. Coming on a herd of antelopes, one of them was quickly unhooded and loosed from his bonds. As soon as he perceived the deer, he dropped quietly off the cart on the opposite side to that on which they stood, and approached them at a slow, crouching canter, masking himself at every bush and inequality that lay in his way. As soon, however, as they began to show alarm, he quickened his pace, and was in the midst of them at a few bounds. He singled out a doe, and ran it close for about two hundred yards, when he reached it with a blow of his paw, rolled it over, and in an instant was sucking the life-blood from its throat. One of the other chetahs was then slipped at the same time, but, after making four or five desperate bounds, by which he nearly reached his prey, suddenly gave up the pursuit, and came growling sulkily back to the wagon. As soon, on these occasions, as the deer is pulled down, a keeper runs up, hoods the chetah, cuts the victim's throat, and, securing some of the blood in a wooden ladle, thrusts it under the leopard's nose. The antelope is then dragged away, while the chetah is rewarded with a leg for his pains.

And now let the reader accompany me once more to a scene among the grandest of the denizens of the wilds—the elephant. The story I am about to relate is chiefly remarkable from the singular presentiment of success that preceded its occurrence, which I not only felt, but announced to several persons.

We had been traveling for the last two or three days in the bed of the Omuramba, and my illness had taken for a time a favorable turn, when traces of elephants became very numerous. Our larder was also all but exhausted, so I determined on replenishing it by a hunt for some of this big game as soon as we could fall in with a fresh trail. I had not long to wait. Early on the morning of the third day after entering this Omuramba, we crossed a fresh spoor of a fair-sized male elephant. In five minutes' time I was in pursuit of the brute, and in less than an hour found myself in his presence. But, as ill luck would have it, he had become aware of my approach, and was, unknown to me, cautiously retracing his steps. We thus suddenly found ourselves face to face in a dense brake, at a distance certainly not exceeding fifteen paces. I felt at first, foreseeing the consequences that might ensue, averse to fire in my awkward position; but there was no alternative. Raising the rifle, therefore, steadily to my shoulder, and taking a deliberate aim at the forehead of the animal, I pulled the trigger. The result was as I had anticipated; my life was probably saved, but my game was gone. With one of those terrific screams so peculiar to his species, the monster wheeled round with the rapidity of lightning, and the next moment was out of sight. I followed his spoor closely up for a long time, but failed in again encountering him. I thereupon rejoined my wagon, both sick and dispirited, yet determined to have another shot or two at some of the fugitive's comrades before the fever should resume its fatal sway over my enervated frame. Turning this resolution over in my mind, I, just before retiring to rest, hallooed out to one of my servants: "Pereira, keep a sharp look-out, for I feel quite certain that elephants will stray this way to-night."

I had soon fallen into a deep but perturbed slumber, my fancy busily depicting, in a broken way, the scene of my day's adventure, and wildly shaping the chances of better success on the following morning, when, at about midnight, I was startled by the cry, "Sir! sir! two elephants are passing us on yonder bank." To spring to my feet and to seize the rifle was the work of an instant; and as soon as my eyes had become sufficiently clear of their sleepy film, I perceived, at no great distance, not two, but three elephants, which, from their towering height, I at once concluded to be males. They were walking with a steady but quick step; and supposing they were about to quench their thirst at some rain-pools hard by, I hastened to intercept them. It soon became evident, however, that they had taken the alarm; while, being afraid myself to lose sight of them in the dimness of a starless night, I deemed it most advisable to postpone my attack on them till daylight. Halting thereupon, I said to Pereira, who was following me with a spare rifle, "No, don't let us disturb them now; to-morrow morning, at break of day, we will take up their spoor." I then added, half speaking to myself and half addressing my servant, "Two of those brutes, as I certainly foresee, must and shall bite the dust before the setting of to-morrow's sun."

Accordingly, the first gray streaks of dawn had

hardly announced the arrival of the blushing day when I was in pursuit of my night quarry. One of these animals had evidently visited a rain-pool in the neighborhood; the excessive rankness, nevertheless, of the grass, and the numerous trails of other elephants of very little earlier date, made it so difficult to follow their spoor, that the sun was high in the heavens before we had fairly tracked them on their way to their daily haunts. Fortunately, they had moved along very leisurely, which enabled me to make up for lost time. Indeed, an uncommonly short tracking brought us in full view of the noble brutes. Two of them were sauntering to and fro; here cropping tender shoots, there thrusting their massive tusks under the roots of trees, in order, by toppling them over, to feed more conveniently on their delicate sprigs and sweet tendrils; while one of the party was loitering in the rear, scooping the sand carelessly out from some favorite and savory root or bulb. Interesting as was the picture, I gave but very few moments to its contemplation. Hiding away my ox and men (with the exception of one of the latter), I lost, as is my wont, no time in coming to the attack. A few minutes' stalk sufficed to bring me alongside the laggard; the instant following, the still morning air was sharply disturbed by the booming of my noble and trusty rifle; a shrill shriek announced its effect, and the brute who had received the shot was, with his companions, immediately lost to view, but not for long—I soon overtook him. Owing, however, to a sudden change in his position while I was taking my aim, and to the great distance at which I fired, the second bullet did not seem to do much harm, for the beast, on being hit, turned quietly round, peered deliberately in all directions with his small sinister-looking eyes, and, before I had reloaded, was once more out of sight. I had not, however, proceeded more than a dozen paces when I caught a glimpse of a huge stern slipping behind a large tree, surrounded by tall, thick bushes. Taking it for granted that this was the elephant I had wounded, I approached the dangerous spot with the utmost caution and circumspection. Well for me it was that I did so, for I had no sooner fairly rounded the tree than I discovered the animal still hiding there. Rubbing his hide against the bushes, he faced me only obliquely. Seeing me, nevertheless, he at once drew back a step or two, preparing to charge, when a well-directed bullet, lodged in his right shoulder, changed instantly his intended charge into a precipitate flight. This shot so effectually crippled the animal that in a few seconds I found myself a match for him. By taking a short cut I managed to intercept his retreat; a second bullet brought him to a stand, while a third, fired almost immediately afterward, stretched him on the ground a corpse. The whole chase and encounter scarcely occupied ten minutes, and I naturally felt pleased and gratified at its speedy and successful issue. Yet, on a near inspection of the carcass, I felt some disappointment at its comparative smallness, while Kamoja, my henchman and tracker, exclaimed, on seeing it, "This is not the elephant you first fired at; that was a larger one." "Impossible," I replied; "I have surely not made the same blunder as at Omanbondè; no, I am sure I have not." "You have, though," doggedly ejaculated the man. "Very well, let us examine the ground," I rejoined, and moved off. And certainly, in the examination we then made, we could discover no trace of any other elephant, either dead or wounded. Kamoja, for all that, continued to look positive, though much perplexed.

Having returned to the carcass, we were shortly joined by the remainder of my party, one of whom called out to me as he approached, "Sir, in coming here, we came across an elephant walking very slowly and stiffly, as if much hurt." "By Jove! Kamoja is perhaps right, after all," I exclaimed; "let us go and see." We had not proceeded above a hundred yards in an opposite direction to that just examined, when we noticed another blood spoor, quite distinct from that of the animal I had killed. Pointing with exultation to these marks, Kamoja, with a smile full of meaning and satisfaction, looked full into my face, and said, as plainly as looks can speak, "Did I not tell you so, sir? For the future, trust to my eyes and ears." To cut a long story short, I will only add that, notwithstanding the serious wound the animal had evidently received, he cost us many hours hard walking and running, much dodging, much suffering from thirst, and exposure to many perils before we finally succeeded in bringing him down. At length, my perseverance being well rewarded, and my presentiment and prophecy fulfilled, the penalty to be paid for all this enjoyment was to follow. The excitement and exertion of the hunt had been too much for me; the next morning I was delirious, and months elapsed before I could again shoulder a gun.

CHAPTER XX.

On the Okavango again.—The Numbers on our Sick-list increase.—Partial Recoveries and Relapses.—The numerous Species of Fish in the River all edible, and some delicious.—Fishing.—Singular Contrivances for catching Fish.—Alligators and Hippopotami, Otters.—My original Project of proceeding northward.—Generosity of Chikongo.—Pereira and Mortar take the Fever.—Obliged to abandon my long-cherished Scheme.—A precipitate Retreat.—The Okavango perfectly unknown to Europeans.—An Excursion toward its Source recommended.—The native Portuguese not aware of the River's Existence.—The Unhealthiness of the Climate confined probably to the Spring Season.—Malaria from the Lagoons.

AFTER many delays and much trouble, we at last found ourselves once more on the banks of the river in safety. But, alas! though hope had by no means deserted me, my feelings were very different from those with which I first beheld it. I was very ill, and there was little or no improvement in the health of my men; rather the contrary, for the numbers on our sick-list increased daily. The inactivity to which I was thus condemned was most distressing. My mind suffered by it still more than my body. At length the fever abated—that is, a temporary and favorable change took place in my health, to be followed, as on a previous occasion, by a return of the malady with increased violence. I had, however, if the truth be told, myself in a great measure to blame for these relapses; for no sooner was I able to crawl about than, instead of nursing myself, I exposed myself, in my usual heedless way, to hardships and fatigues which would task a strong man's best energies.

Nevertheless, I occupied myself a good deal during these convalescent intervals in collecting such information as I could get at respecting the Ovaquangari, their country, their manners, modes of life, their trades and occupations. I endeavored to pick up, besides, some knowledge of the ornithology peculiar to this region, and was particular in inquiring about the various sorts of fish inhabiting its noble stream. Of what I learned, much was to me new. My mind had consequently ample scope for interesting employment, and, had I been blessed with my usual heaith and strength, I might have passed my time both pleasantly and profitably. Yet to me this was but a sorry season; care and anxiety were my chief companions.

The River Okavango abounds, as I have already said, in fish, and that in great variety. During my very limited stay on its banks I collected nearly twenty distinct species, and might, though very inadequately provided with the means of preserving them, unquestionably have doubled this number, had sufficient time been afforded me. All I discovered were not only edible, but highly palatable, some of them possessing even an exquisite flavor.

Many of the natives devote a considerable portion of their time to fishing, and employ various simple, ingenious, and highly effective contrivances for capturing the finny tribe. Few fish, however, are caught in the river itself. It is in the numerous shallows and lagoons immediately on its borders, and formed by its annual overflow, that the great draughts are made. The fishing season, indeed, only commences in earnest at about the time that the Okavango reaches its highest water-mark, that is, when it has ceased to ebb, and the temporary lagoons or swamps alluded to begin to disappear.

To the best of my belief, the Ovaquangari do not employ nets, but traps of various kinds, and what may not inaptly be called aquatic yards, for the capture of fish. These fishing yards are certain spots of eligible water, inclosed or fenced off in the following manner: A quantity of reeds, of such length as to suit the depth of water for which they are intended, are collected, tied into bundles, and cut even at both ends. These reeds are then spread in single layers flat on the ground, and sewn together, very much in the same way as ordinary mats, but by a less laborious process. It does not much matter what the length of these mats may be, as they can be easily lengthened or shortened as need may require. When a locality, then, has been decided on for fishing operations, a certain number of these mattings are introduced into the water on their ends, that is, in a vertical position,

R

and placed either in a circle, semicircle, or a line, according to the shape of the lagoon or shallow which is to be inclosed. Open spaces from three to four feet wide are, however, left at certain intervals, and into these apertures the toils, consisting of bee-hive shaped masses of reeds, are introduced. The diameter of these at the mouth varies with the depth to which they have to descend, the lower side being firmly fastened to the bottom of the water, while the upper is usually on a level with its surface, or slightly rising above it. In order thoroughly to disguise these ingenious traps, grasses and weeds are thrown carelessly over and around them.

This river abounds also in alligators and hippopotami, animals, from the constant traffic going on on the stream, wary and exceedingly shy, consequently difficult to approach. The natives occasionally destroy one of the latter by spearing; they are far, nevertheless, from being bold hunters—indeed, invariably give wide berths to the haunts on the water of these formidable creatures. Otters are also to be found in the Okavango, but of not more, I believe, than one species.

Though both myself and my people still continued seriously ill, I never for a moment lost sight of my original purpose to proceed northward, and had all along been steadily making the necessary arrangements for a start as soon as our health would admit of this movement. I had also communicated my intentions to the chief, and was highly gratified at finding that, instead of making objections to my proposed advance beyond his territories, as is usually the case under such circumstances, he not only readily acquiesced in my scheme, but, of his own accord, offered me guides for a certain distance. Moreover, he considerately undertook the charge of such men and beasts as were either unfit for the journey or not required. Nay, he even went so far as spontaneously to promise my people, should they run short of food during my absence, an abundant supply of whatever they might want. This was, of course, a great relief to me; for, though I ran a certain amount of risk in thus placing myself in his power, it was certainly the least disagreeable of the alternatives before me.

With one or two exceptions, all my native servants were at this time prostrated by the fever, Pereira and Mortar alone being still unaffected by it; and as I had at an early period taken the precaution of administering to these men quinine and brandy, antidotes, I believed, against the disease, I had some faint hopes that they might escape the infection, and thus afford me at least some help in carrying out my plans. But in this hope I was disappointed; for, after about a month's stay on the river, both these men were suddenly confined to their beds. To add to my dismay, the other patients, instead of improving, were rapidly getting worse—in short, sinking into their graves. Had I then, under these circumstances, persisted on prosecuting my long-cherished project, I should certainly have been much to blame, for I had the sad experience and melancholy fate of former explorers, who had obstinately, in a similar situation, persevered in darling schemes, become hopeless, ever before me, ever forcibly present to my mind. What, then, was to be done? To linger where we were seemed certain death, and any visions of future success I might still entertain were too remote to justify me in imperiling so fearfully the lives of my fellow-creatures. A precipitate retreat appeared, therefore, quite imperative. It cost, nevertheless, a severe struggle between duty and ambition before I could resolve upon it. I obeyed at last the monitions of conscience, and bade with a sigh farewell to the pursuit of fame and glory forever. That this act of self-renunciation was not determined on without acute pangs, it would be useless to deny. After such toils, such hardships, such sacrifices, and with the prospect of a final crowning success just dawning upon me, it may well be imagined that I turned my back on the land of promise with drooping spirits and a heavy heart.

Thus ended my short but memorable visit to the Okavango River. I sincerely trust that future explorers of these parts may meet with better success. An excursion up this stream toward its source would undoubtedly prove very interesting, for it is, I believe, perfectly unknown to Europeans;

I doubt, even, whether the native Portuguese are aware of its very existence; they are certainly quite insensible to its importance in a commercial point of view. Navigable it must be throughout a great (if not the greater) portion of its course, even to vessels of some pretension. Numerous tribes, more or less intelligent, more or less traders and acquainted with the art of agriculture, possess permanent habitations along its banks. The unhealthiness of the climate may, it is true, be considered as prohibitive of any frequent or constant intercourse with this country. I strongly suspect, however, that this objection would only apply to a certain season, *i. e.*, to the time when, the annual flow of the river ceasing, exhalations from the surrounding swamps and marshes poison the atmosphere. In the months of June, July, and August, one might, I firmly believe, visit the Okavango with comparative safety. It is only, I think, in the spring, when I was unfortunately in its neighborhood, that the malaria from the lagoons is so fatal.

CHAPTER XXI.

Departure from the Okavango.—Very slow Progress.—The Country retraced devoid of natural Springs.—No Water to be procured for Cattle on our Retreat.—Obliged to halt till the rainy Season set in.—A Return to Ombongo in prospect.—Live-stock getting very low.—Too ill for Elephant-hunting.—Pereira recovers.—He is dispatched with an Attendant or two to Otjimbingué, to inform Friends of my awkward Position, and to procure Provisions.—Visit from Bushmen sent by a Party of the Ovambo encamped about two Days' Journey from us.—Suspicions of the Intentions of this Party.—Spies in the Camp.—Dangers threaten.—The Camp fortified.—Description of fortified Camp in the Desert.

On the 6th of June we took our departure from this most interesting, but to us most melancholy region. On that very morning I had to perform the sad task of burying another of my men. My wagon was now again put into requisition, and, not being large enough to hold our stores and the sick at the same time, I was obliged to send it on each day, first with one portion of our luggage and hospital, and then, on its return, with the remainder. Our progress was consequently extremely slow, so much so that, after a lapse of nearly six weeks, I found myself only about five or six days' journey from my camp on the Okavango. I had greatly hoped, notwithstanding this tardy advance, that change of air and place would have improved both my own and my patients' health, but here again I met with disappointment.

The country, as already stated, was throughout the district we were retracing totally devoid of natural springs; the season, however, not being much advanced, and the rains having fallen abundantly on my way northward, I did not for a moment doubt that our retreat, as far as the Omuramba, might be effected in safety. Nevertheless, I dispatched, while rectifying some rather serious defects in the wagon, a couple of men ahead on our old route to reconnoitre; and, on their return, learned, to my utter surprise and dismay, that for several days' journey no water was to be had for cattle, and scarcely any for ourselves. This blow, for which I was wholly unprepared, totally upset all my present plans. I shuddered at the idea of being cooped up in these dreary solitudes for several consecutive months, and that at a time, too, when we were so completely unprepared for any prolonged stay in a desert which afforded no resources; for five, if not six months, I was fully aware must elapse before the next rain fell, at least in sufficient quantities to enable us to go forward. I anxiously, therefore, and earnestly questioned the Bushmen living in the neighborhood about water, and particularly about the possibility of finding any outlet among the waste lands around us by which we might escape from our difficulties. They, in reply, as earnestly protested their ignorance of any such practicable passage through the country. Unfortunately, I believed them. There was, as we discovered many months afterward, a route of which we might have availed ourselves much more eligible than that by which we had arrived.

In the predicament in which we now found ourselves, we could evidently do nothing but resign ourselves cheerfully to our fate, and quietly await the return of the rainy season. There was still some rain-water here and there in pools around our camp, at a place called Sasseb. This certainly could not last us long; but I was given to understand that, by digging in a certain spot, a permanent sufficiency of water might be obtained; should this report turn out incorrect, and it should come to the worst, we were still near enough to Ombongo to effect a retreat to that locality at any time, when all anxiety about water would be at an end. One thing only gave me a good deal of uneasiness; my stock of cattle for slaughter was fast disappearing, and game, with the exception of elephants, was exceedingly scarce. Indeed, had it been abundant, we could hardly have profited by the circumstance, as but very few of my party were strong enough to engage in the chase. For my own part, I could not yet put a gun to my shoulder.

Pereira and two or three of my native attendants were the first to recover their strength. Why, then, I reasoned, on perceiving this, not send them away? By so doing I shall relieve the larder, and as soon as they get back to Otjimbingué they can inform my friends of my awkward position, and procure me a fresh supply of live and dead stock, with other necessaries; at the same time—not the least important item in the mission—they can convey letters to my friends, and bring me letters from them.

I thought this a very feasible plan; for, though the attempt to return "home" with my whole party would have been utterly impracticable, two or three men, with the same number of oxen, might successfully accomplish the enterprise. Moreover, I felt sure that Pereira would not be disheartened by ordinary difficulties, and would do his utmost to effect the important objects I had in view. I therefore, without much hesitation, decided on this step as the best mode of utilizing the time, and of renewing our scanty supplies, etc.

On the very day fixed for Pereira's departure several unknown Bushmen paid us a visit. They had, they said, been expressly sent on by a party of Ovambo, encamped about two long days' journey from our werft, to ascertain whether this place afforded sufficient water for a herd of cattle. I felt, I confess, a little uneasy at this piece of intelligence; for ever since their memorable and treacherous attack on my friends on the plains of Ondonga, the mere mention of an Ovambo was sufficient to arouse my very worst suspicions. Could, I asked myself—and they were questions that naturally suggested themselves—this party be *en route* for the Okavango for purposes of traffic, or were they spies sent to watch my movements? I was inclined to believe that the former supposition might be the correct one; for not only were the people of Ondonga in the habit of annually making trading trips to their neighbors, but this was actually the season in which they were accustomed to do so. I was, besides, perfectly well aware that I was in the very highway of communication between the two nations. There was also another way of accounting for the presence of the party in these parts; they might be simply an outpost in charge of the remnants of old cattle-folds which abound hereabouts.

Whatever might be its cause, their near neighborhood did not for a moment deter me from dispatching Pereira on his destined journey. I merely warned him from too free or too friendly an intercourse with these men, should he fall in with them; and the necessary preparations being completed, he took his departure (August 3d), accompanied by the hearty wishes of my whole camp, who knew that our comfort, and, in a great measure, safety, depended on his successful and speedy return.

A fortnight since Pereira left us had passed away, and nothing had occurred to confirm the suspicions I had entertained about the Ovambo in our vicinity. Still I could not altogether divest myself of uneasiness; their very silence and avoidance of all communication with us kept me in a constant state of anxiety, till at last my suspicions were so far corroborated as to leave hardly a doubt that our movements were watched by these savages.

Thus it happened: I was tossing to and fro on my pillow one evening in great pain and distress, when Mortar entered the tent, saying half aloud and half in a whisper, "Sir, there are strange people lurking about the camp; I came suddenly upon a fellow just now crouching close to the cattle, and evidently spying into our doings. Shall I give the rascal a shot?" Deadly ill as I was, I could scarcely refrain from a smile at my attendant's readiness for action. "No," I at length gasped forth, "don't fire, but keep a sharp look-out, and let me know the result." Nothing more, however, was seen or heard that night, though from that moment I felt convinced mischief was seriously meant me, and that the spies detected by my servant were emissaries of the Ovambo party. Mortar and two native herdsmen were all the force I could at this time muster, the remainder of my followers having gone out on foraging excursions to cater for themselves. About the safety of these men I naturally felt some alarm; perhaps, thought I, they have already been surprised; and I will not deny that, though not a timorous man, I felt very anxious and restless. Moreover, no news had reached me of Pereira. Might not he too, poor fellow, have fallen a victim to the revenge and treachery of these barbarians? As the sequel will show, I had ample cause, though some of my conjectures may have been wrong, for my very worst fears, which were not far from being realized.

My first care under the apprehensions I now suffered was to recall my foragers or huntsmen, which I happily effected without delay. My next step was so far to fortify the camp as to guard it at least against surprise. This I accomplished by surrounding the encampment with a lofty and dense fence of thorns, piled up in serried order in the form of a square. At each of the four corners of this square I projected similar thorn fences, about eight feet by six, within which, again, I erected stout palisadings, open only on the side facing and leading to the large kraal. I next raised the ground within this paling about three feet, which gave me a command not only of the two sides of the fence joining at each of the four corners, but of the whole camp. I was, of course, aware that but two of these corner projections were necessary, according to the simplest rules of engineering, to enable me to guard the access to our thorny fort—that is, had it been built on a proper scale; but of this the nature of the ground on which our tents were pitched did not admit. It was, in fact, too spacious to be guarded in this manner, especially on dark nights, when the range of vision was necessarily very limited. Close to each of the four watch-towers, for so I may call them, I erected a hut (of course within the great inclosure, my own tent forming one), within which a man or two, well armed, always slept, and were always in readiness, at the first signal of alarm, to hurry to their post. I was thus pretty well defended. But had there been no other barrier to oppose a wild enemy than the fence (it could not be burned, as it was green), it alone would have enabled us to resist the united efforts of hundreds of men. In brief, had it been my fate to die by the hands of savages, they would at least have found their victory dearly purchased, for I had vowed to perish as became a man.

CHAPTER XXII.

Tidings of Pereira.—He falls in with a suspicious-looking Party of Ovambo.—The Country all around on Fire.—Suspect the Ovambo wish to burn me out.—Visit from Chikongo, an Ovambo Chief, Brother of the Chief of the same Name before mentioned.—The whole Neighborhood again in a Blaze within a hundred Yards of the Camp.—Interview with Chikongo, escorted by sixty Attendants fully armed.—The Chief's Professions most friendly.—On my Guard against Treachery.—Showed him I had nothing to fear from him, but he had much to fear from me.—Chikongo's Invitation.—Presents interchanged.—My Illness continues.—Study of Natural History.—A Collection of Birds and Insects.—Partridges.—Antelopes.—Another Elephant shot.—Anticipation of a Feast.

We could now once more sleep in comparative security; and just at this time had tidings of Pereira. A Bushman chief, Kanganda, of whom mention has already been made, unexpectedly made his appearance at our encampment, and brought a few lines from our messenger. He had encountered him in the neighborhood of an Ovambo cattle-post, belonging to a powerful though subordinate captain, by name Chikongo—brother, as I afterward discovered, of the chief of the Ovaquangari bearing the same name. Pereira informed me that thus far he had, though not without difficulty, proceeded successfully, but spoke rather despairingly of the route before him to the Omuramba U'Ovambo, certain Bushmen having assured him that the whole intervening veldt was destitute of water. He also gave me to understand that he had fallen in with a werft of Ovambo, who had not only received him in a very friendly manner, but had presented him with an ox, which he had slaughtered, and was then making a halt in order to jerk and dry it. A thrill of horror shot through my whole frame when I came to this part of his letter. "Poor man!" thought I, "how little you know the nature of savages! Why, if harm is really meant you, this is the very means they would employ to lull you into a fatal security." I cherished the hope, however, that his departure from their werft would take place ere the villains had time to mature their plan for his destruction; for I conjectured that before they put that into execution they must communicate with their paramount chief. But I must not anticipate my story.

Kanganda had left us, and nothing had occurred for some time to divert our attention from our daily monotonous occupations, when suddenly, one morning, the veldt was observed to be every where on fire. Fires of the kind are, however, so usual at this season of the year, that I should have taken no notice of the occurrence had not the almost simultaneous breaking out of many of these conflagrations roused my suspicions, or at least left a very disagreeable impression on my mind. Was it possible that the Bushmen had set fire to the dry vegetation of these torrid tracts for the express purpose of fairly burning us out of the country? This may seem a rather far-fetched conjecture, yet an incident of a similar nature occurred not long afterward, which greatly strengthened my belief in its correctness. I had just had, on the occasion alluded to, a visit from Chikongo (with a number of his followers), the Ovambo chief already mentioned, of whom more anon, when all the remaining patches of pasturage that had escaped the first fire were observed to be at the same moment in a blaze. This occurred at night. On the afternoon of the next day, while amusing myself with mending my camp chair, I was startled by a loud rushing noise at a distance, not unlike that caused by a great whirlwind, which also, at this period of the year, is not here uncommon. My back happened at the time to be turned toward the aperture answering for a door; so, without rising to witness the wind-storm, I remarked only to Mortar, who was employed on some work close to me, "That's a lusty blusterer." "Yes," replied he, "but he won't come this way; the wind is in our favor." We each mistook the other's meaning. A few minutes after, finding the uproar both increasing and apparently approaching, I rose, and looked in the direction whence the noise came. To my astonishment, and, let me add, horror, I then discovered that, instead of a whirlwind, there raged a fearful fire within less than 500 yards of us. Hitherto, as Mortar had rightly judged, the wind had been favorable to us; but at this moment it changed and blew right in our teeth, while, before we had got over our amazement, the fire had advanced with rapid leaps and strides almost to within gunshot. Seizing a blanket, I called out to my men to follow me, and then made a dash at the flames, which drove us back faster than we had rushed forward. Destruction seemed for the moment inevitable. There was no grass, it is true, within the inclosure, and little or none on the outside, that is, within fifteen or twenty feet; there were, however, several huts covered with dry grass and other inflammable substances, and as the flames often bounded at one spring to a distance of forty and fifty feet, there was more than a probability that our camp would catch fire and be destroyed. Fortunately the wind was fitfully changeable, which enabled us, after considerable exertion, to battle with, and in the most dangerous places to subdue, the devouring element. Yet many hours elapsed before we deemed ourselves safe.

To return to my story. One morning, a few days previous to the conflagration just described, I unexpectedly received a first visit from Chikongo. He was escorted by about thirty Ovambo, and the same number of vassal Bushmen—that is, altogether by about sixty followers, armed to the teeth. Eight of these men carried muskets, a weapon, knowing the aversion to, not to say contempt of the tribe for fire-arms, I was totally unprepared to see in their hands. But, though surprised, I took care not to appear so. Chikongo was personally unknown to me; I had, however, heard of him, and he of me often, and that years ago. He had been described to me as a chief possessing much power and influence over his own nation, and one of the very few native potentates well disposed toward Europeans. His friendliness, indeed, to white men had, he assured me, drawn upon him the ill will of Tjipànga, the paramount chief of the Ovambo, and added that the offense he had thus given was so hateful to the majority of his countrymen that he had been threatened, should it be repeated by any endeavor on his part to promote free intercourse between the two races, with immediate expulsion from Ondonga. Of course, I listened with all due deference to this and to many other protestations of his sincerity, coupled with abundant professions of friendship. Not for a moment, however, did I allow myself to be taken off my guard. My comparatively unprotected and helpless position required the utmost circumspection and vigilance. I was not, therefore, to be lulled into a false security by the fine speeches of a barbarian, who, being at the head of a foe delighting in treachery, might, had he found me too confiding, have fatally ensnared both myself and my party. There was, I grant, good reasons for believing in the chief's sincerity, for he was a man of sense, penetration, and judgment, consequently well able to understand the benefits that might result to his country from the establishment of intimate relations between Africans and Europeans. Moreover, his nation had been recently taught, by the severe defeat inflicted on them by Mr. Green, fully to appreciate the energy and determination of white men when once roused to enmity. Thus he might, purely to secure our good-will, and his own and his followers' safety, be really in earnest in his professions of amity toward us. I gave him, nevertheless, clearly to understand, and I begged him to convey this information to his chief, that I neither feared Ovambo outposts, nor their whole national force combined. And this assertion was not idle boast or empty defiance; for I could, in case of need, have confidently reckoned on the assistance of almost all the Europeans in Damara Land, among whom were dare-devils in abundance, to say nothing of the numerous and powerful Hottentot tribes who, under the pretext of aiding an ally, and in order to enrich themselves, would have been but too eager to join in any fray. A signal from me, or from any of my friends, was all they wanted to incite them to imbrue their hands in the blood of their enemies, and of this the chief and his followers could not be ignorant.

Knowing all this, Chikongo pressed me hard to abandon my camp and resort to his village, distant two or three days' journey; but, for obvious reasons, I declined the invitation. With renewed assurances, therefore, of friendly feelings, he, after having enjoyed my hospitality for a couple of days, took his leave. We separated, to all appearance, mutually satisfied with one another. On his departure I presented him with a few articles I thought he would prize, while he, on his part, kindly offered to supply me with cattle for slaughter, should I pass by his homestead before he broke up for his return to Ondonga—a move he contemplated as soon as the rainy season set in.

I continued still to suffer severely from the effects of fever, which seemed determined not to leave me. My debility was indeed extreme; I could not remain standing on my legs for a few moments together, yet, strange to say, I could, though not without much pain, walk a good while. This enabled me to vary the monotony of my solitary life by indulging in my favorite pursuit—the study of Natural History.

Regularly every morning I sauntered out with my fowling-piece, and rarely returned without a few specimens of either birds or insects. It is true I met at first with but sorry success, but on the return of spring, *i. e.*, of vegetable and insect life, the winged tribes became gradually more numerous and varied, and by dint of perseverance I succeeded, in the course of three months, in shooting and preserving no less than nine hundred birds and bats. To be sure, the exertion was sometimes rather too much for my broken health, but, on the whole, I enjoyed the exercise amazingly; so much so that I sometimes congratulated myself on my illness, as, by confining me for a considerable time to one locality, it enabled me to collect many valuable and interesting data relative to the natural history of birds, insects, etc.; I besides became acquainted with many, to me, new species of the winged creation, and learned much of the migratory habits of the birds indigenous to these parts.

Of minor game we saw now little or none, with the exception of partridges, and one or two species of diminutive antelopes. I was too weak, however, to pursue either with any success. On our first arrival in the neighborhood elephants had been rather numerous, but in proportion as the water dried up these animals deserted us. Still a few of them occasionally strayed to our wells to quench their thirst; and Kamapjie, who was at present convalescent, was upon several occasions sent without any successful result in pursuit of one or two of these lingerers in the vicinity. One day he came up with an old bull. and gave him no less than seven bullets from my big rifle, yet, strange to say, he afterward followed up the brute's spoor for nearly two days unavailingly. Want of water compelled him finally to give up the chase in despair.

At about four o'clock in the afternoon, precisely a week after the incident just mentioned took place,

I had occasion to go outside our camp. Now parallel with it, and within one hundred yards' distance, there ran a well-trodden elephant footpath; I had often before noticed it, and was just about re-entering the inclosure, when my eyes chanced to fall upon this very path, along which, to my great surprise, I saw a huge elephant shaping his course at a quick step directly for the water, distant some six or seven hundred yards. Quick as thought I rushed back to my wagon, seized upon my rifle, bullet-pouch, and powder-flask, and was instantly on the animal's track. But the vley whereto he was wending his way was very much exposed—in fact, quite unfit for stalking; consequently, no shelter being near in which to take refuge in case of an attack, I naturally dreaded an encounter with the monster. Recollecting, however, the penury of our larder, I determined boldly to face the danger. It was an anxious and exciting moment, for a single shot was to decide the brute's fate. Stalking cautiously for some time, I succeeded in approaching unperceived to within seventy-five yards of where he stood. He was at that time thirstily taking his fill at one of the wells, with, as ill luck would have it, his snout just lifted up, full fronting me. There was, therefore, no time to lose, and, relying fully on my rifle, I took a deliberate aim at his fore leg, and fired. As I had anticipated, the bullet did its work well, smashing completely the bones of the member it had struck. In an instant the huge animal came down in a kneeling position, his head resting heavily on the ground. Endeavoring, nevertheless, to drag himself away, he exposed his other fore leg, which in another moment shared the fate of its fellow. A few more seconds, and he rolled over on his side a corpse.

The whole scene witnessed by my men from the wagon had afforded them unlimited gratification, derived chiefly from their anticipation of a glorious "blow-out" of meat and fat. For my part, I was not only gratified at my success, but truly thankful, as from this supply I should now be able to fatten both bipeds and quadrupeds, who had certainly, of late, lost very much of the rotund comeliness of their proportions. "Sir," said trusty Mortar, on viewing the enormous carcass, "this is indeed a God-send. It is like the arrival of a long-expected vessel, laden with many goodly things." I heartily concurred in my servant's happy and appropriate allusion.

The dead animal was, on examination, identified as the one hunted and fired at by Kamapjie, but he did not appear to have suffered much inconvenience from the wounds received on that occasion.

CHAPTER XXIII.

Anxiety about Pereira.—His safe Return.—Rejoicings.—He brings Intelligence that Mr. Frederick Green is on his Way to join me.—The extreme Precariousness of my Situation.—Native Politics.—A "Commando" with a numerous Escort dispatched from Ondonga to destroy me.—This fearful Intelligence brings Mr. Green to my Rescue.—An heroic Act of Friendship.—The Expedition sent against me arrives.—The murderous Project abandoned.—The Dangers escaped by Pereira.—Green's Difficulties in advancing.—I go to meet him.—A rather arduous Enterprise.—The joyful Meeting.—Prospects not much mended by it.—Resolved, after much Hesitation on my Part, to proceed to Mr. Green's Encampment on the Omuramba.—Singular Hardships and Fatigues of this Journey.—Scarcity of Water.—Thirst.—Suffering from excessive Heat.

THE time had at last approached when I might look for the return of Pereira and his party. As it drew nearer and nearer, my anxiety naturally increased, for I had never been able to ascertain whether he had succeeded or not in forcing his way through the savage tract he had to traverse back to Otjimbingué. Great God! he might, for aught we knew to the contrary, have succumbed to the physical difficulties on all sides besetting him, or, still worse, have fallen a sacrifice to the treachery of the Ovambo. Either of these suppositions was too painful to dwell upon. Happily, when expectation and hope deferred had nearly reached their climax, our anxieties were removed by Pereira's most welcome appearance; an event which, after he had been absent nearly three months and a half, took place on the morning of the 17th of November. He reached the camp in good health and spirits, having, in almost every respect, acquitted himself to my entire satisfaction. To add to my delight, he brought me the joyful and unexpected intelligence that my friend, Mr. Frederick Green, was in the neighborhood. He had come, as I was assured, and saw at once, to render me, in my jeopardous position, all the assistance in his power. This unlooked-for re-enforcement was indeed most seasonable, for I now learned for the first time the extreme precariousness of my situation. I will describe it as briefly as possible.

At about the time that Pereira reached the southern confines of Damara Land, two distinct parties of Ovambo arrived also in those parts from Ondonga. The former were embassadors from the paramount chief Chjipanga, while the others represented a certain portion of the Ovambo population, dissatisfied at the elevation of Tjipanga, on the decease of his elder brother Nangoro, to the chieftainship. Each of these parties had more than one object in view. The emissaries of the chief were anxious to establish friendly relations with Jonker, to ascertain as spies the temper of the country, and to gather particulars about your humble servant, *i. e.*, to learn as distinctly as possible what my views and intentions, etc., were; while the rebellious embassy, if I may so call them, were bent on gaining Jonker over to their cause, professing at the same time to have come for the purpose of warning my friends of the terrible fate that threatened me. What that fate was they very clearly pointed out by stating that, on their departure from Ondonga, a "commando," with a numerous escort, had been expressly dispatched into my neighborhood on an avowed mission to destroy me or any of my men they might chance to fall in with.

This fearful intelligence reached my friend just on his return from a distant and harassing expedition to the Matibili nation, far to the eastward of Lake Ngami. Its effect upon him was such that, to his undying honor, he determined, without a moment's hesitation, incurring thereby huge hardships and perils, to hurry to my assistance, or, in the worst event, to avenge my death, should he be too late to prevent the execution of the murderous and hellish designs of the Ovambo. Most deeply was I affected by this noble deed. Indeed, this single act of devotion was to me infinitely more gratifying than would be all the wealth the world has to bestow. It was heart-warming to know that at least one human bosom beat genuinely for the solitary wanderer. Dear Green! an approving conscience must be your greatest reward; but, should these lines ever reach you—and God grant they may ere long!—I beg you will here accept my poor but warm and sincere thanks for your spirited resolve to come to my rescue when dangers so great, of which I was unaware, encompassed me. Believe me, this one act of heroic friendship has, in my own estimation, much more than outweighed any trifling service it has been in my power to render you. Whatever may be our future fate, when life itself shall no longer possess the charms and illusions of youth, "hæc olim meminisse juvabit" —it will be pleasant to recall to remembrance the days of yore, and gratefully to dwell on the recollection of your humane and brotherly conduct. God speed you in your present interesting but hazardous pursuit!

Shortly after Pereira had joined us, I learned that the expedition sent against me had actually arrived in my neighborhood. From some unexplained cause, however, its leader had thought fit to abandon his murderous purposes, and to evacuate the country without any attempt to molest me. It appeared certain, nevertheless, that the party he commanded had earnestly sought the destruction of poor Pereira; they had again visited the post where he had been detained under the plea of partaking of their hospitality, a snare, as I had suspected, to lull him into a sense of security till the proper moment should arrive to put him to death. Fortunately, the villains only reached their destination a few hours after Pereira had left it, and, night coming on, they had, deeming farther pursuit useless, retraced their steps to Ondonga. It was thus evident that I and my whole party had narrowly escaped destruction. Had the villains been as prompt and determined as they were viciously inclined, or had they attacked us separately, they might surely have massacred us all.

I said just now that Pereira had brought news of Mr. Green being in our neighborhood; in so saying I was not quite correct, for my friend had unfortunately, in consequence of the drought, been stopped on the U'Ovambo, a circumstance which placed between us a country of no less than eight days' journey in extent—a week's traveling, dear reader, being in the inhospitable regions of South Africa too often a question of life and death. So it nearly proved in the present instance. Indeed, Green was now at the very veldt where I had been stopped four months previously in my endeavors to return homeward. There seemed, therefore, but little chance of his joining us before the rains fell, an event that appeared still very distant. Even Pereira, accompanied by only one or two individuals, and one or two beasts of burden, had nearly perished on his route from want of water. He was on one occasion three days without a drop of the precious liquid, and was actually obliged, in order to obtain a supply, to retrace his steps to the spot whence he had started. How, then, accomplish this transit with twenty men, and thrice that number of cattle?

Thus the situation, both of myself and of my new ally, was, to say the least, at present very unpleasant. Our forces once combined, we should, however, be tolerably secure from any attack our foes might still meditate—nay, strong enough to set them at defiance. Such being the case, I was determined to test to the utmost the truth of the good old saying, "Where there is a will there is a way." Accordingly, I wrote to Green to say that I was on the start to join him, requesting him, at the same time, to make a similar move from the south, that we might, if possible, meet half way. This letter I intrusted to the care of Kanganda, who fortunately happened to be on another visit to my camp. I gave the messenger strict injunctions to use all dispatch, and not to leave my friend (after he had once reached him) till our junction should be effected.

As previously stated, we had been induced firmly to believe that the surrounding country was totally impracticable for a large party at this season of the year. We had been brought, partly by our own explorations, and partly by the assertions of Bushmen, to this conclusion. It was, we now learned, quite a mistake. Pereira, on his return journey, had taken an entirely different route, and had fortunately discovered one or two spots where he was fully convinced a sufficiency of water might, with a little labor and patience, be obtained. On this information, referable only to the first portion of our road—hardly more than a third of the whole distance to be traversed—rested all our hopes of success. But I had made up my mind for the enterprise, and, to use a homely phrase, was determined, "come what come might," at all hazards, to carry it out.

While the necessary preparations for this purpose were being completed, I sent a party in advance to clear a passage and to dig for water, etc.; and on the 23d of November broke up my camp, and proceeded southward with the wagon and the rest of my party. By dint of great exertions, we succeeded in performing several days' journeys in safety, till we came to a dead lock at a place called Orujo. From this point to the Omuramba U'Ovambo there was positively no water for cattle. and little or none for men. Before determining on my future proceedings, I decided, therefore, on awaiting here my friend's arrival. He was longer in making his appearance than was pleasant. Indeed, growing weary of expectation, I dispatched fresh messengers to bring me tidings of his whereabouts. They fortunately crossed his track almost immediately, and in a very little time afterward I had the gratification of once more shaking hands with this stanchest of friends.

I need scarcely say that our meeting was hearty and joyful. It did not, however, materially brighten our prospects. An uncouth country of vast extent, abandoned alike by man and beast, and thickly covered with bush, lay before us. Its soil, moreover, was so soft as to yield most distressingly to the foot at every step, while, to the best of our knowledge, there was no water whatever to be found for our cattle. The transit through this tract, under a tropical sun so broiling as to blister feet and hands, and on the slightest exertion to cover the body from head to foot with perspiration, would require at least four days, including many hours borrowed from the night, for its accomplishment. There were, besides, many other difficulties to be encountered. My driver, for example, had just at this time a most severe relapse of fever, and most of the men were still in a very debilitated state. It may not, therefore, appear suprising to my readers that I hesitated and flinched somewhat in dread of an enterprise that, to say the least, had a very desperate look. It is true I had, as the reader will probably remember, confronted and successfully overcome difficulties quite as formidable as those now facing us—perhaps more so; but in this case there were circumstances which made the undertaking particularly trying and dangerous. Mr. Green, however, accustomed to deeds of daring, urged me unceasingly to make the attempt, and I yielded at last to his solicitations. The journey being determined on, our plan was to push on as fast as men and beasts could travel to a certain point, where it was said we might chance to find a little water. Should this resource fail us, which was highly probable, Green was to advance as rapidly as possible with the loose cattle, and such men as could be spared from the wagon, while I followed at an easier but still unusually quick pace. It was farther arranged that, as soon as my friend succeeded in finding water, and had given a drink to the beasts of burden, he, or some trustworthy servant, should immediately return to me with a portion of the refreshed cattle. But I will not trespass on my reader's patience by entering into all the details of our harassing march. Let it suffice to say that, with immense exertions—suffering the most painful anxiety all the time—we finally reached Green's camp on Omuramba in safety, having sustained no farther loss than that of a dog and two or three new-born goat-kids.

During the five days this journey lasted we had had little to satisfy either hunger or thirst. Its happy issue was, under Providence, mainly owing to the cheerful co-operation and indefatigable exertions of my friend. Nothing less than his energy could have given us so prompt, and, comparatively, so cheap a success.

CHAPTER XXIV.

Homeward Course pursued.—The Omuramba Water-course. —Whence, being sometimes dry, does it derive its frequent Flood of Water?—The rainy Season.—Sufferings from Wetness and Wind.—A Bushman devoured by a Lion Man-eater. —A Lion Hunt.—A marvelous Shot in the Dark.—A Duel in the Desert.—A Lion killed.—A perilous Position.—A wonderful Escape.—A Lion's Grief for the Loss of his Friend.—The History of two Lions, the Terror of the District.—Three Men carried off in the Night from a Village by the Man-eaters.—A hundred human Beings fall a Prey to them.—The Country thereabouts abandoned by human Beings.

AFTER a few days devoted to rest and recreation, our wagons having in the mean time been put in good repair, we diligently pursued our homeward course. Our passage now lay along the banks and in the bed of the Omuramba U'Ovambo, which was several days' journey west of the northern route I had formerly followed. This water-course was the same as the one that has all along puzzled me so much. At this point it had been noted by previous explorers as a current of some pretensions—broad, deep, and running through regular, well-defined banks. Just a year before Messrs. Green and Hahn had found it an almost continuous stream, abounding in water flowing westward, and finally forming the Lake Onondova. It was now quite dry, or, at most, capable only of occasionally filling pits and wells. How, then, or whence does it receive its temporary flood? It appears utterly impossible that such a stream should take its rise in the sandy districts stretching far and wide to the eastward. Nor is it likely that it is fed by the great permanent river Okavango (though this supposition seems at first sight apt to solve the mystery), for at this point the Omuramba U'Ovambo (according to boiling-water observations) is several hundred feet higher than any of those parts of the Okavango visited by me, while the travelers I have just named could not possibly be deceived as to the direction of the flow of water. The configuration of the country, too, equally forbids one to connect this water-course with the Omuramba Ua' Matako, as the main outlet whereby it is drained off is certainly *via* Tioughe. To hazard, then, a last conjecture, let us suppose its chief source to be in the mountains of Otjihejnenne, whence the Omuramba, flowing northward and joining the U'Ovambo in about 19° of S. latitude, is known to spring.

The Omuramba U'Ovambo is a great resort of elephants in the dry season. Mr. Green had some excellent sport in this country before he joined me, and we still had hopes of encountering some of these animals. The setting in of the rains, however, put an end to them completely; for the commencement of this season is the signal for all wild quadruped game to abandon permanent water, of which they have an instinctive dread, and which, knowing well that traps of one kind or another are invariably, in such localities, set for their destruction, they frequent only from necessity.

The rains now fell in torrents for many consecutive days, and the country south of the Omuramba being unusually level, the wagon-wheels sinking often in the soil above their naves, we had some difficulty in getting along. Doubtless we had abundance of water at present; yet, despite this great advantage, the exceeding wetness of the weather was both inconvenient and uncomfortable. Our attendants were the greatest sufferers; as the wagons were too crowded with stores and baggage to give shelter to more than one or two persons, they were exposed to perpetual drenchings.

On reaching the point where my own and my friend's routes joined, I detached three or four men with instructions to push ahead to Otjimbingué. My object in this move was to acquaint our friends of our safety, etc., and to get whatever news there might be from that settlement. This party was to proceed *viâ* Okamabuti and Omanbondè, while we ourselves struck off to the eastward, in order to reach the Omuramba Ua' Matako at Otjituo—a country where we were likely to meet elephants. But here, as elsewhere, the rain had forestalled us. No game of any description was to be seen, though the animals had evidently only lately dispersed.

The fresh remains of a giraffe destroyed by a lion at Otjituo afforded good proof of this.

The place just named was one of those of which mention has already been made, haunted so fiercely by man-eaters. A Bushman chief, who had some time before come to pay Mr. Green a visit, fell a prey to one of them. Here is the narrative of this horrid event, in Mr. Green's own words:

June 20th, 1858. At about eleven o'clock last night I was startled out of my sleep by a dreadful shriek, such as I had never heard uttered by any human being before. The thought at once struck me that the two lions which had given us such trouble on a former occasion were again prowling about, and had perhaps seized some of the Bushmen lately come to pay me a visit, who were encamped at the back of my kraal. Snatching up my rifle and pistol, I bounded out of bed, and soon found my suspicions confirmed by the dismal howls and wailings of several terrified Bushmen whom I met hastening toward my wagon for protection. A poor lad whom we had captured the day before was giving vent to his distress in piteous lamentations for the loss of his father, whom one of the lions had destroyed. Calling to some of my people to follow, I hurried away in the direction pointed out by this poor fellow. The night, in itself intensely dark, received an additional deep gloom from the shadow of a cluster of thick-boughed trees under which we were encamped. In order, therefore, to throw some light on surrounding objects, we set fire to our temporary huts and commenced our search. Mr. Hahn also came to our assistance with a lantern; the dogs meantime kept up a furious barking; yet, with the certain knowledge that the brute was only a few paces distant from us, we could not obtain a glimpse of the cowardly murderer. At length, to the horror of us all, we stumbled on the mangled remains of the unfortunate Bushman who had fallen a victim to the monster. One of his arms was bitten short off at the shoulder, while his hand still convulsively clutched a portion of his "dress." This, and some portion of his intestines, was all that remained of a man alive and quite unconscious of the fate that awaited him only a few minutes before! The sight was both shocking and sickening in the extreme, and as it was now useless to continue a farther search in the dark, we returned to our respective bivouacs. Sleep was of course out of the question. The dreadful scene haunted my imagination unceasingly, and I resolved, as soon as the day should dawn, to pursue the horrible man-eater, and terminate, if possible, his existence.

Accordingly, every man possessed of a gun joined this morning in the chase. At a short distance from the camp the brute was discovered, but, though we followed him up for a long time, we got no shot at him. The cowardly night-prowler took care not to expose himself; and, unfortunately, only two dogs ventured to face him. Had the whole pack assailed him, he would certainly have been brought to bay and dispatched. We were on several occasions close upon him, but the denseness of the bush always helped him to escape before we could get a good aim at him. At length, losing his track, and endeavoring in vain to recover it, we were compelled to face homeward without ridding the country of so dire a scourge.

On a subsequent occasion, however, when returning from the Ovambo journey, Mr. Green encountered this lion, and others of the same species, when his endeavors to destroy them proved more successful. This hunt is thus noticed in my friend's diary of September, 1858:

"On the night of the second instant I made one of the most marvelous shots at an animal in the dark that perhaps has ever been made by any man. I had just arrived at Otjiomavare, the old haunt of the man-eaters, and was nightly expecting a visit from some of them, firmly resolved to kill a few, if possible, when an opportunity of doing so occurred in a rather unexpected way.

"It was about three o'clock in the morning; the moon had sunk below the horizon, and all nature was enveloped in darkness, when the humor took me to have a night ramble. Seizing my trusty double-barreled gun and my revolving rifle, I stood for some minutes a silent and solitary listener to the terrific roarings of two male lions, who after a while passed along the bank of the river opposite to that on which we were encamped, when, suddenly halting again, they commenced another duet in as loud a strain as their lungs could pour forth. I was, by this time, joined by John Mortar, Bonfield, and two of my native servants, all in readiness with their guns, like myself, in case the brutes should attempt an aggressive move. I now advanced a few paces from the wagon toward the river, and, raising my double-barreled gun, called to my Damara Gukub (for, from deafness in one ear, I can not distinguish accurately the direction of sound) to point as near as he could to the quarter whence he heard the lions. This done, I placed the gun on an elevation of about 300 yards, the distance as I supposed of the animals, and fired. No sooner had the explosion taken place than one of the lions abruptly ceased roaring, uttering at the same time a startling growl, such as always announces the receipt of a gunshot wound by these brutes. The "clap" of the bullet against the beast's hide, so well known to sportsmen, was not to be mistaken, and the by-standers simultaneously shouted out, "The lion is struck!" I stood amazed, scarcely able to credit the fact, and might, perhaps, have thought that my hearing had deceived me, had not Mortar, Bonfield, and others present declared with one voice that the lion must unquestionably have been hit.

"After a short interval of silence the roaring

again commenced, much to the left, however, of the spot at which I had directed my shot. We all now listened anxiously for the other brute, from whom, at last, there came a faint outcry, as if from an animal in extreme pain. His unwounded companion, not being able to induce him to flee, appeared to hurry back to his aid, roaring all the while most lustily. All his exertions to remove his sick mate proved nevertheless unavailing, for he remained still on the same spot, uttering occasionally, instead of his accustomed haughty roar, a most sickly moan.

"It was with intense impatience that I awaited the break of day to give me correct information respecting my night's performances. As soon as it was sufficiently light to hunt a wounded lion with safety, I mustered all my dogs, and, accompanied by all my people possessed of guns, proceeded in search of the enemy. They were soon discovered by the dogs both together, trotting slowly away. The banks of the river at this point were somewhat elevated; I sent, therefore, most of my party along their base, and chose the higher ground myself. The dogs flew rapidly past me on the scent, and I followed as quickly as my crippled condition (being still lame from rheumatism) would permit me. One of the lions was some distance in the rear of the other, and I set the laggard, of course, down for the brute I had wounded. Being closely pursued by two of the dogs, he was brought

A HORRIBLE SURPRISE.

speedily to bay. Now was my time, and, stepping smartly out, I was soon within fifty paces of my mark, when, stooping down, I took a deliberate aim with the elephant rifle, and fired. The bullet passed through both the animal's shoulders, and he fell, managing, nevertheless, to raise himself on his haunches, in which position, growling hideously, he lashed alternately his sides and the ground furiously with his tail. I therefore, followed by Bonfield, advanced farther toward him, and was about to put an end to his struggles, when the other lion, who had stationed himself in the rear, in a thick bush a hundred yards or so off, came bounding along with a ferocity of purpose in his royal countenance such as I never saw matched in one of his species. I was then in a kneeling posture, in a perfectly exposed situation, about twenty yards distant from his wounded companion. Charging past his crippled mate, this infuriated brute made directly at me. It was an awful moment, one that required all my self-possession; but, having implicit confidence in my revolver rifle, I did not budge an inch. Leveling at the full, broad chest of my assailant, I pulled the trigger, when—imagine the horror and consternation of the moment—my rifle missed fire! and missed again, and again! His next bound or two would, it seemed inevitable, bring me within the monster's gripe; but, whether terror-stricken at my defiant attitude, or at the click of my weapon, he turned abruptly off to the right, and was in a few seconds back in his former hiding-place, the bush, where he was lost completely to view. While retreating, I once more pointed the rifle at the fugitive, equally in vain. To what was I to attribute these successive failures? I supposed, at first, that the caps had become damp from exposure to the night air, but subsequently discovered an exploded cap between the hammer and its passage, which had prevented the former from striking with full force on the nipple. Bonfield, who stood behind me at the critical moment I have described, raised his gun to fire at the lion the moment he commenced his flight, but I stopped him at once; for, had the beast been merely wounded by the shot, he would, in all probability, have vented his fury upon my defenseless person.

"The reader may well imagine that a thrill of dread ran through me when I found my weapon so unexpectedly failing me. The charge of the lion was so determined, and his eyes were fixed so steadily upon me, that there could be no doubt about the purpose of the brute. My escape I attributed solely to the fact that I did not move, but kept my ground. Any attempt to flee the danger would most assuredly have ended fatally.

"Having put my rifle into good working order again, I went in pursuit of the fugitive, first putting a ball through the disabled animal, who was still defending himself gallantly against a multitude of dogs, assailing him on all sides. I was now joined by the rest of my people, as well as by a crowd of Damaras from the wagons, who, on hearing the report of the big rifle, hastened forward to witness the fall of their much-dreaded enemy. The hunted beast led us through many a thick bush, where we expected every moment to catch a glimpse of him; but he eluded all our efforts to come up with him, and fairly, as we found afterward, doubled on us, returning (such tenderness can dwell in lions' bosoms) to the corpse of his now lifeless companion. Evidently, however, not relishing the idea of sharing his fate, he resumed his flight, and we were never afterward able to overtake him. Seriously afflicted the royal brute must really have been by the loss of his friend, for on the following night he returned again to the spot, and roared most sonorously a loud lament, after which he took his departure, to return no more.

"On examining the dead lion, I was much surprised to find that my night shot had hit him close behind the left shoulder; he must have been then rather facing me, as the bullet had taken a diagonal direction, and had thus not proved fatal. The distance between myself and the lion, on receiving the wound, was, as I ascertained by stepping the ground, somewhat more than three hundred yards. I had the skin of this animal carefully removed, and intend to keep it as a reminiscence of one of the most extraordinary incidents of my hunting experience.

"I learned a few days afterward, from a party of Damaras from the eastern side of the Omuramba, the history of the two lions who had led me such a chase. It would appear from this account that these brutes had followed up the wagons of the Rev. Messrs. Hahn and Rath from their old quarters, Otjituo, and that, on reaching a village of Damaras, where my reverend friends halted for the night, one of them had carried off a native from this werft. The animals were then traced in the direction of the fountain where we found them, and where one of them met with his deserts.

"The Damaras described these lions so accurately that there could not be a doubt about their being the same as those who had been long the terror of this district. The smaller of the two was, they assured us, the one who provided for the other; they added, farther, that this daring monster has been known to attack a village, and seize no less than three individuals successively in one night, returning in the daytime, with his companion, to feast upon the remains of the unfortunate victims. If any credit is to be attached to the report of these people, no fewer than one hundred human beings had already fallen a prey to this pair of formidable man-eaters. Bushmen, we were besides told, had been obliged to fly the country in consequence of the dreadful ravages committed on their ranks by these wild beasts. A Bushman I found in this locality when on my journey northward fully corroborated this statement. On being interrogated as to whether there were any villages of his countrymen along the Omuramba to the eastward, he replied at once that they could not live there, as the lions destroyed so many of them. The Damaras, indeed, when speaking of these formidable foes, always say, 'Those two lions—the smaller alone killing the people—are known throughout this country (pointing north, south, east, and west), and are the dread of all the Damaras and Bushmen, who will, like ourselves, rejoice to hear that the man-slayer is dead.'

"Now it was of the smaller of the two animals that I so happily rid the country, and I consequently felt more pleased at the deed than if I had killed the largest bull elephant that roams the wastes of Africa. I had by this act conferred a benefit on my friends, the 'children of the desert,' and had doubtless been the means of saving many from the horrible fate that had of late fallen to the lot of numbers of their friends and relatives."

CHAPTER XXV.

More Lion Adventures.—A Cow carried off.—An Ambush, baited by a Goat, laid for the Thief.—A Lion Hunt.—Beating up the Country.—Retreat of the Enemy in a Brake.—Courage of a Dog.—The Animal driven out of the Brake by setting it on fire.—Cowardice of most of the Party in running away as soon as the Lion appears.—The Lion attacks his Assailant.—A Shot takes no Effect.—Bodily Encounter with the Lion.—He receives a Shot in the Shoulder while struggling with his human Antagonist, who escapes.—Is precipitated to the Ground by an Accident.—Tussle with the Lion while on the Ground.—Terribly mutilated.—The Lion shot by D—— while mangling his Victim.—The Narrator's Account confirmed by his runaway Party.

As only one of the terrible man-eaters had been certainly destroyed, though it is not impossible the brute shot by me, as already mentioned at Omanbondè, was the second, we were not without apprehension that the survivor might still be lingering in the neighborhood, in which case he was pretty sure to pay us a visit. At least so we thought, and in the apprehension we were not altogether wrong, for at least lions did ere long visit us; whether of the same species as the one so lately killed our experience fortunately did not inform us. As there was, however, a striking incident or two in our encounter with one of these monarchs of the wilds, I will briefly relate the adventure I allude to.

We had one night encamped as usual, and had, previous to retiring to rest, taken care to kraal our beasts of burden and live-stock—a precaution omitted on that occasion by some Damaras possessing cattle, and journeying in our company under our protection. For this negligence they suffered; for, on the morning following, at break of day, a brilliant moon still illuminating the sky, just as I had risen and given orders for a start, I observed one of the dogs darting forward at full speed, and barking in a most excited manner, while his alarmed and startled movements indicated clearly the objects of his fear, and I instantly and instinctively called out, "Lions! lions!" And a lion sure enough there was, within a hundred or two yards of us, in full view of our wagons and bivouac fires. The beast was quietly devouring a cow which he had recently slain. I could at first scarcely believe the fact. How he could have caused the death of his victim on a spot so perfectly exposed, within gunshot of several hundred human beings, surrounded by some dozens of curs, without attracting the slightest notice, seemed to me a perfect mystery. I mentally exclaimed, "Has then man no cause to fear such a creature?" adding promptly, "It will be our turn at you next time, old fellow, and that when you least expect it." Nor was I disappointed; for we fell in with him shortly afterward in the way I am about to relate.

As I had anticipated, the lion just alluded to, or

rather lions—for there were two—followed us up, and on the second night after our encounter played us the same trick as the one above narrated, only on this occasion the victim was slain quite close to our camp, though the fact, as a dense bush hid the assailant from our view, was less difficult than his former achievement.

Being informed of this new invasion of our folds, I said to my friend, "If we do not destroy those lions, they will continue to plague us; and as they have not, it is likely, had time to consume much of the carcass of their last prize, they are sure to visit the spot again to-night. Let us then lay an ambush for them." "Agreed," responded my friend. Accordingly, a few bushes having been cut down, and a sort of skarm constructed, we both ensconced ourselves at nightfall therein, having first tied a goat to a small bush within a few paces of our place of concealment, near the spot where the cow had been killed on the previous night.

The moon had just risen, but was hidden in passing clouds, while the denseness of the surrounding bush threw a deeper gloom over objects than was quite desirable. For a while we strained our eyes and ears ineffectually to catch a glimpse or a sound of the enemy. Suddenly my friend bent toward me, and whispered in my ear, pointing straight before us: "Don't you see something moving there?" Now I rather pride myself on my cat-like sight in the dark; but in this instance, whether it really failed me, or that my eyes did not exactly follow the direction indicated, I saw nothing; the next moment, however, the unfortunate goat began to struggle desperately, and by a sort of instinct I instantly detected the presence of the foe, as instantly —as if Green's warning had only then fallen on my ear—cocking my rifle. My companion cocked his almost simultaneously. And it was high time we did so, for a second had not elapsed, when out sprang a lion from behind a bush directly in front of us, and trotted briskly up to the terrified goat, of whose fate neither of us could entertain any doubt, though we had determined that there should, instead of one, be two victims on this occasion. The old adage, "There's many a slip 'twixt the cup and the lip," was nevertheless, in this instance, rather ludicrously verified; for the brute had no sooner opened his immense jaws to seize on his intended prey than he perceived us, and turned on his heels as quick as lightning. I was, I confess, a good deal taken aback by this sudden balk, and so I believe was my friend; but our discomfiture was of short duration, for the lion had scarcely retreated two or three steps before both our rifles were leveled at him and fired. A growl followed, and then a cloud of smoke hid every thing in darkness, which lasted long enough for the brute to escape out of sight. "Surely," I exclaimed, "we did not both miss." "I certainly did not hear the clap of the bullet," replied Green; "nevertheless, I think your shot took effect, and perhaps mine too." Had I not had a long experience in night-shooting, I should, in all probability, have judged differently; but the more I considered the matter, the more I felt convinced that I had hit my mark. Indeed, a sportsman of any experience knows almost to a certainty when a gun fits his shoulder, however hurriedly raised, whether in broad daylight or in darkness. On arriving at the camp we asked the men about the fugitive, but they were no wiser than ourselves. We then tried, bull's-eye lantern in hand, to obtain a glimpse of his retreating spoor. In vain: the hardness of the soil had left no trace of his flight, neither was there any track of blood to follow up; and as it would have been next to madness to penetrate farther into the bush with such a feeble light, we reluctantly abandoned our search, and threw ourselves on our rude couches till the morning light should enable us to renew it with better success. We were fully resolved, should he not already have received his mortal wound, to hunt our foe to death. Thanks to our trusty rifles, however, we were spared farther trouble; for with the return of daylight the lion was discovered stone dead within thirty paces of our ambuscade. Both bullets had taken effect, mine traversing the entire length of the animal's body, penetrating lungs and heart, and burying itself deep in the neck, while Green's had hit the monster, though perhaps with less deadly effect, on the rump. This lion was not large, but in splendid condition. My friend courteously resigned all claim to the carcass, and its hide now forms one of the *spolia opima* of my African campaigns.

One more story about lion-hunting before I quit the subject. This story was related to me by the gentleman who is really, both as actor and sufferer, its hero, and who exhibited, in circumstances most perilous, a presence of mind and determination of which, on a similar occasion, I only know one other example. The narrative may then be relied upon as strictly true; I have heard it, word for word, from several of the actors in, or rather the spectators of the facts related, for such only, to their shame, as the reader will presently see, they were contented to remain, while their comrade was on the point of being torn to pieces before their eyes by an enraged lion.

"In the year 185—," said the narrator, "while staying with some Europeans and Namaquas in the interior of the country, several lions made their appearance on a certain night, and killed and carried off an ox. We thereupon, on the following morning, determined to get up a hunt in search of the marauders. Accordingly, mounted on such horses and carriage-oxen as we could muster, we were soon in hot pursuit of the delinquents. Having followed their track for a short time, we reached the spot where the ox had been killed, a remnant of the carcass still remaining as a last meal. Continuing on the spoor, we came, in about half an hour's time, upon the enemy, five in number. They were hidden, or rather sheltered in a dense reedy thicket. To this we immediately set fire, while men were placed round about in all directions, so as to command every outlet. For a long time the fire crackled and hissed to no purpose; at length the brake got too hot for its inmates, and out they dashed, one of them passing close to the spot where, followed by a solitary dog—the only one out of about forty that we could induce to follow us—I had taken up my post. Finding himself hotly pressed, and with no suitable shelter before him, the brute soon tacked about, retreating back to his original cover. Before, however, he could reach it, I fired, and apparently with effect. Yet he was shortly afterward again seen escaping, and so successfully this time as to take refuge in a small patch of green reeds; out of this new strong-hold it was now my object to expel him, but my efforts to effect this proved at first quite unavailing. Once, indeed, he showed himself for a moment in a pursuit of the dog, who had followed him into the reeds. But, alas! my canine follower's bravery on this occasion had nearly proved fatal to him, for he received the contents of one of our guns, and was too badly wounded to escape from the thicket. I was determined, however, to extricate him at all hazards from his perilous situation. Accordingly, having, after much persuasion, succeeded in inducing my companions to range themselves within a short distance of the cover, and having handed my piece to a by-stander, I darted into the copse, where, spying my poor dog, I immediately caught him up in my arms, and the next moment found myself and my burden in safety. I could not possibly have been above a couple of paces from the lion when I picked up my dog, as I am confident the whole extent of the reedy patch was not above thirty feet square; I did not, nevertheless, in consequence of the denseness of the bush, see the brute. I only heard his growl.

"Having placed my quadruped companion in safety, we now ranged ourselves within pistol-shot of the reeds, taking care to have a clear view all around us; we then rent the air with deafening shouts, and pierced the brake with numerous bullets. All in vain; the animal remained motionless. The fire which we had originally lighted was now, however, quickly approaching the spot on which all eyes were fixed, and we hoped that it might effect what we had been unable to accomplish, when, to our great vexation and disappointment, a slight veering of the wind drove the flames in another direction. We should now have been fairly baffled if the ingenuity of a Berg Damara had not come to our aid. Collecting a quantity of dry reeds, with other inflammable matter, and setting fire to the same, this intelligent native seized the fagots at one end, and, running at the top of his speed, hurled the whole lighted mass into the very centre of the lion's hiding-place. The effect was almost instantaneous, for in a very few minutes afterward we had the satisfaction of seeing the enemy dash through the flames. It had been previously agreed on that, upon his first appearance, those who possessed double-barreled guns should fire only one barrel, reserving the other for the charge, should he turn upon us. The mere sight, however, of the lion seems to have so frightened several of our party that their barrels were indiscriminately fired in every direction, and some even blazed away in the empty air.

"On receiving our fire the animal made straight for us, on which every one, with the exception of Mr. S—— and myself, took to his heels. The former gentleman, who had never seen a lion in its wild state, became so terrified that he was unable either to fire or to attempt to make his escape. He remained fixed and motionless on the spot, like one entranced. I had by this time taken a few steps backward, yet without ever averting my eyes from our foe, who, having approached to within a few paces of S——, prepared himself to make the fatal spring. I had already fired when he burst out of his cover; but one barrel still remained to me, and, seeing my friend's imminent danger, I no longer hesitated. Clapping the gun to my shoulder, I took a steady aim at the side of his head; unfortunately, just as I pulled the trigger, he made a slight movement, and the consequence was that, instead of smashing his skull, the bullet merely grazed it, passing in the same manner all along the left side of his body. Quick as thought, the enraged animal left his first intended victim, and turned with a ferocious growl upon me. To escape was impossible; I thrust, therefore, no other resource being left me, the muzzle of my gun into the extended jaws opened to devour me. In a moment the weapon was demolished. My fate seemed inevitable, when, just at this critical juncture, I was unexpectedly rescued. D—— fired, and broke the lion's shoulder. He fell, and, taking advantage of this lucky incident, I scampered away at full speed. But my assailant had not yet done with me. Despite his crippled condition, he soon overtook me. At that moment I was looking over my shoulder, when, unhappily, a creeper caught my foot, and I was precipitated headlong to the ground. In another instant the lion had transfixed my right foot with his murderous fangs. Finding, however, my left foot disengaged, I gave the brute a severe kick on the head, which compelled him for a few seconds to suspend his attack. He next seized my left leg, on which I repeated the former dose on his head with my right foot; he once more, thereupon, let go his hold, but seized my right foot for a second time. Shortly afterward he dropped the foot and grasped my right thigh, gradually working his way up to my hip, where he endeavored to plant his claws. In this he partially succeeded, tearing, in the attempt, my trowsers and body-linen, and grazing the skin of my body. Knowing that if he got a firm hold of me here it would surely cost me my life, I quickly seized him by his two ears, and, with a desperate effort, managed to roll him over on his side, which gave me a moment's respite. He next laid hold of my left hand, which he bit through and through, smashing the wrist, and tearing my right hand seriously. I was now totally helpless, and must inevitably have fallen a speedy victim to his fury had not prompt assistance been at hand. In my prostrate position I observed, and a gleam of hope sprung up, D—— advancing quickly toward me. The lion saw him too, and, with one of his paws on my wounded thigh, throwing his ears well back, he couched, ready to spring at his new assailant. Now, if D—— had fired, in my present position I should have run great risk of being hit by the bullet; I hallooed out to him, therefore, to wait until I could veer my head a little. In time I succeeded, and the next instant I heard the click of a gun, but no report. Another moment, and a well-directed ball, taking effect in his forehead, laid the lion a corpse alongside my own bruised and mutilated body. Quick as lightning, I now sprang to my feet, and darted forward toward my companions, whom I saw at no great distance. Once or twice I felt excessively faint, but managed, nevertheless, to keep my head up.

DEATH-GRAPPLE WITH A LION.

"No sooner had D—— so successfully finished the lion than he mounted a horse hard by, and galloped off in the direction of our camp. In the mean time I was lifted on to a tame ox, which was led by a man preceding us. At about half way to our camp D—— and B—— came to meet me, bringing with them, to refresh me, some water and a bottle of eau de Cologne. A drinking-cup we had not, but the crown of a wide-awake hat was a good substitute for one, and I drank the mixture of the two liquids greedily off. A few minutes afterward we were met by some of the servants carrying a door. Exchanging then my ox for this more commodious conveyance, I was carefully borne into camp. Up to this time I had retained perfect self-possession, but the moment my wounds were washed and dressed I swooned, and for three entire weeks remained in a state of complete unconsciousness. I have since perfectly recovered my health, but, as you see, I am totally crippled in my left arm.

"I must not omit to mention that my brave dog, although shot through one of his fore legs, on seeing the lion rush upon me, came forward at the best of his speed, and, in his turn, sprang upon my grim assailant, and clung desperately to him until D——'s bullet put an end to the combat."

CHAPTER XXVI.

Introduction. — Saldanha Bay. — St. Helen's Bay. — The Berg River.—Lambert's Cove.—Cape Donkin and Donkin's Bay. —The Oliphant River.—Mitchell's Bay.—Houdeklipp Bay. —The Koussie River.—Cape Voltas.—Homewood and Peacock Harbors.—Alexander Bay.—The Orange River: Description, Scenery, precious Stones; central Course unknown. —Boundary of British Dominions.—Angras Juntas.—Possession Island.—Elizabeth Bay.—Angra Pequena.—Pedestal Point.—Robert Harbor.—Ichaboe.—Hottentot Bay.— Rae's Bay. — Spencer's Bay. — Mercury Island. — Hollam's Bird Isle.—Sandwich Harbor.

As the present work professes, cursorily at least, to treat geographical subjects, it may be proper for me briefly to describe the west coast of Southern Africa, *i. e.*, that part of it extending from the Cape of Good Hope to Benguela—a country with which I myself am somewhat acquainted, inasmuch as I have often visited and examined its rivers, bays, harbors, islands, etc. It must be borne in mind, however, that the greater part of this coast is still but imperfectly known and surveyed, and that, not having the means of delineating it with the accuracy and detail that would be desirable, I must content myself with laying before my readers such information about it as I myself have been able personally to acquire and collect.

The authorities I have chiefly consulted are Captain Owen, R.N.; Bennet; Findlay; Captain Messum; and Captain Morrell, of the United States, who some years ago published a book descriptive of various sealing voyages along the coast of Africa and elsewhere.

I must premise that, in quoting from this last-named explorer, I have been much on my guard; for, though on many points, more especially such as relate to charts of the coast, he is very accurate, yet on others—and this remark particularly applies to his descriptions of inland localities, scenery, and the like—he is a somewhat unsafe guide; so much so that, had I not been intimately acquainted with the countries of which he speaks, I might have been led into very serious errors.

In Captain Messum, on the other hand, to whom I am chiefly indebted for the information I possess respecting that portion of the west coasts lying between Walwich Bay and Benguela (a part of some importance and very little known), I place every confidence. Captain Messum was for many years occupied in exploring this coast for guano and other valuable products, during which time he surveyed the whole marine tract, from Table Bay to the Portuguese settlements, and has, besides affording me much verbal and written information, kindly placed at my disposal a chart of all his explorations from Walwich Bay to the Cape. Unfortunately, however, time and circumstances prevented the completion of this chart. I have, therefore, not thought it advisable to introduce it in a separate form, but have merely added it to my own map. (See "Lake Ngami.")

Sailing northward from Table Bay, at about seventy miles from the Cape of Good Hope, the first commodious, indeed, the only safe port within the boundary of the colony on this side is Saldanha Bay. This bay, nearly three miles broad (between 33° 3′ and 33° 6′ S. lat.), runs through a ridge of granite which extends north and south throughout its whole length—that is, about fifteen miles. It affords excellent anchorage to ships of every size, and may be safely entered with all winds and at all seasons of the year.

"On entering," says Morrell, "this well-protected harbor, attention should be paid to the following circumstances and localities: On the north of its entrance is a small island called 'Mallagassen;' and on the south, in a bend of the land, near the shore, is another named Jutten. Two miles eastward of the first-mentioned island is a third, called Marcus. Each of these islands has a reef, which juts off from its shore about a cable's length; and as all three of them are low, and can be seen but at a short distance, accuracy in the vessel's latitude is very requisite. The widest passage, and the best for strangers, is on the south of the Marcus island, which may be passed within forty fathoms."

The northern portion of Saldanha, called Hoetjes

Bay, has no fresh water, which may be obtained, however, at no very great distance, and in any quantity. Besides, in the year 1841, a spring was discovered on a small island named the Schaapen, which, having been cleansed, yielded, according to Findlay, no less than ten gallons a minute, or 144,000 gallons in twenty-four hours.

Several farmers reside in the neighborhood of Saldanha Bay, from whom fruits, vegetables, and refreshments of various kinds may be obtained on short notice and at moderate prices. Game, such as small antelopes, hares, partridges, etc., are found in great numbers in the vicinity. The bay itself, moreover, abounds in numerous varieties of fish, of which many have an excellent flavor. At certain seasons the Boers resort to this place with their nets for the purpose of catching and curing large draughts of the finny tribe, which they either consume themselves or sell to inland neighbors. For ships that require refreshments few places offer better accommodations than Saldanha Bay.

From this bay northward the coast is rugged, and beset with rocks stretching a good way from the shore, which makes the navigation both intricate and dangerous. The next place of importance is St. Helena Bay, formed by Point St. Martin (which projects from the coast in a N.W. direction) on the south, and Cape Descada on the north, the distance between the two being nine leagues. The bay itself is about four leagues deep, running E. and

X

S. E. toward the head of the harbor, or south shore. The soundings, from twenty to four fathoms, are very regular.

St. Helena Bay is by far the largest indentation in this part of the coast, but, though well sheltered from S. E. winds, is quite open to the N. W. Nevertheless, from the great depth of the water, the wind seldom reaches the interior of the port with sufficient force to injure a vessel at any season of the year. It is high water here at 2^h 30^m P. M.

At the opening of the bay stands a huge rock. called the Britannia, and in the bay itself the Paternosters. The country in the background is rather mountainous; the Piquet Berg is indeed very conspicuous from its height. From this mountain a river discharges itself into St. Helena Bay, but, like all other water-sheds in this neighborhood, its entrance is crossed by a bar, which is constantly shifting. Once within this barrier, however, the stream, which takes its rise in the mountains that inclose the vale of Drakenstein, is navigable by small craft for from about fifteen to twenty miles. Its water is very pure and wholesome, and more than one vessel used, in former times, to stop here to replenish their empty butts. Casks may be floated about five miles up with the flood, and then filled and floated back to the ship with very little trouble.

Hippopotami are said to have once abounded (one or two still exist there) in the Berg River. The Dutch government, in order to preserve this animal in the colony, imposed a fine of a thousand guilders on any person that should put one of them to death.

From St. Helena Bay the coast is open and almost free from danger. Pursuing a N.N.W. course from Cape Descada, which is a low, sandy beach in front of bluff sand-hills, one comes next upon Lambert's Cove. The entrance to this little shelter, for about a mile, is from the N. to the S.S.E. Small vessels can anchor here in perfect safety in three fathoms' water. Many loads of grain are annually embarked at this place for the Cape market.

Hence, and steering about the same course, Cape Donkin is reached in lat. 31° 54′ S. This cape is the south point of a small bay of the same name, within which vessels may find partial anchorage, with a sandy bottom, in from ten to six fathoms of water.

About four leagues to the northward of Donkin's Bay is the Oliphant (or Elephant) River, which debouches in the Atlantic in lat. 31° 38′ S. Except in summer, the anchorage here is dangerous; and, if I am not mistaken, more than one wreck has occurred on this spot. The entrance to the bay is blocked up by a bar of sand with only about two feet of water on it, and, as a westerly swell is constantly "heaving in" on the coast, there are generally heavy breakers on the bar. Like the Berg River, however, once within, there is plenty of water, and the stream is navigable for a short distance. "This river," says Morrell, "enters from the south.

running N. N. W. for about two miles, when it turns to the E. and E. S. E., carrying a strong current of water for a long distance inland. If there could be a passage cut through the bar at the mouth of this river, it would be the finest harbor on the west coast of Africa."

Fish is found plentifully in the Oliphant River; and at no very remote period huge elephants, as may be inferred from the name, frequented its sandy banks.

Farther north, and near the mouth of the Spock River, is Roodenall, or Mitchell's Bay, a small cove surrounded by cliffs of red sandstone, affording fair anchorage for small craft.

Near the mouth of the Zwarte Lintjie River lies Hondeklipp Bay, which is only accessible to schooners and other small craft—vessels employed chiefly in carrying to the Cape the copper ore brought down from the interior. This bay, which is very unsafe, has been the scene of several wrecks within a very few years. From its proximity to the copper-mines, it has, however, much commercial importance.

The Koussie or Kowsie, not long ago the boundary of the colony, enters the sea at about lat. 29° 40' S. The water of this river is, for a distance of ten to fifteen miles inland, perfectly salt; and, though its channel is accessible to boats, it frequently happens that its mouth is closed up by a bar of sand.

Cape Voltas of the Portuguese, a high bluff point projecting into the sea, with several outlying rocks to the west of it, next arrests attention. From Point St. Martin to this cape the coast is open, and almost free from danger to within half a mile of the land.

South of Cape Voltas, anchorage, though much exposed, is to be found in a small bay in the neighborhood. Immediately to the north, again, we have Homewood and Peacock Harbors, and Alexander Bay; all, however, small, open, and affording but very indifferent anchorage. I once nearly suffered shipwreck in the last-named bay, which, notwithstanding its present deficiencies, may, from its proximity to the Ovambo River, and the lately discovered copper-mines in the vicinity, become some day a place of considerable importance. It would neither be very troublesome nor very expensive to make it a safe and commodious haven.

Between Cape Voltas and the Orange River the coast is strewn with immense quantities of driftwood, carried down by that stream to the sea, and thrown back on the beach by the waves of the Atlantic. The land is very low, sandy, barren, and desolate, characteristics it retains a long way inland. It afterward swells into gentle undulations, and at last rises into lofty hills, which stand out in bold relief on each side of the river.

We now come to one of the most important, as well as one of the most interesting objects on the map of South Africa, the Orange River, or the Garip, as it is called by the natives. Traversing the great continent from east to west, divided in its upper course into three considerable branches—the Nu, Ky, and Maap (the black, yellow, and muddy)—the waters of this river, rolling down from a lofty mountain range to the ocean, intersect a distance of upward of one thousand, while they drain a basin of no less than one hundred thousand square miles. Unfortunately, however, like nearly every other river on the coast, its mouth is blocked up almost totally by a bar of sand, against which the waves of the Atlantic beat with great violence. Its entrance has even more than once, within the memory of the present generation, been closed up entirely, whereby a sudden inundation, overflooding the country, has given it the appearance of a vast lake. Near its embouchure this river expands to a breadth of about four miles, and is dotted over with numerous reedy isles.

Of the Orange River that portion alone is navigable which very nearly adjoins the sea, and then only for small craft, and at certain periods of the year; in the dry season shoals and sand-banks are every where visible in its channel. Even higher up the navigation is frequently impeded by rapids and waterfalls, some of which are very grand and beautiful.

Mr. Thompson, the South African traveler, has thus described the impression a first view of one of these cataracts made on him:

"At length we halted, and the next moment I was led to a projecting rock, where a scene burst upon me far surpassing my most sanguine expectations. The whole water of the river (except what escapes by the subsidiary channel we had crossed, and by a similar one on the north side), being previously confined to a bed of scarcely one hundred feet in breadth, descends at once in this place in a magnificent cascade of fully four hundred feet in height. I stood upon a cliff nearly level with the top of the fall, and directly in front of it. The beams of the evening sun fell full upon the cascade, and occasioned a most splendid rainbow; while the vapory spray arising from the broken waters, the bright green woods which hung, as it were, from the surrounding peaks, the astounding roar of the waterfall, and the tumultuous boiling and hissing of the headlong flood, rending and crushing its way through precipitous cliffs, then striving with agony to escape along its deep, dark, and narrow cavities, formed altogether a combination of beauty and grandeur such as I have never before witnessed. As I gazed on this stupendous spectacle, the following splendid lines from Childe Harold burst spontaneously from my lips:

"'The roar of waters! from the headlong height
Velino cleaves the wave-worn precipice;
The fall of waters! rapid as the light
The flashing mass foams shaking the abyss;
The hell of waters! where they howl and hiss,

And boil in endless torture; while the sweat
Of their great agony, wrung out from this
Their Phlegethon, curls round the rocks of jet
That gird the gulf around, in pitiless horror set,

'And mounts in spray the skies, and thence again
Returns in an unceasing shower, which round,
With its unemptied cloud of gentle rain,
Is an eternal April to the ground,
Making it all one emerald: how profound
The gulf! and how the giant element
From rock to rock leaps with delirious bound,
Crushing the cliffs, which, downward worn and rent
With his fierce footsteps, yield in chasms a fearful vent.'"

Notwithstanding the barren and arid nature of the ground about the lower course of the Orange River, it is an exceedingly fine stream, and becomes more and more so as one ascends its current to the eastward. "The Orange River here," says the Rev. Mr. Moffat, "presents the appearance of a plain, miles in breadth, entirely covered, as it were, with mimosa-trees, among which the many branches of the river run, and then tumble over the precipices, raising clouds of mist when there is any volume of water." Again: "All those who have had the good fortune to see the Garip," writes Sir James Alexander, "agree in praising its beauty—its broad stream at one time rushing tumultuously over a rocky and shelving bed, now spreading out into a translucent lake, then hurrying over a rock four hundred feet high, thus forming a grand cataract, which sweeps in its course round numerous islands, some of them inhabited by banditti, and others by hippopotami."

The banks of this mighty stream are indeed every where clothed with a broad belt of thorn and mimosas, with willow and a species of rhus and ebony, and are quite alive with the notes of birds; while the strangely wild and fantastic-shaped hills, which so frequently involve the river in their embraces, form one of the most picturesque and exciting scenes it is possible to conceive.

Even Burchell appears to have been in raptures with the Orange River: "The first view to which I happened to turn myself in looking at the stream," says that distinguished traveler, "realized those ideas of elegant and classic scenery, at once fantastic and romantic, which are created in the minds of poets. The waters of the majestic river, flowing in a broad expanse resembling a smooth translucent lake, seemed with their gentle waves to kiss the shore and bid it farewell forever, as they glided past in their way to the restless ocean, bearing on their limpid bosom the image of their wood-clothed banks, while the drooping willows leaned over the tide, as if unwilling to lose it, and the long pendent branches, dipping their leafy twigs in the stream, seemed fain to follow."

Almost from our earliest acquaintance with this river rumors were rife, and they still prevail, of the existence of precious stones in its bed, but I believe there is no well-attested instances of any having been found there. It abounds, it is true, in opals, agates, carnelians, etc., of every hue and form, but, though often very beautifully variegated, these curious pebbles are coarse and imperfect. Cart-loads of them might be collected in some parts of the river in a very few hours.

In its lower course the banks of the Orange River consist of sand, clay, and mica, intermixed with very considerable portions of oxide of iron; the latter, in a particular form, has been mistaken for *pulverized rubies!*

Until quite lately our knowledge of the central course of this stream was very scanty. Mr. Moffat, son of the worthy and well-known missionary of that name, has, however, very recently followed its course from its junction with the Vaal to the sea, and, I am informed, sketched a very interesting and instructive chart of his explorations.

During the guano fever (of which more anon), the British government at the Cape, in order to secure to themselves the right of granting licenses to the crowds of adventurers that flocked to this coast in search of guano, endeavored to prove that the English dominion really extended as far as the Portuguese settlements; but it is now known that the Orange River is the boundary of our colony on the west coast.

"Beyond this boundary, and at the place called Angras Juntas," says Morrell, "there is a small bend in the land, a mile and a half wide where it commences, running about a mile to the eastward. Here, when the wind is southerly, ships may find tolerable shelter. There is also a small rock that stands about two miles to the S.W. of this point which has deep water all round it.

"At the entrance of this bay there are fourteen fathoms of water, which gradually lessen to five within about half a mile from the land. The bottom is sandy. The best anchorage is under the south shore (one fourth of a mile from the point to the S.W.), in six fathoms of water." This is the account given of it by Morrell; but Captain Messum, who visited the spot at a much later period, informs me that the cove has since filled up.

Hence, with the exception of a few small islets, or rather rocks, viz., the "Plum-pudding," and the "Albatross," there are scarcely any more points to be noticed on the coast until we arrive at the "Possession," an island situated (according to Captain Owen) in 26° 56′ 30″ S. lat. This island, about three miles in length and one in width, has been long known to navigators for its good anchorage and as a depository for guano—a manure which at one time abounded there. The place was formerly a favorite resort of seals. It affords at present a good shelter, as I have said, to vessels at all seasons, though the navigation is not without danger; for there are sunken rocks off its south point, and a reef, about three miles in extent, projects from its N.E. extremity, over which the sea often breaks with great fury. The rocks and reefs, however, to the eastward, keep the sea pretty well out of the harbor. Between the extreme points of this reef and the main land the channel is three miles wide, with a depth of water of from eleven to seven fathoms, and with a sandy bottom, making altogether a safe haven. It is much exposed, nevertheless, both to northerly and southerly winds. On the east side is a landing-place for boats. Ships intending to anchor while the south winds are fresh should approach the anchorage from the south, and leave it by the opposite passage.

In the months of August, September, and October, vast quantities of penguins' eggs may be obtained in this island; along its shores there is at all times an abundance of fish of excellent quality.

Elizabeth Bay, a small indentation of the coast, is exactly fronted by Possession Island. "Between this place and Cape Voltas there are many small islets and reefs, lying half a mile from the shore, but at double that distance from the land there are no dangers to be encountered, and ships, if becalmed, may anchor five miles from the coast in from fifteen to twenty fathoms, on a sandy bottom: these soundings extend along the whole range of coast."

About five leagues north of "Possession," in lat. 26° 38′ S., Angra Pequena (a small bay) forms a very conspicuous break in the coast. The extremity of the little peninsula forming the southern portion of this harbor is called Pedestal Point (lat.

26° 38′ S.). It derives its name from a marble pedestal, said to have been erected here by Bartholomew Diaz in 1486. This monument of the perseverance and skill of that great navigator has, however, long since disappeared; the tradition is that it was destroyed by some ignorant or mischievous person, in the hope of finding treasures beneath its foundation.

The aspect of Angra Pequena is as dreary and melancholy as it is possible to conceive. Scarcely a vestige of vegetation is to be found within some miles of the place; dry sand and rocks, time-worn and buffeted by centuries of bad weather, constitute the whole landscape. Moreover, there is no fresh water to be had here. To remedy this deficiency, an attempt was made, some time ago, to sink a well in one of the granite rocks, but the task proved a failure. Yet, despite these disadvantages, Angra has long been resorted to by traders, who have a depôt here, which is occasionally visited by the natives of the interior, who bring with them for sale cattle, fur skins, ostrich feathers, etc. For these goods they receive in exchange clothing, tobacco, guns, ammunition, etc., but more especially spirits, to which the Namaquas, who have once tasted the fiery liquid, are fearfully addicted; they will sacrifice their last ox or sheep to procure intoxicating drinks. Indeed, this portion of the country, which never could boast of much wealth, has been nearly ruined by brandy.

The sailors of the different whaling, sealing, and guano ships that have touched at Angra for fresh provisions have frequently, it is affirmed, taken advantage of this failing of the natives to cheat them of their property in the most scandalous manner. By promises (probably never intended to be kept) of presents, etc., they have been in the habit of inducing the poor savages to come on board with their cattle, when, either by frightening them to part with their live-stock for trifles, or by making them drunk, they usually contrived to take possession of the property of their simple guests, and to send them on shore without any remuneration.

There are several islands about Angra Pequena, such as the "Penguin," the "Seal," the "Shark," etc. (none exceeding a mile in length), which, together with the neighboring bays and inlets, afford most excellent anchorage.

"Between the main land, Penguin and Shark Island, Robert Harbor has also a good sheltered anchorage, in five fathoms of water, with clay bottom. This harbor may be entered and left with perfect safety, either from the N. or S. end of Penguin Island, but the southern entrance is to be preferred. The best situation to cast anchor is on the east side of the bay, near its centre, about two cables' length from the shore, leaving a single rock that lies level with the surface of the water, and nearly in mid-channel, about half a mile to the north of this passage."

At Angra Pequena, before noon, light northerly winds are prevalent, and in the afternoon fresh S.W. breezes. At $2^h\ 30^m$ P.M. on full and change of moon it is high water; the spring tides rise eight feet.

Many years ago specimens of copper ore were discovered in the neighborhood of Angra Pequena, and a company was shortly afterward formed in England for the purpose of working the supposed mines; after some time and much money had been expended, the speculation was found, however, to be a losing one, and the establishment was in consequence broken up.

From Angra Pequena a dangerous reef extends along the coast to near the island of Ichaboe (lat. 26° 18′ S.)—once so famous for its guano, of which more anon.

The first place one meets of any consequence after leaving this reef is Ichaboe itself. Hottentot Bay, which is situated about fifteen miles north of that island, is spacious and well-sheltered from the prevailing southerly winds. It has a moderate depth of water, gradually shallowing toward the shores; the bottom is a mixture of clay and sand, and forms, in consequence, most excellent holding-ground. In the summer time a vessel may be hove down here with ease.

On the authority of Captain Livingstone, it is stated that an excellent bay, not previously marked in any chart, was discovered by Mr. R. Rae, master of the "Gallovidia" schooner, in 1844. It has been called by the name of its discoverer; its position is laid down in lat. 26° 8′ S.

"This bay," says Mr. Findlay, "is three and a half miles long, with a breadth of about three miles. A point, somewhat similar to that which runs out to the southward of Ichaboe, stretches out from the main land, and shelters the haven from the southward. It forms, on the whole, a secure anchorage, having a clean bottom of blue sand and mud, with gradual and regular soundings of from eleven to three and a half fathoms.

"The point just alluded to is in part rocky and cliffy, but near the main land low and sandy, so that Ichaboe may be seen from the mast-head of even a moderate-sized vessel anchored here. On the south side of the bay is a small islet or rock, and a reef connected with the shore.

"A reef also, partly rock and partly sand, extends from the point to the westward. It has two fathoms water almost close to the point, but may be considered as dangerous for a mile and a half farther on, or even in eight fathoms water, where the sea has been seen to break heavily on the bar. This bay is completely sheltered from the S.W., round by south and east to the N.W., and may afford a refuge to any vessel overrunning Ichaboe harbor, and till a favorable opportunity occurs of returning to that island."

Near the 26th degree of S. lat.—between lat.

25° 40′ and 25° 45′ S.—lies Spencer's Bay, which presents toward its south point several high-peaked rocks, almost six hundred feet perpendicular at the water's edge. This bay, with a rocky bottom, and scarcely any shelter from the sea, is, when a strong southerly wind prevails, a very unsafe place of anchorage. In July and August it is frequented by whales.

Nearly at the middle of the entrance to Spencer's Bay, at about three quarters of a mile from the S.W. point, and at one mile and a half from the N.E. end, the voyager comes upon Mercury Island. This is a bleak, rugged rock, of an oblong shape, about one mile in circumference, bearing N. and S., and rising about two hundred feet above the level of the sea, which at times beats against its sides with indescribable fury. In the face of this rock there is an immense cavern, into which the sea rushes through several apertures or rents, causing thereby an awful noise and commotion.

This rock is the favorite resort of the penguin, the gannet, and other birds; seals also haunt it in abundance.

Considerable quantities of guano have been brought away from Mercury Island, and merchants at the Cape continue still to draw from it small supplies, though the manure is said to be of a very indifferent quality. On one of my voyages up the coast I visited the place, which was then occupied by some laborers stationed there to collect guano.

Y

It is impossible to conceive any thing more wild and dreary than this isolated spot, and nothing but the hope of great profits could, I imagine, ever induce men to imprison themselves in so wretched a dungeon; a sentence of transportation could not certainly be more severe and more penal than the banishment and confinement the guano gatherers impose upon themselves.

Between Spencer's and Walwich Bay, at about nine miles from the main land, we next encounter Hollam's Bird Isle, situated in lat. 24° 37′ S. This is a small rocky island, not above a quarter of a mile in circumference, possessing but very indifferent anchorage at its northern extremity, while a reef of rocks, on which the waves frequently break heavily, runs out in a S.W. direction. Indeed, there is almost always much sea hereabouts, which renders landing difficult and even dangerous.

During the months of July and August, the reef just spoken of is frequented by numbers of those whales which seafaring men term the "right whale." Whalers were, and I believe are still, in the habit of occasionally resorting to the islet; and, if provided with chain cables, may lie at anchor on the north side of it (in ten fathoms water) the whole season.

Hollam's Bird Isle is largely resorted to by penguins, gannets, and seals. A few turtles are also reported to frequent the east side of it, where the beach is of a sandy nature.

Sandwich Harbor—the Porto d'Ilheo of the Portuguese, in lat. 23° S., or about thirteen leagues from Walwich Bay—though honored with so high-sounding a name, might perhaps, with more propriety, be called a lagoon, two leagues or thereabouts in length, with a depth of water varying from seven to two fathoms. It is formed on the east side by a high, white, bluff sand-hill, and on the west by a low sandy peninsula, nearly level with the sea, with shoal water for more than a mile on the sea-board. The entrance of the lagoon, formed by two low sandy points, is very narrow, and not more than a quarter of a mile wide.

On the beach at Sandwich Harbor there is a copious fresh spring, yielding most excellent water. Pasturage for cattle may also be had in the neighborhood. Yet, despite these advantages, it is deprived of the importance it would otherwise have by the immense hillocks of soft yielding sand which cut off its communication with the interior.

Sandwich Harbor abounds so much in fish, that some years ago a Cape merchant established a fishery here, which was and is conducted with considerable success. The fish taken, being salted and dried, are exported to the Mauritius, where they always command a ready sale, not unfrequently fetching the high price of £30 to £35—nay, they have even realized £38 per ton, that is, for one kind of fish called "snook." Other kinds scarcely fetch more than one half of this high price.

The next point of interest—and probably the most important of all north of the Orange River—is Walwich Bay; but as this place has already been so fully described in a former work of mine ("Lake Ngami"), I need not here dwell on the subject farther than just to state one or two facts. First, since my last publication, an important fishery has been established here. It has not, it is true, yet proved remunerative; the prospect of its being so is nevertheless extremely hopeful. Secondly, the exports and imports of this "port" have very considerably increased, and promise to increase still more when once the regions newly discovered and explored by me have been sufficiently laid open to commercial enterprise. Lastly, the ivory trade of the lake districts, which formerly found an outlet on the east coast of South Africa, has been almost entirely turned into this channel, to the direct and substantial benefit of the commerce of the Cape.

CHAPTER XXVII.

The Swakop River.—Half-moon Bay.—The Omaruru River. —Cape Cross.—The wrecked Vessel.—Mount Messum.— Berg Damaras.—Hogden's Harbor.—Cock's Comb and Sugar Loaf.—Supposed permanent Stream.—Fort Rock Point.—Cape Frio.—The Cunenè, or Nourse River.—Great Fish Bay.—Formation and Disappearance of Bays, etc.— Excursion inland from Great Fish Bay.—The Nourse River again.—Bembarougi.—Port Alexander.—The River Flamingos.—The Natives.—Fossil Shells.—Summary.—Concluding Remarks: Rivers, Harbors, Islands, etc.; Winds, Temperature, Rollers; Scarcity of Rain.

SAILING northward from the anchorage at Walwich Bay, the voyager finds the shore clear of all dangers until he arrives at the mouth of the Swakop River. Here a slight indentation is formed by one reef jutting off from its southern, and another from its northern extremity, with a distance of about two miles and a half between them. The bed of this river can be plainly traced E.N.E. for a mile and a half; it then makes a curve to the S.E., and is at once lost to view. At its mouth, Mount Colquhoun, a most conspicuous mass of rock, distant about eighteen miles from the shore, may be seen towering up to an elevation of three thousand feet above the level of the sea. On both sides of this embouchure are also several sand-hills; those to the south presenting a dark brown appearance, while those to the north, containing bright specks of mica, have a lighter tint, the two ranges ascending together with a gentle slope to the base of the mountain just named.

The soundings from Walwich Bay to the mouth of the Swakop, *i. e.*, to within three miles of the shore, are sixteen fathoms, with scarcely any variation, for the bottom consists of sand; but about three quarters of a mile from the coast, the bottom becoming rocky and foul, the water runs only to a depth of nine or ten fathoms.

North of the Swakop is a low, sandy foreshore,* thirteen miles or thereabouts in extent, with occasional clusters of shrubs. Here a reef, projecting from a sandy point, forms a half-moon bay, where landing can be effected. Several reefs besides, twelve or thirteen miles long, shoot out almost from the shore, which is level, and devoid of all vegetation except a few bushes. Inland, the country, after an hour or two's walk, becomes rugged; and at five-and-twenty or thirty miles' distance, a chain of black rocky mountains, extending as far as the 16th degree of S. lat., comes in view. The southern extremity of this range is conspicuously marked out by a hill of considerable height, shaped exactly like a dome.

From about lat. 22° 15′ the shore trends somewhat to the northwest for nearly five miles, when

* A low shore backed by higher ground.

another small half-moon bay is found partially protected by a reef off the point to the westward. This place affords some facility for landing with boats, so that the reefs to the north may be satisfactorily examined. Three miles farther on along the coast-line—though by the beach not till after two hours' irksome walking—one comes upon a river, and a considerable patch of swampy ground close to the sea, where fresh water may be had and flocks may feed. Captain Messum found numerous tracks of the gnu and the gemsbok in this district. Not above two miles farther north, he discovered, too, the mouth of another river, where he noticed vast quantities of drift-wood, composed often of trees of considerable magnitude, piled above each other in regular tiers. As there is very little vegetation of any kind in the neighborhood, he conjectured that the timber must have come from some distance; and, moreover, that the current must occasionally, at least, be very powerful, as it had forced a passage through a sandy table-land, elevated about one hundred and fifty feet above the level of the sea, and extending to within a few miles of Cape Cross. This, no doubt, is the Omaruru River, briefly described in the first chapter of this narrative.

From the Omaruru to Cape Cross the shore has a fine bold outline, and is quite free from danger. Captain Messum sailed along it within a distance of from three quarters to half a mile, and found a depth of water varying from seven to eight fathoms.

Cape Cross, a rocky headland, projecting about a mile to the westward of the southern line of seacoast, forms a bay to the northward of from two and a quarter to three and a half miles in depth. From the point of this promontory there is a reef, about one hundred yards long, which terminates abruptly in a depth of ten fathoms of water. On rounding the Cape, fair anchorage is immediately found in six fathoms, but the best anchorage is to be had—after passing a slight projection from which another reef extends—about a mile and a quarter farther on. To within half a mile of this second point the bottom is clear and sandy, with a seven fathoms depth of water. In attempting, however, to effect a landing, Captain Messum's boat was swamped, for a heavy swell from the S.W. sweeps round the points, and throws sometimes immense rollers on the beach. One must therefore, in disembarking, watch one's opportunity. The best moment to make a push for the shore is while the lull lasts, which takes place after seven or eight successive seas have spent their force. *The best landing is abreast of a red sandstone rock.*

At this place Captain Messum discovered a wrecked vessel, the remains of the one, no doubt, mentioned in "Lake Ngami," of which Jonker Afrikander went in search. From finding an iron cooking range in good preservation, and other signs of late habitation on the coast, he conjectured that the crew, or at least part of it, had been saved, and had for a while remained here. The vessel, which he supposed to be of American construction, was deeply imbedded in the sand at the head of the bay; nothing of her was visible but a few timbers.

Directly inland (from Cape Cross), the highest and most conspicuous peak of the whole black mountain range, recently mentioned, rears its head very loftily. It rises, indeed, to the height of about 3200 feet above the level of the plain. Its western and eastern faces are abrupt, while its southern extremity is nearly perpendicular. My friend has given to this peak the name of Mount Messum. The Berg Damaras in the neighborhood call it Dourissa.

From the bay to the foot of this mountain runs a level, sandy plain; but to the north, and near the shore, are high sand hillocks, with an extensive salt plain to the eastward. "After journeying ten miles," says Captain Messum, "we saw the tracks of human beings; and Robinson Crusoe was not more astonished at perceiving the traces of a man's foot in his desert island than we were at seeing the like traces in the hardly less desert region we were now traversing. Close under Mount Messum we, according to these indications, found a village of Berg Damaras, consisting of about fifty families, possessing goats and a few sheep, but no large horned cattle. We found also several wells of good water. The appearance of the people was not very prepossessing; they looked as if they had been just shaken out of a bag of soot. Their hair, though woolly, hung long, from some artificial constraint, down their backs. The men's dress consisted of a square piece of skin depending from the waist in front, and tails hanging behind, with a broad leathern strap wound several times round the body. The dress of the women was rather more ample; it was fastened round the waist with a girdle, and they could at pleasure cover their shoulders and breasts. I saw no kind of European ornament among them; but one man, who appeared to be a chief, was decorated with two blown bladders at each ear.

"The food of this people appeared to consist of nara seeds and small bulbs.* From poles in their huts parts of gemsboks often depended, and as the huts themselves were usually covered with the skins of the same animal, I should suppose that this game is very plentiful in this place. The natives were not the least afraid of us, but jabbered away in a language which, having only an occasional click, was rather more musical than that of the Namaquas.

"Vegetation is very scanty in this country; yet the goats and sheep were in excellent condition.

* Seeds of grasses contribute also largely to their nourishment, more especially one kind, which they are in the habit of taking from a certain species of small black ant, who, as usual with the industrious, store them in large quantities for hard times.

Flocks of these animals, and a few spears tipped with the horn of the gemsbok, seemed to constitute all the property the natives possessed. I saw no iron of any description among them." This last circumstance is very remarkable, for the stranded vessel was so near that they might have easily obtained almost any quantity of that metal from the wreck.

"From the anchorage at Cape Cross the coast is for about eighteen miles uniform, and free from every kind of danger, with the exception of one, which may be incurred from a shoal patch nine miles to the north. The soundings, from half a mile to upward of a mile from the shore, are pretty regular, varying only from seven to ten fathoms. The high sand-hills terminate just before the eighteen miles alluded to end. Here a bay is formed, in which landing can be effected. North of this the low shore, running four or five miles inland, is but a continuation of the salt plain already mentioned.

"Passing northward, the coast runs almost in a straight line, free of coves, creeks, or indentations of any kind, until the 21° of S. lat., when there commences a series of bays, reefs, rocks, and recifs[*] or bars, which extend as far as twenty-five miles, *i. e.*, to lat. 20° 39' S. The most southerly of this chain of coast dangers is a bay of some depth, beset with many shoals, over which the sea, when

[*] A recif implies a bar running parallel with the shore.

agitated, breaks with great fury. From this point a recif stretches about five miles northwest, until it almost reaches another point (having a similar bay) fronted by another recif, which runs three miles in a northern direction, till it nearly joins a reef to the westward, a full mile and a half from the shore, when, bending to the north on a line with the coast, it forms a third bar, inside of which the water appears smooth.

"In lat. 20° 47' S. there is a remarkable break of about three quarters of a mile in the sand-hills, evidently caused by an immense body of water at times rushing through their heavy heaps.

"This twenty-five miles (just spoken of)," continues Captain Messum, "formed the most interesting portion of our exploring cruise. The Portuguese, in their charts, place a harbor, named Angra de St. Ambrosia, on this part of the coast, near the 21st degree of lat. Morrell, the American navigator, also discovered a bay here, which he calls Hogden's Harbor; after fifteen days' search, however, both with the vessel and with the boats, we could not find it. The harbor, if it really existed, has, I conjecture, been filled up by the encroachment of sand; for the wind blowing almost always one way, or from S.S.W., similar events are not unfrequent on this coast. I have known even localities where, at one time, mountains of sand met the eye, reduced in the course of a few months to level plains."

There seemed to be more vegetation hereabouts than in any other place we had yet visited. We also saw natives, and at Double Point Bight a great quantity of fish hanging on poles and stakes to dry; but the sea beat with too much fury along the whole extent of coast to allow us to land. I nevertheless, on two different occasions, spent a considerable time at this point, and traced the recif twelve miles in a whale-boat, in the vain hope of discovering an opening through which one might get into safe water. Yet I would not say that an anchorage may not be found in the vicinity; in which case, or could a passage be effected through the reef, this place would be, from its central situation, more adapted than most others for a trading establishment.

From the part of the coast of which I am at present speaking, at some distance inland, two remarkable rocky mountains may be seen—the Cock's Comb to the south, and the Sugar Loaf* to the north. These names, given them by me, mark them out so distinctly, that the moment they are seen they must be recognized.

North of the recif just alluded to, the coast, assuming a bold outline, is very little varied by coves or embayments, and is pretty free from danger. The sea here, in some places dashing perpetually

---

* In my journey through western Damara Land I obtained a glimpse of these peaks on two or three different occasions.—*Author.*

against the base of the sand-hills, gives them the form of almost perpendicular cliffs. Close in-shore Captain Messum obtained no soundings with a hand-lead-line twenty fathoms long.

In lat. 19° 19′ S., the shore is fronted by a bar or recif, about a cable's length distant. Twelve miles farther north, 19° 7′ lat., a river is seen meandering through a low, sandy flat, which, as it appears to be a permanent stream,* may be a most important and interesting discovery. At its mouth Captain Messum observed a great deal of vegetation, and much drift-wood on the beach. He also hit upon a village of natives, who possessed a few goats. The black rocky mountain range already mentioned loses gradually at this spot its regularity, and at last strays and stumbles into the direst confusion. Another range, dividing the main chain, then runs off to the eastward, along the southern base of which the river, no doubt, finds its bed.

* When in the Ovambo country, Mr. Galton and I visited one day a kind of vley river—that is, a succession of vleys or pools—which the natives gave us to understand flowed westward. The Damaras also stated that a considerable running stream existed in those parts, but as their accounts were rather obscure and conflicting, we took no notice of them. There can not be much doubt, however, that the river discovered by Captain Messum is the one we saw, or some other not far off.

Since the discovery of Lake Onondova, I am rather inclined to think that the river seen by Captain Messum is a continuation of, or rather an outlet from the said lake, which is said to flow westward between the Ovambo and Ovagandjera country.

This range does not reappear again to the northward for a long time.

Six miles north of this locality is a remarkable headland, situated at the extremity of a low sandy point. Close to it, detached indeed from its side, is a large round block of granite (called by Captain Messum Fort Rock Point), which thus forms between the cape and the rock a considerable chasm. Round the sandy point is besides a cove, with a bar inclosing smooth water extending across its entrance. There is here every facility for landing with boats. Vessels may anchor, too, in five fathoms, bringing the rock to bear W.S.W., but, except in fine weather, it would be dangerous to do so. The place is particularly worthy of notice as well suited to the formation of a trading establishment or a missionary station. I do not mean to say that a better might not be found, though the good landing for boats and the fair roadstead for shipping it affords are great recommendations. About half a mile eastward of the cove we moreover saw reeds, and other evident indications that there is no lack of water in the neighborhood.

The natives here differ in some respects from the Berg Damaras of Cape Cross. They are not so dark colored as their compatriots in that country, but were similarly clad. Their huts were built in the conical style, and covered with the coarse grasses and reeds which grow abundantly in the vicinity. I observed much dried dog-fish, some made up into portable bundles, as if ready for transportation to some other place. It may possibly be that some larger village is situated higher up the bed of the river.

One mile and a half north of the Fort Rock Point is a shoal, but, the water inside appearing quite smooth, it may probably afford better anchorage than can be found immediately under the point. North of this shoal the shore is high, rugged, and not dangerous. The sand-hills here rise to a considerable height; that they, however, have no great depth, is shown by the black rock peering occasionally above their lower surfaces. Eight to ten miles inland, the range of the rocky mountains continues to run at a moderate elevation, N. by E., as far as lat. 18° 42′ S., where the low narrow foreshore begins to expand, leaving a space of about two miles between the beach and the sand-hills. Captain Messum again observed natives here, and a quantity of fish drying on stakes, but did not succeed in landing.

The coast-line northward is from this place quite uniform, until a point emerges about lat. 18° 27′ S., between which and Cape Frio it makes a half-moon sweep, forming a bay five miles or thereabouts round. "Under this point," says Captain Messum, "which I called False Cape Frio, temporary anchorage may be had in five fathoms of water and sandy bottom, by bringing the point to bear W.S.W. The shore here is low, a high block of rock, a detached mass from the main mountain range, forming its background."

Cape Frio is also a low sandy point, under the lee of which tolerable anchorage is to be had. We passed within half a mile of this headland, in from six and a half to nine fathoms of water, with a sandy bottom, the point bearing W.S.W. "This," continues Captain Messum, "is a most interesting locality, and would be a good place to land in order to explore the coast northward to the Nourse River. There is every appearance of water near the landing, and there is little doubt that natives reside in the neighborhood. I did not examine the spot so thoroughly as I should do on another occasion. I was anxious to ascertain whether an immediate disembarkation could be effected there, or at the River Nourse, knowing that, if not, Great Fish Bay (the southern part of which is nearer the river than Cape Frio) would at least afford me a safe harborage.

"Leaving Cape Frio, the coast runs nearly due north and south. When I passed it the weather was so hazy that the land in the background could not be distinguished. We coasted along within a mile to a mile and a half of the shore, and found the waters quite safe, excepting only where a small shoal patch, in latitude 17° 50' S., extends about half a mile from a low beach studded with rocks."

In lat. 17° 30' S. by account (and long. 11° 46')

Z

we came upon the mouth of the Cunenè River, probably the same as the Nourse.*

"This river (the Nourse) lies in a bight, and appears to flow into the sea through two rocky heads. Off the most southern of these is a reef extending several hundred yards to the westward, sheltering, it would seem, a landing-place, as the water inside was smooth quite up to the river. When I first saw the reef it was blowing a gale of wind, with a heavy sea on, so that the break occasionally stretched quite across to its northern head. Under these circumstances it would have been madness to attempt a landing, and we could see but a little way inland, for immense masses of sand, whirled about in eddies by the wind, filled the atmosphere, and hid all the features of the interior country; we observed, however, that the beach to the north was covered with large timber-trees, and noticed a palm-tree quite green, which could not have been many days in the water."

In a Lisbon paper (*Diario do Governo*) of March, 1855, appeared an account of an expedition to the Nourse, or Cunenè, undertaken by the Governor of Mossamedes, in order, it is to be presumed, to ascertain how far the descriptions of this river were

---

* The Nourse River was discovered by Captain Chapman, of the *Espiègle*, in 1824; it had then nine feet of water on the bar, and was described as navigable for small craft. Subsequent surveying expeditions under the *Leven* and *Barracouta* could, however, discern no traces of such a river.

true, and with the farther view, it is probable, of forming a settlement in its neighborhood. The article alluded to is headed *Relatorio da Viagem feita do Rio dos Eléphantes em Novembro de* 1854, and is, in substance, as follows:

"Having sailed in a schooner from Mossamedes, the governor and his party landed at Great Fish Bay, which struck them as the most dreary and desolate of scenes. Hence they traveled on foot along the beach until they arrived at the Cunenè, which they reached after two days' fatiguing march, without water. They found the mouth of the river entirely blocked up by sand. Some little way up its course, its right bank, they say, became rocky, and, after a while, so steep and rugged that the party could not proceed farther. The left bank, as far as they could see, consisted of a succession of sand-hills, and the stream itself is described as narrow and full of cataracts. They met no natives, but supposed the country might be inhabited a little higher up. Game, however, was abundant, more especially elephants; and on the return of the expedition to Mossamedes, elephant hunts to these regions were promptly got up by adventurous sportsmen."

"From the Nourse northward," says Captain Messum, in continuation, "the shore is fronted by a low sandy beach, at first narrow (about half a mile), but gradually widening until it reaches Great Fish Bay, where it is three or four miles in breadth.

The sand-hills at the back of this low fore-shore are about 500 feet high, and present as barren and desolate a prospect as any part of the coast. According to a rough calculation (presuming the Nourse River to be in lat. 17° 30′ S.), the distance between this stream and Great Fish Bay will be nearly forty miles by the coast.

"Great Fish Bay is formed by the Tiger peninsula, a long sandy tract of land, in no place ten feet above the level of the sea, and toward its southern extremity so narrow that the sea occasionally washes over it. The north end of the Tiger, which is somewhat broader, perhaps two miles, is placed in lat. 16° 30′ S., and long. 11° 41′ E. The anchorage we took up was, according to my observation, in lat. 16° 50′ S. This calculation will give the bay a length of about twenty-one miles. In many parts it is rocky; its head, approaching from the south, may be seen several miles off. The water on its eastern side washes the base of the sand-hills, and contains several fine mussel-beds.

"In the survey (made, I think, by Captain Owen) the bay is represented as perfectly safe; yet about ten miles south from the point is a shoal, on which we struck, and knocked off thirty feet of our false keel.

"Many of the coves and inlets on this coast possess the same features as that of Great Fish Bay. Thus Angras Juntas, Hottentot Bay, Sandwich Harbor, Walwich Bay, and Port Alexander, are protected by narrow banks of sand accumulated by the S.S.W. wind. This wind, taking the sand-hills at an angle, has leveled them into a low sandy beach, which has gradually been, by the same besoming, elongated to the northward. But these bays are slowly undergoing great alterations. Angras Juntas is already completely filled up, though the Portuguese still note it as a place of good anchorage. Sandwich Harbor is also wonderfully changed; while, with respect to Walwich Bay, its peninsular form and its southern part, as surveyed by Owen in 1826, are quite transformed. The latter, entirely filled in, has become a series of shoals that at low water are now dry, while Pelican Point has extended to the north, and is still extending farther in the same direction. Owen lays down deep water off this point, whereas there is now there but fifteen feet of water at most, hardly covering the break. Great Fish Bay has also undergone similar changes. Its southern extremity has evidently been blocked up, and many small bays are in this manner, from year to year, appearing and again disappearing along the coast."

From Great Fish Bay Captain Messum made an excursion inland, which he thus describes:

"Starting from the head of the bay, we traveled about ten miles E.S.E. over immense sand-hills and curiously formed ravines, when we came suddenly upon a native village, consisting of about fifty families of the finest-looking negroes I ever saw. Scarcely one of them was under six feet high, and such open and prepossessing countenances I had not before seen in Africa. The women, despite their color, were particularly good-looking, and, moreover, remarkably plump and well fed. Their language sounded very much like the Kafir spoken at Natal; yet I do not think they were of the same tribe as the negroes we afterward met at Port Alexander. We saw among them neither cattle nor goats. They seemed to live by hunting and fishing; at least the remains of numerous species of bucks and zebras, besides piles of large mussel-shells and fish-bones scattered about, appeared to indicate as much.

"During our visit to these interesting natives, a tall, athletic young fellow brought in a young buck. The weapon by which it had been killed, the one chiefly used by these wild huntsmen, appears to have been a very powerful bow, rather more than six feet long; the arrows belonging to it were beautifully made, and barbed, or, rather, tipped with iron. The assegais with which our new acquaintances were also armed were similar to those of the Kafirs. With respect to ornaments, so indispensable to savages, the chief woman, or matron of the family we visited, wore in her hair several buttons, and round her neck a Portuguese coin (a half millreis) and some beads. They had all on their arms and ankles copper rings, so bright, and in weight and color so much resembling gold, that,

GROUP OF NATIVES NEAR GREAT FISH BAY.

until tried with aqua fortis, they could not be discriminated from that valuable metal. To my surprise, they got their water exquisitely pure, but not very abundant, from out a solid granite rock. They received us at first very timidly, and must have been watching our approach for some time, as the women and children were all hidden, and the men repeatedly drew their fingers across their windpipes, as if to know whether we intended or not to cut their throats. Our guns especially frightened them; they would not touch any part of them; we therefore thought it advisable to pile arms under a rock. After that the women and children gradually made their appearance. The little ones would not allow us to touch them, but the grown women soon gained confidence, and began to examine our skins with the greatest curiosity. After remaining with these people about four hours, we resumed our journey E. S. E., or in the direction of a certain rocky mountain four or five miles ahead of us.

"Although there was not the slightest symptom of vegetation at the village where we had just stopped, we soon got among stunted brushwood, and the footmarks of game at once became abundant. We now lit a fire and endeavored to get a little rest, yet had to keep watch, for in all my travels, before or since, I never heard such doleful howls as the hyenas, who were prowling around us from the time we commenced our bivouac till just before daybreak, kept up all night. The next day, sloping our course more to the south in order to strike the Nourse River, the bush became thicker, and we saw in the distance numerous herds of springboks and gemsboks, so shy, however, that we could not get within range of them. On the evening of this day we reached the foot of a rather low chain of rocky mountains, running N.E. and S.W. Here we found water, but brackish. On the other side of this range we hoped to get sight of the river. By calculation we were now about twenty-five miles from the bay.

"The next day, traveling onward, we made a good progress, but saw not so much game as before, and found no water. The heat was intense. We had hitherto had a fine refreshing breeze, but there was not a breath of air now stirring, and the sand was so hot that it burnt our feet. Our sailors, four in number, began to give in. However, we continued to push on for another day, and toward evening had the satisfaction of seeing the Nourse. At the distance from which we caught sight of it, it appeared to be a considerable stream. But we could not get any positive knowledge on this point, for, having again failed in finding water on the road, and our cans being nearly exhausted, the men refused to proceed farther; we were obliged, consequently, to retrace our steps without delay.

"In this excursion and in subsequent rambles we met with the same kind of gum-tree as we had noticed at Ichaboe, and with nara fruit in abundance.* We saw also the natives grind a small seed, something like that given to Canary-birds (probably the grass-seed alluded to in a foot-note in page 5), between stones, and afterward make it into a paste mixed with honey. They had, too, a vegetable like a small cucumber in appearance, but not in taste. The vessels in which they carried their water, etc., were made exactly like those of the Zulus of Natal, but the workmanship of these vessels was much superior to that of the Natalists. We noticed, likewise, baskets of honeycomb and innumerable bees. We did not see a single tree, not even a bush, above three or four feet high. This led me to conjecture that the Nourse River, which brings down the large trees we saw on the beach, must have a considerable course, winding, according to our observation, to E.N.E.

"From the time we left the village already spoken of till we returned to the vessel we did not see a single human being. We had been absent ten days, and during that interval had probably walked considerably above one hundred miles, though, in a straight line, perhaps not the half of that distance. Yet this is farther, I believe, than any white man

---

* In "Lake Ngami" I have stated that the nara was pretty much confined to the neighborhood of Walwich Bay; but, according to Captain Messum, it would seem that it is to be found along the west coast, though certainly not in any great abundance.

has penetrated in that direction—at least was at the time of my incursion.

"I tried to prevail on some of the natives to come on board with me; they all refused except one young man, who was willing enough had he not been held back by his parents—in fact, by the whole village. From this I conjectured that these people had heard of, or perhaps had some experience in, the Portuguese system of slave-trading."

But to proceed. Captain Messum describes the line of coast between Great Fish Bay and Port Alexander as so free from danger as to allow a vessel to approach it within half a mile. One small indentation is alone to be found between the places just named. A river, however (Bembarougi), of which the captain could find no trace, is laid down here in some maps. He is inclined to believe, nevertheless, from observing a good deal of vegetation scattered about in a ravine, that a water-course may at times run through the country.

On arriving at Port Alexander, this persevering navigator again made an excursion into the interior, the result of which he thus briefly relates:

"Having anchored late in the afternoon, we did not land till the following morning. During the night the natives had evidently been reconnoitring the vessel; of this fact their numerous footprints in the sand left no doubt. We did not suffer them, however, to delay us, but started immediately in a northern direction. We had not journeyed far when we came upon a party of fishermen paddling about near the shore. This was the first time, from Port Natal completely round Southern Africa, that we had seen the natives attempting any thing like navigation. The craft in which they were now embarked (catamarans) consisted of pieces of wood fastened together, about six feet broad and twelve long. We distributed some snuff among them, gave them a whiff or two from our pipes, and they provided us with two young fellows to act as guides.

"Passing over the bluff which forms the eastern head of the bay, we arrived at the dry bed of the River Flamingos, and, ascending its course about five miles, came to a native village. Here I was delighted at finding, for the first time since I had left the Cape, something like real vegetation. The natives of this place cultivated gardens, which produced maize, calabashes, pumpkins, etc. We saw, likewise, frequent herds of cattle, looking in excellent condition; and the farther we proceeded up the exhausted water-course, the more numerous the villages became. The huts of which they consisted seemed built, too, for permanence, and were very comfortable dwellings. It was pleasant, after toiling through so much sand, to sit down at last under the refreshing shade of the palm-tree. We remained three days in this locality, in order to enjoy ourselves and to take notes of every thing noteworthy.

"Besides large herds of cattle, the natives here possessed elephant and hippopotami ivory, whence obtained I could not ascertain. I saw also knobkieries, made from rhinoceroses' horn, and honey and beeswax in great abundance.

"It was evident, however, that we had not the confidence of the poor savages; they approached us with the greatest timidity, and would not allow their women and children to come near us. On one occasion, when we were examining some cattle, the herd were driven away in great haste. They would not let us either sleep in their huts; we had to 'bunk' it out on the sand, while they kept an anxious watch over us all night. They gave us, nevertheless, all we wanted, and asked for no payment. We feasted at their expense sumptuously on milk, maize, and 'balls' of unknown ingredients, compounded with honey. We gained, however, in some degree, the confidence of our guides, who consented to come on board with us. Great was their surprise when there at seeing their faces reflected in a looking-glass; and the cat coming into the cabin sent them on deck precipitately. They asked for *aguadente*, but, after tasting, would not drink it. They often made motions, indicating their fear that we were going to cut their throats and eat them; while the knives laid out for dinner made them tremble so much that I had to remove these suspicious-looking implements from the table. They would not sleep below, but remained awake on deck all night. In the morning we sent the poor creatures away, rigged out in shirt and trowsers, with other presents too, to them of inestimable value. We gave them also some copper pieces, with the name of the vessel and the date of our visit stamped on them. They had never before, I suspect, been so courteously treated by white men.

"On the northern side of the River Flamingos, on the summit of a high table-land of about from 500 to 600 feet above the level of the sea, I gathered some beautiful fossils, exactly, to all appearance, in the same state as when they were originally submerged; that is, the different strata in which they were imbedded seemed to have just arisen out of the ocean. A very fine collection of these fossils was afterward lost with the vessel; but Mr. Wilson, of Cape Town, is still in possession of some given him by me."

Captain Messum's exploration of the coast extended as far as Benguela; to follow him farther, however, would be to transgress the limits of this work. The gallant captain thus sums up the result of his voyage:

"I had now examined well-nigh every part of the coast, every islet, every creek, from Walwich Bay to Benguela, and had not found what I was in search of, namely, guano, or nitrate of soda. Pelican Point seems to be the extreme northern haunt of the penguin (the principal depositor of guano), the gannet, and the shag; but Hollam's Bird Isle is the chief rookery, toward the north, of these birds. Round the different bays, it is true, there were numerous flamingoes and pelicans, but these wild fowls, we know, never congregate in sufficient numbers to form large deposits.

"I do not say that nitrate of soda does not exist in this region, but only that I did not find any, though I traversed salt plains, not a few of many miles in extent. Words can hardly describe the suffering such traveling occasions. Every step one takes plunges one ankle-deep into a saline crust of several inches in depth; then the tropical sun, without a cloud, blazing on the white surface of the salt plain—how painful to the eyes! Imagine, farther, an atmosphere broiling hot, the thermometer standing frequently at 100° to 110°, and even 120°. Add to this a burden of provisions and ammunition, forty or fifty pounds' weight, carried by each man, and you may understand the truth of the saying, that, to travel in Africa, one should have the endurance of a camel and the courage of a lion."

In concluding his remarks on the west coast, Captain Messum thus writes:

"If asked my opinion as to the best landing-place for a start on an exploring expedition into the interior, I should have no hesitation in saying at once Port Alexander; albeit the Portuguese here are, I shrewdly suspect, trying on the slave-trade, which they can do with all the greater facility as the very existence of the port is unknown to the inhabitants of Messambedos (Little Fish Bay), in the neighborhood. There has been much talk, too, about establishing a factory here; yet, when I spoke to the Portuguese governor on the subject, he told me he should discountenance any such project unless it had the sanction of his government.

The Portuguese settlements extend on this coast to the south as far as Cape Negro, on the southern side of the River Flamingos.

Annoyances from these settlements might, it is true, deduct a good deal from the advantages Port Alexander would otherwise offer. If so, I should then recommend Cape Frio, or some spot a little south of it. Natives of a very docile character are permanently settled in this place, and a little kindness could not fail to gain their confidence. Ride and pack oxen, too, may be obtained there, while water is abundant, and the country to all appearance accessible.

Could, indeed, any harbor be found between the 21° and 20° 39′ S. parallels of S. lat., the situation of Cape Frio would combine all advantages—a central position, native inhabitants, and security against all interference on the part of the Portuguese.

The Nourse River is no doubt also a promising point for explorers to commence operations. I am strongly of opinion that a fair landing is to be found close to its mouth; and, should the stream be at all navigable, even of ever so light a draught, how easy access to the interior would be!

A A

With a few general remarks, more or less applicable to the whole shore-line, I shall now conclude my description of the west coast of Africa.

This extensive coast is singularly deficient in navigable rivers, sheltered bays, and safe harbors. Many, indeed, of the rivers so called, which intersect it, are merely periodical torrents, having, during the rainy season, strong rapid currents, but leaving, on the approach of summer, their deep sunken beds almost completely dry. The rivulets, too, supplied by the mountain springs, scarcely escape from their lofty sources ere they are either absorbed by the thirsty earth, or evaporated by the heated air. Even the permanent rivers, some of which contain sufficient water for the navigation of small craft for several miles up the country, are all, more or less, rendered inaccessible by bars across their mouths.

The whole littoral portion of Southern Africa, from the Cape of Good Hope to Walwich Bay, presents one wearisome picture of bleak, barren rocks or arid sand-hills. Vegetation is everywhere extremely scanty; here and there may be seen a few stunted bushes, about two feet high, a few geraniums, and one or two kinds of gum plants, all of a sickly, grayish-green color; add a few species of wiry grasses growing among the sand, and you have the whole vegetable product of this coast. The desolation of the scene is completed by a turbulent surf beating against the shore with a terribly monotonous constancy.

The prevailing winds at the Cape are S.E. and N.W.; the latter blows in hurricanes, and generally brings on foul weather. The other wind, which, from the peculiar formation of the mountains on either side of the so-called Cape flats, rushes through from the S.E., instantly takes the direction of the line of coast, but is never met with after passing a little to the northward of Table Bay. Yet, as I have already said when speaking of Namaqua Land, this wind is not, during the cold season, uncommon in the interior, and when it does blow the whole atmosphere is at once changed, the air becomes insufferably hot, and respiration is so impeded that one pants instead of breathing freely.

The prevailing local wind, extending from sixty to two hundred miles from the shore, along the whole length of this coast, is from S. by W. to S.W. by S. Indeed, the south wind, varying considerably, of course, in strength, blows for about nine months in the year. During this time the sky overhead is clear and cloudless, though the horizon, with a space of from fifteen to twenty degrees above it, is often enveloped in so deep a haze that the land from seaward is completely hidden, and the approach to the coast thus rendered extremely difficult and dangerous. The sound—ay, even the sight of the surf, is generally the first intimation seamen have of their vessel's proximity to the land. During the remaining three months of the year the sea is often calm, or light breezes prevail from the

N.N.W. These northerly winds are generally accompanied by dense and very damp fogs.

In the summer season, when the weather is calm and the sky without a cloud, the sun is very powerful; but, generally speaking, and more especially during the prevalence of the southerly winds, the temperature is very low. Thick woolen clothing is even necessary, for the wind is at times so keen as to peel off the skin of the face, and to make the lips sore. The temperature never varies much, averaging during the year in the shade 50° to 60°.

On all this coast it rarely or never rains. The dews, however, during the nights, are heavy, and the thick fogs in the winter season saturate every thing with moisture. After one of these fogs water will frequently drip from the riggings of vessels almost by pailfuls.

CHAPTER XXVIII.

A Contrast.—Discouragement with respect to Settlement in one Part of Africa counterbalanced by the Encouragement it meets with at 250 miles from Table Bay.—Establishment on the River Knysna.—Dangerous Entrance to the Harbor. —A tremendous Surf.—Perils incurred in getting into safe Water.—Description.—Fine Scenery.—A fatal Act of Daring.—A noble and diversified Prospect.—Delicious Climate. —Description of Landscape.—Salt Marshes.—Government Dock-yard.—A Night Scene.—European Visitors.—An English Gentleman-Farmer.—Plattenburg's Bay.—Forest Scenery.—Birds of gorgeous Plumage not Vocalists.—General Prospects of the Settlement.

DISCOURAGING as the survey of the S. W. coast of Africa, with a view to the formation of settlements in that part of the world, may appear in the preceding chapters, yet discouragements as great as those pointed out have been, in the accomplishment of a like object, already in that country overcome, and may be again. I allude particularly in this remark to the original Dutch establishment on the River Knysna, about two hundred and fifty miles eastward of Table Bay. This place, which some time ago attracted much attention, was visited a few years back, merely as a traveler, by Captain W.; and as the account he gives of it very much resembles in some respects the pictures we have just sketched, while in others it offers a complete contrast to them—a hopeful one, nevertheless—I will conclude the coasting part of my subject by placing the captain's narrative, very slightly modified and abridged, before my readers. It will be pleasant to avert one's eyes for a while from savage sterility to behold the desert "blossoming as a rose," *i. e.*, barbarism yielding its place to civilization, though not, alas! by the improvement, but by the expulsion or extinction of barbarians.

"Proceeding," says our traveler, "from Port Elizabeth (Algoa Bay) to Cape Town, we had occasion to touch at the Knysna. After beating on and off for nearly a week to discover the entrance, we at length perceived the pilot's signal, which was any thing but favorable to our enterprise. We had been previously informed that it was customary to hoist a *red flag* upon the pilot's tower, which is erected on the east cliff at this notable entrance, at periods of danger; and lo! the discouraging signal; but, notwithstanding this serious obstacle to our wishes, we had the temerity to risk all hazards, and to steer direct to port. Our captain was doubtless an excellent seaman, and we fully confided in his skill; he pleaded the hour of the day and a fair wind, which was most essential, in order to justify his neglect of the pilot's signal. We neared, therefore, the coast, and it became evident that the entrance was rather narrow—in truth, a mere rent in the cliff, effected by some sudden convulsion and subsidence of the intermediate rocks; but of this I could obtain no information, as there is no existing record of the catastrophe. Our attention was arrested by a glimpse of the picturesque interior; and, nothing daunted from the confidence which we derived from the calm bearing of the crew, I devoted myself to making a drawing of the object before me—the entrance of the Knysna, with mountain scenery in the background. It was impossible to look around without feelings of awe and admiration; the whole line of coast eastward and westward was literally fringed with huge broken masses of rock, over which was breaking a tremendous spray. We could descry a species of 'Scylla and Charybdis,' on either side whirling and bellowing with convulsive shocks; now emerging from the foam, and presenting a bare, black, broken surface, which fancy might depict a many-headed hydra form; then, drinking up the coming sea, it would vomit forth the frothy spume into a thousand fantastical cascades, shedding the prismatic colors of the iris. 'If the wind slackened now,' said the captain, 'we should fall an easy prey to one or other of these monsters.' A heavy swell of the sea appeared now to raise us nearly perpendicular, and suddenly precipitated us forward with fearful velocity to the critical point of the navigation. Every thing previously had appeared to harmonize with our wishes. 'Steady!' was the word, and 'port! port!' oft repeated. At length the captain took the helm; all the hands were in a bustle, and looked anxious. 'Now, my lads, hold on,' was loudly vociferated; the vessel trembled under our feet. I looked anxiously abaft; a sudden shock threw most of us along the deck, when I beheld with terror an appalling sea spreading the whole length of this celebrated entrance, full half a mile, now lifting up its head close to our stern, and mantling with rage that we had escaped, and beginning to curl upon us its mighty volume, as if it would ingulf the vessel. A momentary thrill of horror seemed to paralyze all on board; we felt the final shock of its rage in safety; it fell powerless in our rear, and with one deep, long sweep, at least a quarter of a mile, which seemed to reach the very bottom, propelled us securely over the bar. 'All's well! Steady, my lads! port! port!' was hastily said as we dashed into the rapids of conflicting currents, occasioned by the tide now settling outward with race-horse speed through the contracted passage. Being fairly entered, we perceived the pilot anxiously awaiting us, and motioning with his flag, endeavoring to direct us through the intricacies of this mazy and eddying gorge. This we effected with admirable precision, and swiftly passing on to a considerable distance, we at once glided into a smooth, tranquil, mirror-like basin, aptly and comprehensively termed the sailor's 'Feather-bed Bay.' In our precipitate passage, every object appeared 'magically' to run past us, as we almost brushed the branches of the flowing foliage of this delightful fairy region.

"We had leisure now to look about us, and to reflect upon the dangers we had so suddenly and recently passed. At this moment the pilot boarded us, and angrily remonstrated with the captain for his folly and temerity in disregarding his signal of *dangerous;* adding, 'You have risked the lives of your passengers as well as the property of the owners; but I suppose you are pretty highly insured!' Assuredly, if the last sea had broken upon the vessel, she might have foundered at once, or, at any rate, have swept us all overboard. We shuddered at the incautious manner in which we had been left to our own discretion; we ought to have been lashed to the bulkheads for security. The pilot added that he had nearly lost four of his best hands (those who now manned his boat) by similar daring. They had shipped a sea upon the bar, and were clean precipitated into the eddy, when, fortunately for them, another sea safely lodged them all on deck again; a fact which the men themselves afterward confirmed to us. The captain, to justify himself, said that, perceiving our self-possession, he was fearful of unnerving us by too much parade of caution, although he well knew we were likely to get a ducking; and, truly enough, the last fearful breaker had given us ample proof of his discernment by a most copious shower of spray, which drenched us to the skin. It is not unusual, in such dangerous and critical moments, for seamen to affect show of hardihood and misapplied courage. We were informed that a short time after the pilot had been appointed to this station, three or four persons connected with the naval establishment determined to try their powers in stemming the current without the bar, when the tide was setting out with all its velocity. They had been cautioned not to hazard their lives in such a useless and foolhardy experiment; but, strong in their own opinion, advice was fruitless. They manned their boat, and proceeded to the current, which speedily put the metal of these brave fellows to the test, who, when it was too late, discovered that they had been over-presumptuous. All human effort proved unavailing and ineffectual against the potent stream; the conflicting currents baffled their endeavors, and fear and remorse overwhelmed them in the vortex of destruction. Their distress was but too evident; their uplifted hands spoke their hearts' grief and despair; they were beyond the reach of human aid, and their agonized screams were mocked in the turmoil and unceasing din of roaring billows. The boat was soon carried aloft amid the breakers; it soon after appeared at a considerable distance from the land, like a speck upon the ocean, and, melancholy to relate, these courageous and once useful members of society were, in the prime of life, hurried away by their precipitate bravado into a lingering and horrible death—carried out to sea, without the smallest provision, and never heard of more.

"But, notwithstanding all that has been said of the narrow entrance, the iron-bound coast, the rocky obstructions, and the mighty surge which beset this river, there is no doubt that, by duly attending to the instructions and signals of the pilot, the navigation of the Knysna may be as readily and safely effected as that of any other barred river. A delightful tranquillity succeeded the excited feelings which such perilous encounters as we had passed through seldom fail to produce. We had now a noble and diversified prospect before us, and therefore an ample field for inquiry and contemplation. Like the still waters of the Cumberland lakes, the distant hills and surrounding woods gave deep interest to this novel scene; every object before us was faithfully reflected in the placid bosom of the liquid mirror, and we continued to glide along its smooth surface for a mile and a half, when the rattling cable gave notice that we were soon to be transferred to *terra firma*, a change to which we looked forward with considerable impatience, and which we found, as soon as we pitched our tents on shore, really delightful. . . . .

"We will now take a peep outside: the delicious climate invites us to enjoy every moment that remains of daylight, and we have a magnificent panorama to inspect. Yonder, to the south, stand two pyramidal rocks of granite, faithful sentinels at the mouth of the Knysna. The westward heights are fringed with splendid foliage, descending to the margin of the stream. Eastward, the pilot's tower betokens the care which the Admiralty takes in giving security and confidence to those who live on 'the profound deep.' Its site is well chosen, upon a lofty promontory, and may be seen at twenty miles distance. How highly picturesque are the sides of its elevation, covered with every variety of evergreen shrubs, spangled with blossoms of every hue, and fragrant as beautiful! Huge masses of rocks intersperse the shrubbery, and these of various romantic shapes, some with well-formed arches, Oriental, Gothic, and Roman; others, deeply caverned, reiterating, with thundering yells, the stunning sound of never-ceasing breakers, appear the abode of the Furies, and, foaming with ire, forbid approach or investigation.

"The pilot's house, at the foot of the eastern heights, to which access is given by a zigzag foot-path, next commands attention. Its position is pretty well sheltered, having a 'stoop' before it, *i. e.*, a raised terrace-walk, that affords a pleasant lounge for the enjoyment of a cigar. Adjoining is a boat-house and sheds, well supplied with grappling-irons, cordage, spars, and fishing-tackle. But what is that great bulk which encumbers the view in front of the dwelling? Alas! the remains of the first vessel that dared encounter this navigation —the 'Emu.' The Emu rocks were pointed out to us just as we entered, juttting into the channel, nearly under the pilot's tower. To avoid these wreckers large posts are fixed upon the heights above, which mark the proper bearing to escape all danger, so that what was once truly difficult and hazardous is now rendered easily accessible and perfectly free from danger.

"The salt marshes which form the great basin are altogether very extensive, and cover many thousand acres. They are occasionally flooded, and then we have a noble expanse of inland water, as fine as any of the most celebrated lakes of Europe for picturesque beauty, though not, perhaps, of so great extent. On the west bank of the river we perceive a farm, under Dutch cultivation, the possession of Mynheer Barret, whose flocks and herds browse as far as the western cliffs. On the opposite bank, beyond the marshes, is Milk Kraal Farm, with the modest but comfortable residence of George Rex, Esq., an English gentleman; and on the north of our marquee is the government dock-yard, with sheds, mould-lofts, other buildings, and the residence of the master-builder.

"Beyond these several objects rose an undulating background, studded with forest-trees, natural plots of flowering shrubs, an infinite variety of evergreens, rare plants, and singular-looking grasses, large plots of wild geraniums, and heaths of a thousand species, winding round the extensive basin, and traversing the banks of the river far away, even to the distance of the Uitenbegtta range of mountains, and possessing numerous localities of great beauty and interest, which a transitory visit to Knysna could not afford an opportunity to inspect, much less to describe with justice. Suffice it, therefore, to say, that this is the most park-like and beautiful district which I have visited in South Africa.

"We had lovely weather, and the soft, refreshing air whispered the near closing of a day never to be forgotten. The long, distant shadows of the hills now approached us, and spread their gray mantle over the valley; white fleecy vapors flitted across the bosoms of the distant hills, and almost sudden night involved us in darkness. Pending our brief daylight, we had the good fortune to get our stores and boxes on shore, while abundance of provisions poured in upon us from all quarters. We here found every thing we could wish—wood, water, and stock of various kinds—so wonderfully do supplies generally exceed the demand. We had blazing fires between the river and our marquee, and they were soon put in request by all our followers. The glaring ruddy light, and the busy spectacle of numerous persons quickly passing to and fro, was a singular contrast to the calm scene we had so recently witnessed. This, again, soon gave place to silence—all hands had reveled and dispersed. The stars twinkled in their spheres; the crickets and the hosts of the marshes sent forth their sonorous and incessant din to lull us into sleep. But soft! we hear sounds which 'murder sleep,' and restlessness appears in every animal around us. My horse and my goat had been made fast near the entrance of my marquee, and their anxiety and instinctive watchfulness was but too apparent. I cautiously looked out, and numerous eyes glistened on every side, while streams of phosphoric sparks swept over our roof and almost brushed my face. These I had happily seen before. The little fire-fly was a familiar visitant, and harmless; but how shall I secure my poor horse and goats if they are attacked? thought I. There was danger in the attempt to save them. We could form no resolution, and therefore, as usual (after the precaution of increasing the number of our lights, and making as many shadows as possible), resigned ourselves to the guardianship of the All-merciful for the night. Our rest was frequently disturbed with woo—woo —woo, as the thousand wolves grew bolder, and my horse plunged so dreadfully at times that we feared our walls would give way. Daylight, however, and the 'Yo, heave ho!' of the sailors sent these voracious neighbors bootless home to their fastnesses.

"The morning ushered in a host of visitors to our marquee of every grade, chiefly Dutchmen, in the hope of purchasing stores. Fire-arms, gunpowder, tea, groceries, and hardware were chiefly in request; but of these I had previously disposed of all that I could spare, which caused great disappointment. All these visitors were remarkably frank, civil, and familiar, freely partook of our fare, and politely praised every thing they beheld. But these boors (improperly so called) were in truth remarkably *courteous*, inviting us to their homes, and offering to send wagons for us. With these Mynheers it was all 'mocy,' 'plenty,' and 'pretty,' 'mocy frow,' 'mocy kent,' 'mocy picanni'—'plenty pretty,' 'pretty fine,' 'plenty funny.' After satisfying their curiosity, they civilly withdrew, apparently well pleased with their reception, for they repeated their visit every morning during our stay. . . . .

"After the departure of the last visitor our attention was arrested by the cry of 'A sail! a sail!' We hastened to an elevated spot, and had the satisfaction of seeing the 'Durham' enter, with a press of sail, in capital style. She had the tide in her favor, and the pilot had boarded her outside the bar, giving us a fine elucidation of the safe and easy navigation of the entrance.

"And whence comes yon cavalcade of white mettled palfreys, mounted by ladies of no common bearing, habited in Parisian costume, and attended by servants carrying green gauze flap-flies to catch the papillons? A tall, genteel young man now directs his way to us, bearing a pretty native basket: he will inform us. It proved to be a basket of delicious fruit, which the proprietor of the Milk Kraal Farm had kindly sent us by his son, with an invitation to visit him. The gentleman, after delivering his message, rejoined his sisters. It was gratifying to become acquainted with him, and he was afterward our frequent guest and companion. As our sojourn in this blissful vale must necessarily be short, we had determined to make good use of our time, and I had arranged my plans, which I carried the next morning into execution, for a trip through the forest to Plattenburg's Bay.

"The country which on this expedition we passed through was every where delightful as far as the eye could reach; and the deep, green woods, with their fine umbrageous foliage, gave us a grateful shelter from the heat of the sun, which, as the day advanced, began to be oppressive. Nothing could be more striking than the stateliness of the trees, most of which were flowering evergreens, presenting to our view a great variety of beautiful pendent bunches of flowers of all colors—blue, white, scarlet, and yellow—yielding at the same time a most delicate fragrance, while the ground beneath was studded and enameled with a multiplicity of curious wax-like little stars, daisies, and harebells. The road was well defined, and nearly straight for a considerable distance, having very much the appearance of a nobleman's park. It was in this secluded spot, but a few years ago, that the Caffres committed fearful ravages and murders. After passing through the forest we soon obtained a fine view of Plattenburg's Bay, which, being distant from Knysna about fifteen miles, we reached in two hours and a half. Here we observed the extensive ruins of a considerable range of warehouses, the original depôt of the Dutch East India Company; and having made the circuit of the bay, which has a fine roadstead for shipping, we retraced our road home, which we reached soon after sunset, being highly satisfied with our excursion.

"We felt it our duty to acknowledge the generous present of George Rex, Esq., the gentleman who had deputed his son to visit us, by paying him a visit in return. He is an English farmer on a large scale; his vineyards, tobacco-plots, and fields of wheat and pulse all bore testimony to a neat and clean system of agriculture; in fact, the whole establishment gave evident tokens that every thing was under the direction and guidance of an active and cultivated mind, while his numerous family spoke of a state of filial and fraternal affection, excellent social discipline, and refinement of manners rarely to be met with in places so far removed from the thoroughfares, or even by-ways of civilization. We had passed several very pleasant days in making short excursions into the neighborhood, when the skipper announced that he had completed his cargo, and that his intention was to put to sea on the following morning. We therefore soon dispatched matters for striking our marquee and our tents, which, with our luggage, were soon put on board. We embarked before sunset on Christmas Eve, taking a last farewell of a scene which has left an indelible impression on our hearts and minds. The river, which forms its chief feature, of great beauty, though not of great extent, is calculated to be of vast importance to future generations in a commercial point of view; it abounds with a great variety of delicious fish, particularly the mullet; here, too, the paper nautilus has a safe retreat, yielding specimens of the largest and most beautiful kind any where to be met with; nor can I forget the feathered tribe, which impart additional interest to the groves. Without pretending to describe the different species, I will merely intimate that I have seen examples of the most rare and curious formation and habits, and others of the most gorgeous plumage, but no vocalists. In this respect the woods are mute, except from the singular and dolorous bird which distinctly and continually breaks the dull monotony with his loud cry of 'fifty dollars,' and is hence called the fifty-dollar bird! With respect to the wild animals, and multitudes of pernicious reptiles, they are known to swarm in South Africa, and require no place in this brief memoir."

CHAPTER XXIX.

The Guano Trade.—When Guano was first used in Agriculture.—Its Discovery in Africa.—The Island of Ichaboe: its Anchorage; its Rollers.—The Treasures of Ichaboe made known by Mr. Livingstone.—First Attempt to reach the Island a Failure; a second succeeds.—Vessels arrive in Numbers.—Immense Deposits of Guano.—The Penguin.—The Penguin's Lament.—Stages for loading Vessels.—The "Flying Railway."—Committee of Safety.—The Guano Pits.—Squabbles among the Captains and others.—The Guano Fever versified.—The Island is properly divided.—Ichaboe presents an animated Scene.—Bad Doings on the Island.—Sir John Marshall.—The Guano Pits exhausted.—Concluding Remarks.

In my description of the west coast of Africa, its rivers, harbors, bays, etc., allusion has been frequently made to guano, and to the trade in that article, carried on some years ago on so large a scale, and even yet not quite extinct. Before, however, I speak of this trade, it may be well to say a word of the manure itself.

Guano, or *huano*, as it is also spelt in Spanish (either letter being used at the discretion of the writer), is, it is said, a Spanish name; but, whether Spanish or Peruvian originally, it is now, by adoption, a good English word.

As a manure, this ordure has been known and used in Peru from the date of the earliest records

of that country—
to any written hi
teemed in ancient
made its removal fr
of its depositors, wit
ishable by death. Ha
appreciated so long, it
was only yesterday we he
agricultural virtues in Europ
of the Spanish government, wh
ascendant in South America, and
olutions — almost prohibitive of co
which it has since been exposed, may par
haps, account for this. However that may be, it
is certain that the credit of the first introduction
of guano into England is due to a French gentleman named Baopoillet, and to Mr. Bland, a partner in the firm of Meyers, Bland, and Co., of Valparaiso. These gentlemen sent several cargoes of this manure to England in 1839 and 1840. They had at first much difficulty in overcoming the prejudices of agriculturists against any thing new. The intrinsic value, nevertheless, of the importation soon overcame all opposition; and shortly after, an English mercantile house, in connection with the gentleman just named, obtained the exclusive privilege of shipping the precious ordure from the coast of Peru and Bolivia—a reward well merited by the enterprising perseverance of Messrs. Baopoillet and Bland.

...rs becoming speedable properties of ...es of this valuable ... Pacific Ocean were ..t, and the world was search of other deposits. ...coast of Africa, hitherto ...pt to the whaler and the sealarly visited with this object in ... not in vain.

...of guano on this coast, just then a ...one created, when first known, from ...many commercial resources it offered, quite a sensation in England. It opened to our agriculturists a sure means of relief from circumstances ...h had depressed them to the lowest point, and ... the same time, an impetus to our mercantile ...ne, never before reduced to so lamentable a state of stagnation as at that period. A vast number of vessels now found employment in the guano trade, and freightage all over the world was thereby greatly improved.

At first, it is true, mercantile men were slow to credit the good news; but after a while their doubts disappeared, and whole fleets, instead of single vessels as at first, were dispatched to the land of promise. Many individuals, possessed with the conviction that Ichaboe would prove a second El Dorado, embarked the whole of their fortunes in one venture to that island. Some of them certainly acquired great wealth, but others, it is to be feared, suffered very heavy losses.

Though guano was imported from several of the rocky islets bordering on the western coast of South Africa—namely, from those at the mouth of Angra Pequena harbor, from Mercury, Hollam's Bird, etc.—it was chiefly from Ichaboe, situated in lat. 26° 18′ S., and long. 14° 58′ E., that the bulk of this valuable deposit was obtained; and it is therefore more especially of the guano trade in that island that I am now about to speak.

Ichaboe, a rock thrown up, no doubt, by a volcano, is about three quarters of a mile in circumference, and at its highest point not more than thirty feet above the level of the sea. It is surrounded to the N. and S.W. by outlying rocks, extending in some places as far as a quarter of a mile from the shore, and is distant three quarters of a mile or so from the opposite main land, that is, five miles or thereabouts from the outer part of a dangerous reef, off a tongue of land to the S.E. of the island. This reef, many parts of which are under water, and not to be discerned when the sea is smooth, is very extensive and very dangerous. There is, it is true, a narrow channel through it, but it is an extremely perilous one, never resorted to, except from necessity, by vessels unacquainted with the safer passage.

Ichaboe has no harbor whatever; even the anchorage, embracing the whole space between the island and the main land, is greatly exposed. The depth of its water varies from three to nine fathoms, and the rise and fall of the sea at spring tides is not above six feet. The bottom is throughout rocky, uneven, and covered with kelp. The holding for anchors is therefore decidedly bad; two, indeed, are generally required, with an ample scope of chain to enable vessels to ride with any thing like safety in strong southerly winds. This extra length of chain often caused serious damage to the guano fleets, more especially at a sudden shift of wind. The vessels would then swing round, and, before the chains could be hoved in, or the ropes got out to steady them, would dash against each other, and, being pitched about by a constant heavy swell, do one another much injury. On one night, for instance, in the month of October, 1844, fourteen vessels, from the cause I have just mentioned, lost bowsprits, one or two became partially dismasted, and two were so much damaged that they were condemned immediately afterward as unseaworthy. A very great number of anchors and chains, moreover, have, from their forelocks and pins coming out of them, been lost at various times off Ichaboe. This has been by some attributed to a peculiarity in the water, causing oxydation in an extraordinary degree, and so loosening the jointures and fastenings of iron-work. It is, however, much more probable that the losses I allude to were occasioned by the forelocks breaking, or the pins working out, from the constant friction of the chains against a rocky sea bottom. There was no instance, nevertheless, of a chain becoming unshackled when its pins were made of wood, well and carefully driven in.

The proper entrance to Ichaboe anchorage is from the southward, where there is plenty of water, and the channel is wide and safe. The opposite entrance is, on the contrary, very narrow, and the water insufficient for any deeply-laden craft. Many ships have struck in going out; and all over the northern part of the anchorage rocks have been discovered by vessels unexpectedly striking on them.

To add to the dangers and discomforts of a bad anchorage, the enormous rollers, so often described by parties visiting St. Helena and Ascension Island, are also prevalent here, and often assail the coast with great violence during a calm. "One fine afternoon, for instance, when the guano fleet was lying at anchor, the water quite smooth, and the boats busily loading at the stages, a heavy sea came rolling in, which swamped, in a few minutes, six boats, and seriously injured several of their crews. These rollers, huge sea mountains, gathering volume in their advance, and tumbling in, one after another—their crests broken into white foaming masses of water—formed an awfully grand spectacle. One might expect—though the cause of the phenomenon is as yet quite unexplained—incursions from these monstrous columns of billows at any change of, or at the full of the moon, when, sweeping every thing before them, they would, on reaching the beach, expend their fury in a noise like thunder, and, breaking up, spread over many a furlong of sand and rock, out of the reach of the regular tides. These formidable rollers are always heaviest across the northern entrance to the anchorage, where the water is shallow. Many vessels, anchoring too much in that direction within their sweep, have been greatly damaged; and one, the 'Guernsey Lily,' was in 1845, when freighted and ready for sea, unfortunately driven on shore. At the times when the rollers set in, there is no perceptible change in the barometer, nor any unusual appearance in the sky; the weather continues entirely the same as before—that is, a heavy, thick, and almost impervious haze hangs over the horizon, as it does nearly all the year round."

The existence of guano on the African coast was first brought to the knowledge of British merchants and ship-owners by Mr. Andrew Livingstone, of Liverpool, a gentleman well known to the nautical world. He got all he knew about Ichaboe from the work of Captain Morrell, of whom mention has been already frequently made.

At first, however, Mr. Livingstone endeavored in vain to get a well-known firm in Liverpool to send out vessels to Ichaboe; they did not even believe in the existence of the island; and some considerable time elapsed before other parties were induced to send out to that place a small schooner of their own, with two equally small chartered vessels. These ships sailed with sealed orders; one of them returned without attempting to find Ichaboe; but the schooner arrived at Angra Pequena, and came to an anchor in the outer roads. From this point she was driven to sea by a strong S.S.W. wind, evidently in consequence of those on board not knowing the anchorage-ground, though an excellent Admiralty chart of it exists. The vessel drove to leeward so far that, on standing in to the land, she only fetched Hottentot Bay, at about twelve miles to the northward of Ichaboe. From this bay the master of the schooner pulled up to Ichaboe in a small jolly-boat, and succeeded in landing (at least so says the schooner's log-book), though he nearly knocked his boat to pieces in the surf. On returning to the schooner, it was discovered that she had only thirty gallons of water on board, while none was to be obtained on the coast. Under these circumstances, her skipper bore up for St. Helena, where, his original destination being entirely ignored, the vessel was freighted for the West Indies.

Of the chartered brigs I have mentioned, one, the "Ann, of Bristol," Captain Farr, touched at the Cape of Good Hope, took in water, and duly reached Ichaboe, where she remained during the months of March and April, 1843. Having, however, no materials on board with which to construct a stage, her lading proceeded but slowly, and was attended with much difficulty, for it was only on fine days that the boats could approach the rocks to receive the bags of guano. When about three fourths laden the brig began to drive before one of the strong southerly winds which prevail on the coast, and, having parted his chains, Captain Farr determined to bear up for England. Arriving there in safety, he was sent, with a view to secrecy, to discharge his cargo at Dumfries. The news, nevertheless, soon spread, though all possible means were resorted to to prevent its getting abroad, and to mystify the public. Captain Farr now made a fresh arrangement with a house in Glasgow; his crew communicated what they knew to others, and Mr. Livingstone, considering himself perfectly at liberty to do so, gave all the information he possessed on the subject to a Liverpool firm. It appears that this gentleman had been most unjustly treated by his employers when in charge of their vessel, the "Gallovidia." They had refused to abide by their original agreement, which was a verbal one, and have never given to Mr. Livingstone, to this day, the slightest remuneration for his valuable services. Their speculations on the coast, however, have been so conducted as to bring upon them, to the full, their due reward.

Toward the middle of November, 1843, several vessels arrived (principally from Liverpool and Glasgow) simultaneously on the African coast. One of them went by accident direct to Ichaboe;

ISLAND OF ICHABOE.

others to Possession Island and Angra Pequena, where guano was, it was believed, also to be found. Very few of the parties first sent out were aware of the existence of Ichaboe. They knew only of the islands laid down in the charts and mentioned in books of directions. It was, however, promptly brought to their notice, and many who had freighted their vessels at Possession Island and Angra Pequena threw their cargo overboard, in order to reload at Ichaboe, where the guano is superior in quality to that any where else to be obtained.

This island, when first visited, was literally covered with guano, immensely accumulated toward the north, but in less dense heaps at its southern extremity.* In its northern pits, the manure measured, when operations were first commenced, forty feet in depth, and decreased gradually to about ten feet at its opposite end. From data which can not be very incorrect, the whole quantity, varying greatly in quality, removed from the islet was, at the period alluded to, about 200,000 tons, the best being decidedly obtained from the northern pits. The N.W. corner of the rock contained, too, a considerable quantity of the deposits of the gannet and cormorant, while its southern end was covered with decayed seals and their droppings. The bulk of

* The cause of this is probably to be found in the fact that the north is the lee-side of the island, to which the feathery tribes naturally retreat for shelter against the inclemency of the weather, and the prevailing strong southerly winds.

the guano, however, at least the one half of it, came undoubtedly from the penguin, while the remainder consisted chiefly of the dead, decomposed bodies of that bird.

It may be as well here to mention, that of the 200,000 tons of guano shipped from Ichaboe, only eight small cargoes were carried off by foreign vessels; of these eight, moreover, only two were obtained from the pits; the others, of a very inferior quality, were picked up wherever they could be got.

"On first landing, in November, 1843, on the island which enjoyed for a time so odorous a celebrity," says a certain writer, "the place was literally alive with one mass of penguins, etc., which were so tame, or, rather, so unaccustomed to man's appearance that they would not move without compulsion. Thousands of the eggs of this bird, collected by the sailors, formed a savory addition to their usual rations of salt meat." They are hardly fewer at present; for, notwithstanding the numbers of penguins shot every year, and the enormous quantity of eggs and young annually carried off and destroyed, these birds still continue to resort to their favorite haunt in almost undiminished multitudes, while the constant presence of man for nearly a quarter of a century has not in the least affected their social habits, or diminished their fondness for their wild oceanic home.

The following lines from the Cape Press show how much this bird occupied the fancy or the fingers of Cape Town scribes when the guano fever was at its height, and conversation in every society turned in that settlement upon the all-absorbing topic:

"One evening it chanced, as I strolled by the shore,
This saddest of ditties the cool night-breeze bore
Distinct o'er the surf, with its gruff sullen roar:

"THE PENGUIN'S LAMENT.

"Tormented for aye be the pitiless breast
That drove me afar from my home,
A desolate bird o'er the broad billow's breast,
In search of a country to roam.

"Fiends ever torture the cold, ruthless heart
That robbed my warm nest of its young,
And made a poor heart-broken penguin depart
From the land whence his forefathers sprung.

"May Conscience's thorns on his death-bed be strewn,
His friends in adversity flee;
Was Martin's Act made for the jackass alone?
Extend not its mercies to me?

"Then in Albion, no longer the land of the just,
The penguin's lament shall be heard,
And those miserly wretches lie low in the dust
Who spared not a poor ocean bird."

None of the vessels, on arriving at Ichaboe, were on their first voyage provided with materials for erecting platforms whereby to take in their cargoes with facility; yet, as a heavy surf breaks at some distance from the shore, stages or platforms of considerable length were required for this purpose. With a rich treasure, however, before them, the energy and emulation of the adventurers soon overcame the forbidding difficulties of Nature's interposition. Some clubbed together their spare spars, studding-sail-booms, top-gallant and mizen-top-masts, and, by erecting a stage, commenced operations, while others, less amply furnished with means, or more enterprising, constructed a sort of "flying railway" with fewer materials, but with an equal, if not a greater amount of labor. In proportion, however, as the difficulties of loading became known, and fresh vessels arrived from England, spars and planks for staging were imported in great numbers, and were, toward the close of the year 1843, completely at a discount.

A high surf, deep water, and a bottom entirely composed of rocks covered with sea-weed made the difficulty of erecting stages two or three hundred feet from the shore very great. These stages, besides, in consequence of the irregularities of the rocky bottom, and the necessity of finding smooth water for the boats at their termination, could never be constructed in a straight line. Those first set up were swept away by the sea almost immediately, and more elaborate inventions had to be resorted to to give stability to the contrivance.

For this purpose, a position being chosen, which could only be on the north or east side of the island, a heavy bower anchor, having a length or two of chain attached to it, to prevent its chafing against the rocks, was laid down outside the surf; to this chain was affixed a stout hawser, secured at its extremity to the shore, in order to serve as a ridge-rope for shears, which consisted of two spars lashed together and driven into holes among the rocks. A tackle from the coast was then made fast to this construction; and one pair of shears being established, the others, each successive pair being well fastened to the ridge-rope, were got up with less difficulty.

All the shears, amounting often to fourteen or sixteen pairs, being erected, small spars were lashed longitudinally to each of them at about twelve feet above the surface of the water. Cross spars were thereupon well cleated, fore and aft, between the shears, and upon these spars, planks, sometimes nailed and sometimes lashed, were made fast and steady. At the extremity of each stage was slung a swinging platform, which could be lowered or raised as the rise or fall of the tide might require.

The railway method of taking in cargo, as it was called, was an imitation of the plan adopted for lading ships freighted with salt at one of the Cape Verde islands. To those who had no spars or planks to form a stage it was the only resource left, and was as follows:

A spar or main-boom, from forty to fifty feet long, was, by means of a pair of shears, erected on the shore as near the surf as possible, and about twenty feet above the water's level. A heavy bower anchor, with a chain attached to it, and a stout hawser to that, was then laid down outside the surf, in thirty or forty fathoms or thereabouts. A powerful tackle, fastened to a well-secured anchor, was thereupon lashed to the hawser, which was carried on shore through a snatch-block. This hawser was now set up quite taut, with a block, hook downward, at its extremity, to which was attached a small line for easing away and hauling up, etc. The long-boat being then moored to the hawser where it entered the water, two or more bags of guano were either hoisted or heaved up to the derrick-head, where a man was stationed to hook them on to the traveling-block. The bags, having arrived safely so far, were eased down the first part of the hawser, to prevent their acquiring too much velocity, and then, with a "let go," reached the boats conveniently enough. Empty bags, stores, etc., were then hauled up, and other full bags sent down. Improvements on this plan, which were certainly original and ingenious, but too tedious and laborious, were attempted, but did not succeed.

The rapid increase and constant arrival of vessels occasioning differences between their captains, it soon became evident that some system of maintaining order and a good understanding among them must be adopted. A committee of shipmasters and others was therefore formed, and certain rules were laid down which had this object in view. These rules were strictly enforced by the commanders of her majesty's ships of war, who occasionally touched at Ichaboe; and very severe police regulations, rendered necessary by the numbers of dissolute characters—sailors as well as laborers—who frequented the island were also put rigorously into execution.

The guano to the north of the islet being, as I have already said, deepest, driest, and best, and the water smoother there than at any other part of the coast, the parties first arriving commenced their lading operations in this quarter. Without any measurement or rule, they chose such part of the soil fronting them to gather their spoil as they thought fit, and for the first two months disputes rarely occurred among them, for there was room for all. The spots selected by these adventurers to work upon were called pits—why, it would be difficult to determine—possibly from some casual remark of a sailor or laborer.

The number of vessels present at Ichaboe toward the close of the year 1843 amounted to nineteen, and the arrivals went on increasing, though, from this time, a good many ships were constantly leaving with full cargoes. As the claimants for freighting-places became, however, more numerous, the difficulty of satisfying them became greater in the same degree. At first, every new-comer chose a new station, until the whole northern frontage of the island—the only part of it adapted for lading —was occupied. Another system was, however, now absolutely necessary, and masters of vessels, instead of choosing new pits more remote from the landing-place, made arrangements with their predecessors to succeed to their pits or stations on the condition of assisting them in shipping their cargoes, and paying a fair valuation for the stages.

During the months of July and August the vessels arrived at Ichaboe in such numbers that nearly three hundred were at anchor off that island in the latter months. Freighting-places, as may be supposed, became consequently extremely valuable, and were bought for money, all eagerly desiring a northern frontage in preference to the neutral ground. Under these circumstances, many shipmasters, and other parties from the Cape, established themselves on the rock, obtained possession of the pits, stations, and stages, and sold them at prices more or less exorbitant, according as the demand for them rose or fell. Much murmuring was occasioned by this seizure by a third party on privileges and property to which they had no legal claim whatever, and several attempts to put the practice down were consequently made in the committee—in vain, for the majority of its members were more or less interested in the iniquitous gains of the new system.

It was while this enormous fleet was lying off Ichaboe that another Cape Town scribe showed in the following verses the universal interest taken in guano speculations, and how completely the subject engrossed all conversation in the colony.

"A thousand fine vessels are plowing the main,
With their white sails all spread till their lofty spars strain;
But what are they seeking, and where are they gone?
Attend to my lay, and I'll tell you anon.
There's an island that lies on West Africa's shore,
Where penguins have lived since the flood or before,
And raised up a hill there a mile high or more.
This hill is all guano, and lately 'tis shown
That finer potatoes and turnips are grown,
By means of this compost, than ever were known;
And the peach and the nectarine, the apple, the pear,
Attain such a size that the gardeners stare,
And cry, 'Well! I never saw fruit like that 'ere!'
One cabbage thus reared, as a paper maintains,
Weighed twenty-one stone, thirteen pounds and six grains,
So no wonder guano celebrity gains.

"If business cause you to walk down the street,
A group of old fogies you're certain to meet,
Rigged in chokers, frock-coats, and boots, all complete;
Except that the latter are large for the feet,
But that is apart from the subject I treat:
Their broad-shouldered figures, their weather-bronzed features,
Convince you at once that they're seafaring creatures.
One pulls out a snuff-box and hands it about,
While each one in turn puts it up to his snout,
But none of the party will take a pinch out:
You're puzzled till some one says, 'Here's an example
Of Malagas guano; it's not a bad sample.'

"You speak a strange sail—ask her where she is bound—
She answers, 'Wherever guano is found.'

"At dinner some gentleman, helping a dish,
Says, 'A little guano, sir?—beg pardon—fish?'
And so the word's dinned in your ears, till you wish
Those foreseeing penguins had never laid by
(Without speaking before) such a precious supply."

One good effect followed from the dissensions just alluded to. The neutral ground, containing, it was found, as good guano as any on the island, now began to be occupied. The manure from this locality was shipped from and to the northern stages, and a good deal of the ground had already been nearly worked through when the parties engaged in clearing it were warned that, according to regulations to that effect, they could not proceed farther in a certain direction. Had they been allowed to do so they would evidently have encroached upon the property of those who had possessed the side-pits, either from the beginning or by purchase, and who naturally wished, requiring them no longer, to sell them to some successor at a good price.

The places for embarkation were, as I have already stated, all on the north and east side of the island. In order, therefore, that the other frontages should be able to take advantage of them, the whole islet was divided by a line from east to west. By this division it was probable all the pits would be worked out at the same time. That it might be so, a longitudinal line was drawn north and south, and a series of pits from the east and west was made up to that point.

Ichaboe at this period presented a scene perhaps the most singular, the most grotesquely picturesque, and the most animated that ever was beheld.

"Imagine," says Sir John Marshall, who commanded her majesty's frigate "Isis," "a fleet of about two hundred and twenty-five sail, some of them old and rigged out for the occasion, many with masters of irregular habits and insubordinate crews, seamen and laborers amounting to about 3500 men of the lowest and most drunken class, crowded together in certainly the most boisterous anchorage in the world. It is a proud sight, nevertheless, to see so many craft all lying with their anchors ahead, amid dangers of no ordinary kind, and evincing, in coolly riding under difficulties that would appal most others, the daring and superior seamanship which so strongly characterizes our people. No wrecks have occurred since I have been here; but, though we saved one vessel when on the rocks, much mischief has been done. Bowsprits, stern-frames, and boats have chiefly suffered; yet I believe the damage is trifling compared with what might have been expected. Fancy so many ships at only an average distance from each other, of from twenty to thirty fathoms, amid rollers in which the 'Isis,' the lower cells of whose ports are nine feet and more above the water, has dipped her main-deck guns, and where, moreover, there is no protection from a gale from the west, and but very partial shelter from any wind."

At the commencement of October there were altogether present at Ichaboe about six thousand seamen and laborers, of whom at least three fourths were located on shore. At that time the part of the island which had been cleared of guano was completely covered with tents, in which much skulking during the day, and much rioting at night took place. These tents were pitched so close together that it was almost impossible to detect a truant laborer or seaman hiding among them, and the scenes of drunkenness and debauchery they sheltered would have disgraced the lowest haunt of vice. Spirits, in much greater quantities than were allowed by the regulations, were issued to the men, with the connivance of the mates, though not with that of the masters; and Bacchanalian orgies were held in the encampment, abominable beyond belief, which would call up a blush even on the face of the most abandoned.

Things came at last to such a pass that the committee, supported by Sir John Marshall, ordered every tent on the island to be struck on the day following their sitting.

Many a curse, not loud, but deep, was heaped that night on the heads of the "—— committee," as they were called, not only by the seamen and laborers, but by the masters themselves, many of whom, I am sorry to say, indulged themselves in the camp revelries with quite as much zest as their crews. On the morning of the day on which the tents were to be struck some opposition to the injunctions of the committee was attempted, but Sir John was too well prepared to leave it the least chance of success. At one o'clock P.M. he pulled toward the landing-place, with the frigate's boats completely manned and armed; and, disembarking half the marines, with a few blue jackets, went round the island, overawing, by his presence, the disaffected, and effectually quelling, by a judicious display of force, every thought of resistance that had been previously entertained. At five P.M. not a man remained on the island except the marine guard who landed every evening to clear it, and to prevent any disembarkation until the morning. From the time of his arrival up to the time of his departure, Sir John Marshall, by his unwearied energy and perseverance to promote the interests of all concerned in the guano trade, by his urbanity and kindness, by his ready access to seamen and laborers, and his unremitting attention to the whole wide circle of his duties, rendered himself universally respected and beloved, and certainly deserved, in the amplest measure, the thanks of the merchants and underwriters of Great Britain.

The removal of the tents and the clearing of the island every evening was assuredly one of the best measures adopted while the merchant fleet remained at Ichaboe; it tended to keep up discipline, which had been seriously relaxed, among the various crews, and prevented an encampment being turned into a rendezvous for the indulgence in every sort of horrible excess.

Up to the autumn of 1844 not more than 90,000 tons of guano had been removed from Ichaboe; but from that time the valuable deposit began to disappear rapidly; from September, 1844, to the middle of February, 1855, so great was the number of vessels taking in cargo that, in the month of January alone, four hundred and fifty were at anchor off the island, and such the activity of the crews that the remaining 110,000 tons of manure were entirely cleared away.*

"The wealth obtained from Ichaboe," remarks a certain writer, "the ingenious machinery by which the guano was removed, the enormous fleet of vessels and number of men employed, with the huge hinderances of nature's interposition they had to contend with and to subdue, must strike every intelligent observer as presenting a very extraordinary example of commercial enterprise and hardihood. Though the surf, thundering toward the shore, washed down stages at intervals as fast as they were set up—though the wind and the sea in the anchorage rendered communication between parties engaged in the same task often difficult, and the boating off of guano frequently impossible, yet there was no relaxation of effort for one moment, and in an incredibly short space of time complete success crowned these strenuous exertions.

* The price of guano at Ichaboe varied according to the demand, at one time being 5s. per ton, and at another from 15s. to 20s. The freight paid to chartered vessels was £4 per ton. On an average, the price of good guano received by the importers was £6 10s. to £7 10s. per ton. The farmer, however, never obtained it under £8, and then often adulterated by the holders.

"The weather only permitted, on an average, three good boating-days in the week; on the other days it was generally impossible to land. When, however, a landing could be effected, all hands were occupied with the spade, or in filling and carrying bags to the stages for shipment. On a fine calm day it was pleasant to stand on the summit of the rocky islet, and look down on the busy hive below. One might then see one party in a pit, amid clouds of dust, digging guano, while another was shoveling it into bags; and farther on, perhaps, a band employed in wheeling or carrying sacks to the shore, where a long row of men would be seen running along with others on their shoulders, tossing them into the boats at the stage ends, and returning rapidly for more. Then, again, the deeply-laden boat pulled off to the vessel, and the crew on board, heaving up the cargo to their well-known measured chant, just reaching the ear of the listener on land, and contrasting well, by its lulling sound and effect, with the stirring life which it so softened and harmonized, added greatly to the picturesqueness of the scene. On some of the fine days referred to, which occurred generally after bad weather, not less than two thousand tons have been shipped in the course of twelve hours. I need not say, therefore, that, generally speaking, the men worked well, and, if at times they were somewhat noisy, this might easily be tolerated when the nature of their labor was considered. It was, on the whole, a proud sight for any Englishman to contemplate. The vast mercantile fleet assembled—the energy and perseverance of its commanders and crews—the toil and difficulties encountered and overcome—the immense value of the shipping—the expense of the entire equipment—the worth of the homeward cargo—its importance in a commercial as well as in an agricultural point of view—all this constituted a spectacle for the eye and for the mind such as the British nation alone can furnish, and which probably has, in the history of commerce, never had its parallel."

THE END.

www.ingramcontent.com/pod-product-compliance
Lightning Source LLC
Chambersburg PA
CBHW022111290426
44112CB00008B/638